Private Oceans

Anthropology, Culture and Society

Series Editors:
Jamie Cross, University of Edinburgh,
Christina Garsten, Stockholm University
and
Joshua O. Reno, Binghamton University

Recent titles:

Private Oceans

The Enclosure and Marketisation of the Seas

Fiona McCormack

PlutoPress
www.plutobooks.com

First published 2017 by Pluto Press
345 Archway Road, London N6 5AA

www.plutobooks.com

Copyright © Fiona McCormack 2017

The right of Fiona McCormack to be identified as the author of this work has been
asserted by her in accordance with the Copyright, Designs and Patents Act 1988.

British Library Cataloguing in Publication Data
A catalogue record for this book is available from the British Library

ISBN   978 0 7453 9915 7   Hardback
ISBN   978 0 7453 9910 2   Paperback
ISBN   978 1 7868 0138 8   PDF eBook
ISBN   978 1 7868 0140 1   Kindle eBook
ISBN   978 1 7868 0139 5   EPUB eBook

This book is printed on paper suitable for recycling and made from fully managed
and sustained forest sources. Logging, pulping and manufacturing processes are
expected to conform to the environmental standards of the country of origin.

Typeset by Stanford DTP Services, Northampton, England

Simultaneously printed in the United Kingdom and United States of America

Contents

Series Preface

Anthropology is a discipline based upon in-depth ethnographic works that deal with wider theoretical issues in the context of particular, local conditions – to paraphrase an important volume from the series: *large issues* explored in *small places*. This series has a particular mission: to publish work that moves away from an old-style descriptive ethnography that is strongly area-studies oriented, and offer genuine theoretical arguments that are of interest to a much wider readership, but which are nevertheless located and grounded in solid ethnographic research. If anthropology is to argue itself a place in the contemporary intellectual world, then it must surely be through such research.

We start from the question: 'What can this ethnographic material tell us about the bigger theoretical issues that concern the social sciences?' rather than 'What can these theoretical ideas tell us about the ethnographic context?' Put this way round, such work becomes *about* large issues, *set in* a (relatively) small place, rather than detailed description of a small place for its own sake. As Clifford Geertz once said, 'Anthropologists don't study villages; they study *in* villages.'

By place, we mean not only geographical locale, but also other types of 'place' – within political, economic, religious or other social systems. We therefore publish work based on ethnography within political and religious movements, occupational or class groups, among youth, development agencies, and nationalist movements; but also work that is more thematically based – on kinship, landscape, the state, violence, corruption, the self. The series publishes four kinds of volume: ethnographic monographs; comparative texts; edited collections; and shorter, polemical essays.

We publish work from all traditions of anthropology, and all parts of the world, which combines theoretical debate with empirical evidence to demonstrate anthropology's unique position in contemporary scholarship and the contemporary world.

Jamie Cross
Christina Garsten
Joshua O. Reno

Acknowledgements

Thanks are due to so many people for their support in multiple ways during this project. I extend heartfelt appreciation to all my collaborators in New Zealand, Iceland, Hawaii and Ireland, who over the years have participated generously in my research. Particular thanks go to Angeline Greensill, John Hikuwai, Margaret Mutu, Waldo Houia, Katarina Edmonds, Níels Einarsson, Craig Severance, Kale Langlas, Kathy Kawelu, Siobhan McCormack, Marge McManus, Pearse Doherty, Seamie McIntyre, Gerry Early and John O'Brien. I am grateful for the encouragement of my very dear colleagues in the Anthropology Programme at the University of Waikato, Aotearoa/New Zealand: Tom Ryan, Fraser Macdonald, Keith Barber, Michael Goldsmith, Judith Macdonald, Des Kahotea and Apo Aporosa. Jacinta Forde, Luke Oldfield, Lily Brown, Steve Webster and Jon Altman have also dedicated their time to this project. I am especially thankful for the support of my husband, David Scott, and my father-in-law, Lawrie, who built me a garden office so I could write in peace. My children, Oisín, Ciara and Mila deserve special acknowledgement for their tolerance and empathy. Also, David Castle of Pluto Press has expertly guided me through the publishing process. Finally, my father, Patrick Joseph McCormack, deserves the utmost thanks. He has cast his critical eye over every word in this manuscript. I dedicate this book to him and to my mother, Renata McCormack.

Various ideas in this book have appeared previously in some of my published essays and chapters. In this present form, however, both the data and analysis have been hugely extended and represent a new direction in my thinking.

Abbreviations

ACE **Annual catch entitlement**: the tonnage of fish that the quota owner is able to harvest in a year. This entitlement can be fished by the owner or leased to others.

ACL **Annual catch limit**: this demarcates an overall amount of a fish species, or a total quota, that when reached in a fishing year triggers a closure.

AFL **Aotearoa Fisheries Limited**: the company established to maximise the value of Māori fisheries assets for the benefit of its *iwi* and Māori shareholders (now Moana New Zealand).

CFP **Common Fisheries Policy**: the fisheries policy of the European Union.

EU **European Union**

EEZ **Exclusive Economic Zone**: the sea zone prescribed by the United Nations Convention on the Law of the Seas. It stretches from the baseline to 200 nautical miles from its coast. Under the EEZ states have perpetual rights over the exploration and use of marine resources, including energy production from water and wind.

FCV **Foreign charter vessels**

HDAR **Hawaii Department of Aquatic Resources**: the department which manages Hawaii's aquatic resources and ecosystems.

IFQ **Individual fishing quota**: a different term for ITQs, used, for example, in Iceland.

ITQ **Individual transferable quota**: the dedicated portion of the TAC allocated to individuals.

LEP **Limited entry permit**: a system used to limit the amount of vessels in a fishery. Restrictions also typically pertain to gear and vessel length.

MBI **Market-based instruments**: policy instruments that use markets, price and other economic variables to provide incentives for users to reduce or eliminate negative environmental externalities.

MIO **Mandated *iwi* organisation**: an *iwi* organisation that has met the governance criteria set out in the Māori Fisheries Act 2004. MIOs are entitled to receive fisheries assets. There can be only one MIO per *iwi*.

MPI   **Ministry of Primary Industries**: the department in New Zealand under which fisheries are governed.

MSY   **Maximum sustainable yield**: the largest long-term average catch or yield that can be taken from a fish stock under prevailing ecological and environmental conditions.

NGO   **Non-governmental organisation**

NOAA **National Oceanic and Atmospheric Administration**: a scientific agency within the US Department of Commerce focused on the conditions of the oceans and the atmosphere.

PES   **Payment for Ecosystem Services**: schemes in which the beneficiaries, or users, of ecosystem services provide payment to the stewards, or providers, of ecosystem services.

QMA   **Quota management area**: geographic areas within the EEZ.

QMS   **Quota management system**: the type of individual fishing quota system used in New Zealand to manage fish stocks.

TAC   **Total allowable catch**: a species-specific total amount of fish stock that can be harvested. It is set typically by weight and for a given period of time.

TACC **Total allowable commercial catch**: the portion of the TAC that the commercial fishing industry can catch in a given year.

TFC   **Transferable fishing concessions**: the nomenclature used for ITQs in the CFP.

TGH   **Tainui Group Holdings**: the commercial entity of Waikato Tainui.

TOKM **Te Ohu Kai Moana**: formerly the Māori Fisheries Commission.

Glossary

Māori words	English translation
Aotearoa	New Zealand
hapū	sub-tribe, tribe (also: pregnant)
hui	assembly/gathering/meeting
iwi	tribe (also: bone)
kaimoana	seafood
kaitiakitanga	guardianship, stewardship, trusteeship, trustee
kaumātua	elderly/aged
koha	gift/offering
mana	prestige/power
marae	literally courtyard, the open area in front of the *wharenui* (meeting house). Also used to describe the complex of buildings around the *marae*
pakeha	New Zealander of European descent
rāhui	to put in place a temporary ritual prohibition, closed season, ban or reserve
rohe	boundary/territory/border
rohe moana	customary sea area owned by iwi and hapū/seascape
rangatiratanga	chieftainship/right to exercise authority/chiefly autonomy
runanga	tribal council/iwi authority
takiwā	territory
taonga	treasure
tapu	sacred/prohibited/set apart/forbidden
Te Reo	Māori language
tikanga	correct procedure/custom/habit/rule
tupuna	ancestor
waka	canoe
whakapapa	genealogy
whānau	extended family, though also to be born/give birth

Hawaiian words

ahupua'a	land division extending from the uplands to the sea
haole	white person/foreigner

'ohana	extended family
konohiki	headman of an *ahupua'a* land division under the chief; *konohiki* control land and fishing rights
kupuna	grandparent/ancestor
lū'au	Hawaiian feast
poke	raw fish salad
tūtū	grandparents of both genders

Introduction: Neoliberalising the Environment – the Case of Fisheries Quota

The individual transferable quota (ITQ) system in fisheries is but one approach to managing marine environments, albeit an approach that is becoming increasingly hegemonic on a global scale. New Zealand in 1983 and Iceland in 1984 were the first countries to begin the transformation, followed by the Netherlands and Canada. The model has now been rolled out in at least 18 countries (Chu 2009) and there are approximately 150 ITQ programmes worldwide (Costello et al. 2010). It is an ever-expanding regime and is, for instance, the preferred management option currently advocated at the federal level in the United States and among the highest policy ranks in the European Union (EU). Member states in both places are at various stages of compliance, transition and, in some cases, resistance. That countries as spatially and culturally distinct as South Africa, Australia, Mexico and the Cook Islands have implemented ITQs and others such as Russia, Japan and Norway are moving in this direction indicates two main possibilities: ITQs successfully work to reverse the notorious sustainability crisis in the world's fisheries; and the economic thesis on which the system is based is everywhere applicable, being compatible with local biophysical and cultural contexts, existent economic forms and human values. Both suppositions can be challenged. I suggest, instead, that ITQs are rooted in fantastical imaginings about the superiority of private property rights in generating 'good' environmental governance and economic efficiency; and that a belief in the virtues of 'the market' as the optimal space through which to distribute fishing rights may be radically misplaced.

In fisheries economics and policy literature ITQs are proposed as a pragmatic response to over-exploitation as well as innate and universal human behaviour (see Arnason 2008). The narrative can be summarised as follows: it is the human condition to over-exploit common resources, to 'race for fish'; to rationally harvest as much as possible today in the knowledge that every other fisherman will behave similarly. Each fisherman, mindful of establishing a competitive advantage, will also be incentivised to invest in more expensive gear, faster fishing vessels, and newer and more sophisticated technology in a continuous effort to capture a larger share of the total fish harvest. Instead of increasing a fisherman's share of the catch, however, such investments lead to a growing imbalance between harvesting costs and profit, that is the fishing enterprise will become overcapitalised, resulting in an economically inefficient operation. In most cases, neither state regulation of gear or vessel size nor the setting of a limit on the total amount of fish that can be harvested works to stymie the immanent logic of fishermen racing or overcapitalising. Rather the panacea lies in privatising fishing rights and allocating these rights through market mechanisms. Market-based approaches to marine environments, it is argued, have the advantage of optimising economic efficiency and are a means of securing conservation objectives. Such approaches reach their pinnacle in ITQ systems.

In ITQ fisheries fishing effort is limited by the establishment of a total allowable catch (TAC) which is set (ideally) yearly by central governments for each fish stock based (ideally) on the research, data collection and rec-ommendation of fishery scientists. This TAC is then divided into quota shares which are distributed to various fishermen in the fishery based on criteria which change over time. When the system is first introduced, quota is typically freely gifted according to fishing history and/or the amount of capital invested in the industry. Subsequently, quota is distributed via 'the market', where it can be bought, sold and/or leased, often with the help of quota brokers and online trading systems. Owning quota guarantees a share of the TAC, and the more quota owned the larger the share. This assurance, it is anticipated, incentivises sustainable fishing practices, reduces the danger of overfishing and solves the problem of fishermen racing for fish. Quota owners have a direct interest, it is theorised, in the preservation and sustainability of the fisheries since their wealth increases in conjunction with the health of the fishery, and this is particularly the case when quota is constructed as a permanent, private, freely tradable, property right. The fishery becomes economically efficient as less efficient operators leave the fishery, selling their quota to their more efficient counterparts. Excess capacity is thus reduced. Further, there is an increase in economic rents from a previously underproductive common property fishery.

While my concern with the overall consequences of ITQ systems will be detailed throughout this book, it is pertinent at this point to provide a snapshot. The following list of impacts, with a proviso that not all consequences appear in all cases, emerged from a global interdisciplinary working group[i] on ITQ fisheries, the first meeting of which was held in the Institute of Arctic Studies, Dartmouth College, USA, in September 2015.

Socio-cultural impacts:
    Alienation and loss of individual fate control
    Increased social stratification and class barriers
    Loss of lifetime investments in homes and other infrastructure
    Outmigration and gender imbalances
    Loss of community viability

Political-economic impacts:
    Lack of fair returns to owners/stewards of the resource
    Cartelisation of the fishing industry
    Barriers to new entrants in a neo-feudal setting
    Concentration of wealth and power
    Transformation of 'paper fish' into financial derivatives
    Institutional lock-in/irreversibility

Environmental-biophysical impacts:
    Incentives for high-grading
    No rewards for low-carbon environmentally sustainable fishing
    No focus on ecosystem-based management

In many ways what has happened, and is happening, in fisheries is a particular manifestation of the onshore destruction of industrial and manufacturing capacity in the name of economic progress, but with some new departures. These particularities can be best understood by situating ITQs within the broader neoliberal reorganisation of the political economy that occurred in the 1980s and, more specifically, through exploring the reconfiguration of human–environmental relationships that have transpired under market environmentalism. These two conceptual and policy frameworks provide a critical lens throughout this book. I argue that ITQ fisheries embody a quintessential neoliberal approach to human and natural worlds and while mindful that 'neoliberalism', like 'globalisation', and, as I suggest later, 'sustainability', has become a somewhat all-embracing concept, its use as a descriptor of ITQs has, I think, heuristic value. By honing in on a particular industry, that is fisheries, in very different ethnographic contexts (Iceland, New Zealand, Ireland and Hawaii), a calibrated analysis of the social complexities, contradictions and consequences of neoliberalisation can be suggested. This is a task urgently required given the growing academic disquiet with the seemingly indiscriminate manner in which neoliberalism has been applied, the call to ethnographically ground the concept, and the need to specify both the linkages with and the disconnections from older systems of capital accumulation.

Situating neoliberalism

Anthropological engagements with neoliberalism as a descriptor of global restructuring over the last three decades have produced critical works on the materiality of everyday existence. Yet there is a growing disquiet that the term may have morphed into a catch-all descriptor of the current condition and thus lost much of its diagnostic power in accentuating the distinctive (Allison and Piot 2014). This unease is based around three main critiques: a perceived lack of accounting in published work for the differences and similarities with capitalism and/or late capitalism (Ganti 2014); a growing awareness of the variegations of neoliberalism, which may simply be too immense to be usefully captured by one analytical category; and theoretical divergences in approaches to neoliberalism such that there is no agreed upon definition of the concept, thereby making it a slippery subject of analysis (Goldstein 2012). Wacquant (2012) broadly compartmentalises these divergent approaches as economistic ones and those to do with governmentality. Whereas the former is concerned with state withdrawal and the deregulation and privatisation of formerly state domains, the latter, underwritten by Foucauldian thought, speaks of neo-liberalism as a 'flowing and flexible conglomeration of calculative notions, strategies and technologies aimed at fashioning populations and people' (2012: 69).

Nonetheless, few authors are ready to abandon the concept in its entirety and a number of journals have recently committed to developing a more robust anthropological account. *Cultural Anthropology*, for instance, announced in 2014 that it would devote one issue per year to what it calls the 'futures of neoliberalism' in an effort to thicken and nuance the term's meaning; the debate section of *Social Anthropology* published a stream of articles in 2012 dedicated to problematising Wacquant's 'actually existing neoliberalism'; and the 2014 *Annual Review of Anthropology* includes Ganti's article underscoring the epistemological value of the concept.

In light of this work, I outline below six basic tenets which guide my usage of neoliberalism:

Neoliberalism as hyper-capitalism

Neoliberalism is well captured by the descriptors 'hyper-capitalism', 'capitalism with the gloves off' or 'naked capitalism'. It cannot be collapsed into 'late capitalism', which is a temporal and descriptive indicator, a term devised to describe transformations in the nature of capitalism (Ganti 2014). Neoliberalism is, as oft-declared, an ideological and philosophical movement, a 'thought collective' (Ganti 2014; Mirowski and Plehwe 2009). It is also much more insidious than this. It is decidedly concrete, having been written into policies, laws and resource management regulation, and the new wave of market-based instruments in environmental management.

In his analysis of neoliberalism, Neveling (2014) reminds us that it is but one of several possible manifestations of capitalism, past and present, and should be treated as such. Neoliberalism, he asserts, does not signify a radical social rupture (Neveling 2014: 7). Like earlier conceptions of globalisation or modernisation, neoliberalism is a phenomenon of lower analytical reach than capitalism, both diachronically and synchronically (Neveling 2014). Kalb (2012) contextualises the relationship as analogous to that between law and the broader political economy: that is, between neoliberalism as a formal framework of governance and capitalism as the relational field of forces that champions, enlivens and regulates it. While I concur that the theoretical subjugation of neoliberalism to capitalism is analytically valid, the practical consequences of neoliberalisation may, in fact, be utterly radical. The implementation of ITQs in many places has had rapid, and sometimes overnight, social repercussions. In this respect ITQ fisheries provide an ideal site where the specificities, and indeed extremities, of the relationship between capitalism and neoliberalism can be revealed. In other words, ITQ fisheries are epitomic to understanding neoliberalism in, for instance, New Zealand or Iceland, or more exactly, the workings of neoliberalism in capitalist New Zealand or capitalist Iceland.

The context in which neoliberalism became entrenched as a credible intellectual doctrine was contingent on problems within the capitalist mode of production. The 1970s were witness to an over-accumulation crisis, the re-emergence of international finance, increasing and

system-wide indebtedness, and escalating popular demands for redistribution (Kalb 2012). Neoliberalism was deployed to address stagflation (that
is, a combination of high inflation and stagnant economic growth in a
situation of growing unemployment), to impose debt repayment strategies
on indebted sovereign states and to stifle a rising tide of collectivism.
It provided an intellectual corpus that benefited the holders of capital.
Ganti identifies four main referents of this corpus: (a) a set of economic
reform policies concerned with the deregulation of the economy, the
liberalisation of trade and industry, and the privatisation of state-owned
enterprises; (b) a dogmatic development model that prescribes very
different roles for capital, labour and the state in comparison to previous
models, the consequences of which are political, economic and social; (c)
the reification of market exchange and its extension to all social realms,
displacing all other forms of exchange and ethics; and (d) a governance
model rooted in a self-regulating free market, competition and self-interest
(2014: 91).

There is a complex relationship between liberalism and neoliberalism.
As a form of governance neoliberalism is distinct from liberal philosophy,
although the 'neo' is suggestive of a relationship. Merlan, for instance,
assumes a continuity between liberal democracy and neoliberalism and
considers the latter, characterised by an extreme emphasis on market
freedom to the exclusion of other values, to be simply a one-sided, 'evil
twin'-like development of the former (2009: 314). Yet liberal democracy
is itself critiqued by the left for its hypocrisy and ideological trickery, and
for engendering an idea of inclusion that is never fully realised in practice
(Brown 2003). Vázquez-Arroyo asserts that, over time, liberal democracy
leads to depoliticisation, democracy in form rather than substance and
that it stifles the democratic politics that once gave credence to it. More
importantly for the present discussion, it opens the door to neoliberalism,
and provides it with 'a cloak of legitimacy' (2008: 127). The discontinuities
between liberalism and neoliberalism may, however, be more portentous
than the continuities. Although it shares with classical liberalism a belief
in markets as a more effective mechanism for dispatching information
about supply, demand and prices than the state, its visualisation of the
state is not one that seeks its elimination. Rather, neoliberalism works to
redefine the nature and function of the state. It is rooted in the conviction
that its perception of a good society cannot occur naturally and can only be
achieved through concerted political effort and organisation (Ganti 2014).

While the global fiscal crisis in 2007 evoked euphoric declarations predicting the end of neoliberalism, it is now evident that the crisis is actually strengthening it. This is because the crisis was a crisis of capitalism, not of neoliberalism. It is also, significantly, a result of the cementing of neoliberal ideology into law and policies, a process which has facilitated its enduring stickiness. It is, for instance, extremely difficult to reverse privatisations, particularly when these are bound up with international financialised capital and debt. In the post-crisis collapse of Iceland, this intractability confronted the left-leaning Green Party when it attempted to change fisheries governance in line with election promises, popular demand and a United Nations Human Rights Committee ruling.

Neoliberalism and neoliberalisms

Neoliberalism is not only spatially variegated but also temporally, having entrenched itself in different locales and biophysical environments in different ways, it also re-entrenched itself anew after the global fiscal crisis. This chameleon-like configuration is reflected in the view of neoliberalism as 'messy', a thesis advanced by scholars who approach neoliberalism within a governmentality framework. Thus, it is purported, there is no single package of policies or guiding principles, rather neoliberalisation 'displays a lurching dynamic' characterised by opportunism, improvisation and 'on-the-hoof recalibrations' (Peck and Theodore 2012), it is consequently decidedly messy both in terms of theory and practice (Kalb 2012). Similarly, McCarthy and Prudham note the difficulty in defining neoliberalism as any one thing since the term stands for 'a complex assemblage of ideological commitments, discursive representations, and institutional practices, all propagated by highly specific class alliances and organized at multiple geographical scales' (2004: 276). There is no one primeval neoliberal doctrine against which its implementations can be tested.

This understanding of neoliberalism as somewhat chaotic and hyper-variegated is reflected, on the one hand, in the distinctive contours of neoliberalism in resource management and in market environmentalism, and, on the other hand, in the heterogeneity of these processes. Gómez-Baggethun and Muradian (2015) point to the different technologies, markets and property ideas informing market-based instruments in environmental management; Bakker (2010) highlights the existence of a diversity of neoliberalisations in nature, a consequence, she suggests, of different 'socio-natures', a term used to capture differing biophysical characteristics, behaviours and the co-constitution of these with labour and consumption practices. In the marine environment, Mansfield (2004: 314) notes that neoliberalism has a particular dynamic centred specifically on the linkage of property rights, market behaviour and the perceived proper use of ocean resources. The analysis of neoliberalism as messy also denotes a flexibility – that neoliberalism(s) is prone to mutate and able to adjust and readjust itself to capitalism's crises – a conceptualisation that can usefully account for the evolution of ITQ regimes, their changing dynamics over time including that in the current phase of financialisation. It is also suggestive of singular localisations, of qualitatively different varieties of practices on the ground.

While I am convinced of the importance of challenging a view of neoliberalism as monolithic, as immutable over space and time, it is equally the case that there are constant features. These broadly include the near idolisation of a self-regulating market as the governing mechanism for allocating all goods and services (McCarthy and Prudham 2004); an intensification of programmes of privatisation and commodification; an accelerated extension of economic rationality to formerly non-economic domains and the individual subject; and the subjugation of social institutions and social action to the demands of market values. Albeit neoliberalism has undergone many theoretical modifications since its first deployment, it is still heavily rooted in the fiction of the spontaneous order of the market (Hilgers 2012). And while ITQs have been implemented at various points over the past three decades in a multiplicity of spaces and have been confronted by culturally distinctive actors, there is a definite coherence to these configurations and a commensurability of social consequences. This is not to deny that there is also diversity.

Hilgers' (2012) consideration of neoliberalism as a coherent political 'utopia' that turns into a plurality of neoliberalisms as it hits the ground running, foregrounds this spatio-temporal dimension and neoliberalism's global propagation as a political project. This understanding enables a coherent account of theoretical neoliberalism at the same time as the recognition of practical localisations (see also Ferguson 2010; Harrison 2010; Harvey 2007). Hilgers (2012: 89) argues that the historicity of any particular state redeployed under the constraint of neoliberalism seriously affects the way in which these redeployments are carried out. The resistances and struggles, the multiplicity of double movements, that confront structural adjustments and neoliberal experiments are another important set of factors that may help explain neoliberal diversities.

Neoliberalism and the opening of spaces

A singularly striking feature of neoliberalism is that it cannot be identified with a particular political ideology as both social democratic and conservative parties embrace it when in power. In New Zealand, for instance, it was the fourth Labour government which enthusiastically adopted neoliberalism in the 1980s and began a rigorous restructuring of the state sector. Labour's implementation of deregulation, privatisation, competitive tendering and contracting for public services left only the task of breaking the (already) attenuated power of the union movement, through reform of the labour market, to its conservative successor. This job was rapidly implemented in the 1990s when the National Party government consolidated the emergent understandings of the state and the economy. Since the 1980s, New Zealand, while fully committed to neoliberalism, has oscillated between a New Labour and a neoconservative version, with the latter currently holding sway. There is in fact little that is inevitable about neoliberalism. It articulates with, for instance, indigeneity in highly creative, often surprising and spatially uneven ways. As an alternative political cultural formation, indigeneity may be just as likely to appropriate neoliberalism for its own ends as the other way round (Kingfisher and Maskovsky 2008: 115).

This 'opening of spaces' for historically marginalised groups, although seemingly contrary to the central tenets of the free market and individualism, is nevertheless consistent with neoliberal practice. Hale (2005: 12) argues that an emphasis on the development of civil society and social capital, and the granting of cultural rights is what 'give[s] the "neo" its real meaning'. This recognition of rights, however, may strengthen the capacity of the state 'to shape and neutralize opposition' (Hale 2005: 10). I argue in chapter 1, for example, that the resolution of Māori indigenous claims to the seascape in New Zealand was accomplished by the attempted realignment of Māori ways of owning with individual property rights; a type of privatisation built on creating new forms of property and one that enabled the fulfilment of conflicting goals simultaneously. It is, however, the transferability aspect of ITQs, described in chapter 3, that has the added propensity to create new forms of dispossession.

Neoliberalism and lived realities

My concern with neoliberalism is foregrounded by a concern with lived realities.

Over three decades of socialisation into neoliberal policies, their entrenchment and re-entrenchment, has had its effects. Alongside massive social disruptions, this process includes a forced realignment of the individual as an 'enterprising self', able to adapt to a market ordered by competition. This restructuring of personhood implies that neoliberalism is involved in the quotidian. It is implicated in the concrete structure of everyday life, in human bodies and experiences, in kinship structures and in our most fundamental social relationships, and it plays a real part in the ways in which people think about and problematise their lives. For, as acknowledged by Margaret Thatcher, the British neoliberal pioneer, the objective is to change the heart and the soul.

Neoliberalism as critique

I use neoliberalism as a form of critique, as an oppositional badge (Castree 2010b). Although the term 'neoliberalism' was initially coined to signify an ideological separation from classical liberalism, economists and other proponents had discarded the latter usage by the late 1950s. In contemporary commentaries neoliberalism is most commonly associated with an oppositional stance, with 'ideologically and theoretically charged' scholarship (Ganti 2014: 93). This book, then, is a rebuttal to proponents of market environmentalism or 'green neoliberalism'. Neoliberalism is popularly contested, increasingly so. The current guise of global capitalism in its neoliberal manifestation is universally more socially polarising, less democratic, less accountable and less controllable, let alone civilisable, than the majority of humankind finds acceptable (Kalb 2012: 328).

I am writing days after an unprecedented public protest in New Zealand's capital Auckland to the signing of an international trade agreement, the TPPA, that is the Trans Pacific Partnership Agreement, or in the protesters' acronymic inversion, Taking Peoples' Power Away. This agreement, in terms of fisheries, is likely to further offshore processing. The protest was unprecedented both in terms of numbers (estimates range from 10,000 to 43,000) and organisational stealth. Teams of young people scaled hastily erected bamboo tripod structures at key traffic intersections, causing major traffic jams and diverting cars from the central business district. Such opposition was echoed in the 12 signatory Pacific-rim countries.

Neoliberal limits

Finally, there are definite limits to neoliberalism as an explanatory tool. Presenting neoliberalism as characteristically all-encompassing overshadows the many ingredients that it contains. Financialisation, privatisation, deregulation, marketisation and commodification, for instance, each of which is entangled in neoliberalism, but, which hit the ground differently and at different intervals, in different parts of the world. The ethnography used in this book, drawn from New Zealand, Hawaii, Iceland and Ireland, contradicts the notion of neoliberalism as an ideal type. Neoliberalisation is, moreover, limited by nature and culture. As Bakker points out 'the articulation of labour and accumulation strategies with ecological processes in specific biophysical settings ... creates barriers and constraints to capital accumulation' (2010: 270). The ocean, given its fluidity, opaqueness and unpredictability, is perhaps more resistant to accumulation than most natures. Similarly, neoliberalism is limited by the political economies with which it antagonistically articulates. The rebuttal of ITQ systems in commercial fisheries in Hawaii, as described in chapter 4, attests to the ability of people to proffer a different vision of their relationship with the seascape. While Māori had little option but to accept the implementation of the quota system in New Zealand, the current ownership of quota by tribal groups is not conclusively neoliberal. The settlement of indigenous claims to fisheries, using privatised quota as compensation, has a definite social justice character. While the objective was 'to get Māori into the business of fishing', the property returned to tribal groups also signals interdependence and the distribution of wealth to tribal members.

Marketising the environment

A second departure from prior programmes of modernisation is the concurrence of ITQs with the proliferation, since the 1980s (McCarthy and Prudham 2004), of market forces in environmental policy; a trend backed by powerful international bodies such as the United Nations, the World Bank and the International Union for the Conservation of Nature. Nature, in this paradigm, has been reconstructed as a package of quantifiable ecosystem services and environmental problems are caused, it is surmised, by a failure to price these services.

A shift to market environmentalism is apparent in the replacement of government regulatory standards with voluntary schemes, the growth of market-based mechanisms such as pollution permit trading schemes, the substitution of taxpayer-subsidised public goods services, such as water, with full-cost consumer pricing and the growth in cost–benefit evaluations of environmental policies. The latter created the demand for monetary valuation schemes, such as wetland banking, carbon trading and biodiversity offsets (Kallis et al. 2013).

A toolkit of market-based instruments (MBIs), developed by economists to promote the use of financial incentives, has gained prominence in the field of biodiversity conservation and in the provision of ecosystem services. In procedural terms these seek to address 'the market failures of externalities [for instance pollution] by incorporating the external cost of production or consumption activities through taxes or charges on processes or products, or by creating property rights and facilitating the establishment of a proxy market for the use of environmental services' (Brauer et al. 2006: 11). MBIs include, for instance, Payment for Ecosystem Services (PES), Markets for Ecosystem Services, environmentally related taxes, charges and subsidies, emissions trading and other tradable permit systems, deposit refund systems and mitigation or species banking.

The classification of this diverse array of tools under the umbrella of MBIs is the subject of contention (Pirard and Lapeyre 2014), from those both supportive of and opposed to their implementation. There is, in addition, an ongoing debate as to what constitutes a PES, with some policy makers and scholars identifying ITQs as a marine exemplar (see for instance Agardi 2008; Forest Trends and the Katoomba Group 2010; Johannsen 2012) while others characterise ITQs as Markets for Ecosystem Services (Gomez personal correspondence 2016) and/or a tradable permit system. However, what is important here is the overarching logic driving the programme not the validity of the MBI classificatory details and reach, which, according to Pirard and Lapeyre (2014), may simply be the association of monetary values with nature. This logic stems from the transposition of market analytics (narrowly conceived) to the realm of nature. Once nature becomes identified with this paradigm, the point where it has been reimagined solely as an economic phenomenon, it is seemingly logical to assume that an economic instrument is needed to correct what is constituted as a failure. Thus, the dominant theoretical stance for PES is that ecosystem service degradation is the result of market failures to account for externalities, and that valuing and paying for such services will mitigate these effects (Kallis et al. 2013). The payment is assumed to function as an incentive to reduce negative environmental externalities.

The construction of the environment as a package of ecosystem services to be assigned a monetary valuation and for which an appropriate market-based tool can correct degradation, powerfully privileges market rationality over any other human–environment relationship. It also neatly circumnavigates the critique of capitalism and, in particular, its mani-festation under neoliberalism, that the capitalist mode of production is itself heavily implicated in environmental destruction (Castree 2010a; Sullivan 2013). Capitalism as a system is inherently driven to expand, to invent new outlooks for accumulation, rendering apparently natural the internalisation into capital of previously uncommodified aspects of nature and society (Castree 2010b; Escobar 1996; Sullivan 2013). As Eriksen (2016) so poignantly asks, can the world capitalist system and the 'system earth' accommodate this accelerating relational, institutional and ecological 'overheating'?

There is an obvious conceptual convergence between neoliberalism as a system of political economy and market environmentalism as a specific means for its realisation in the natural domain. ITQ systems in fisheries are an early manifestation of this union and provide an ideal setting to scrutinise the marriage of a new wave of concern for the environment with the ideology of neoclassical economics: that is, the assumption that sustainability will emerge through the incentivised bargaining of those with private property allocations. It is important to note, however, that although neoliberalism and market environmentalism are interconnected processes they are not necessarily contingent. Gómez-Baggethun and Muradian write, 'in fact, the ascent of market-based approaches in environ-mental policy and conservation has paradoxically coincided with a relative downturn in the international agenda for market liberalization' (2015: 218). As illustrative of this downturn, they point to the death of the Doha round for the global liberalisation of trade in 2010 and the subsequent prioritisation of bilateral or multilateral treaties. Further, they argue, if the global fiscal crisis in 2007 shook the era of market triumphalism, it did little to damp down the interest in MBIs, which have become increasingly popular among economists, policy makers and natural scientists over recent years.

This is not to suggest that market environmentalism is without its critics, or that the nature of the surmised relationship between the state, private enterprises and citizens is fully determined. The rolling out of MBIs in general, and of ITQs in particular, is an incomplete process and the potential exists for humans to intervene, resist and reshape their expansion. It is these possibilities, experiences of alternate relationships between people, and between people and their resources, the framing of economic and social lives at variance with that presumed universal in economic orthodoxy and the cultural creativity of fishing people in their struggle to make sense of new opportunities and constraints, that provides the starting point for this book.

Ethnographically, I draw on long-term fieldwork in New Zealand and more recent fieldwork in Hawaii, Ireland and Iceland. As field sites they are historically and culturally distinctive, yet, in terms of the pivotal role of the sea, and a perceived peripherality of their economy and society, they are markedly similar: they collectively demonstrate the tensions and contradictions that arise at the nexus of global and local economies, social orders and struggles over environmental governance. Each field site has variously engaged with ITQ systems and responded differently, and at different times, to privatisation, commodification, financialisation and other forms of dispossession: New Zealand boasts the most long-standing and comprehensive version, and highlights the articulation of ITQs with indigeneity; the potential for ITQs to be turned into financial derivatives is exemplified in the case of Iceland, as are struggles to soften the often extreme social consequences of market environmentalism; in Ireland ITQs have not been fully rolled out and there is concerted resistance to making quota transferable. Dispossessions, however, exist and these are largely articulated as a consequence flowing from the encompassment of Irish fisheries under the EU quota system; Hawaii offers an alternative case. In thus far rejecting privatisation models in fisheries and instead situating value in local cultures and economies, Hawaii sheds a comparative light on human–environment relations and the consequences of neoliberalising nature.

While each site's development of fisheries is unique, there are commonalities in terms of broader processes of enclosures. Here I use New Zealand's development of fisheries, up to the implementation of the quota management system (QMS), to draw attention to some of these trends.

New Zealand has the fourth largest Exclusive Economic Zone (EEZ) in the world and the ninth longest coastline. The seascape in general, and fishing in particular, is part of New Zealand's national identity and has a deep indigenous significance. This is expressed, for instance, in

Article 2 of the 1840 Treaty of Waitangi guaranteeing to Māori the full and ongoing possession of their fisheries, and in the tenacious struggle over fisheries engaged in by Māori since colonisation was formalised in 1840 (McCormack 2010). Fishing also has significance for the settler population and generational, commercial fishermen in coastal communities such as Leigh have deep attachments to their seascape (McCormack 2012). It is historically a preferred pastime – some 30 percent of New Zealanders fish recreationally harvesting about 25,000 tonnes of fish annually (Bess and Rallapudi 2007; Ministry for Primary Industries 2010). Indeed, the spatial geography of New Zealand lends itself to fishing; the 200-mile EEZ, at 4 million square miles, is 14 times the area of the land mass, thus most of its territory is salt water.

ITQs became entrenched as a credible management option contingent on problems of over-accumulation. Until the 1960s, commercial fishing was a relatively small-scale activity in New Zealand, less important than agriculture, the backbone of the economy. Most of the domestic fleet tra-ditionally concentrated in the inshore sector and distribution was largely confined to the local market. A desire for expansion became prevalent in the early 1960s, as indicated by the establishment in 1963 of a Fishing Industry Board mandated to champion economic growth. This desire for expansion was further stimulated by a number of international events, including the entrance of Britain into the EU in 1973 and Britain's consequent development of new agricultural trading arrangements that were less favourable to New Zealand's exports, and the two oil crises, which led to a large contraction in the New Zealand economy. The extension of state property, from 3, to 9, to 12 miles, culminating in the declaration of the EEZ in 1977, was also a significant driver. Much of the incentive for these expansive property claims came from the perceived encroachment of foreign fishing vessels into sovereign waters and the desire to recapture this fishing wealth.

The 1970s marked a rapid growth in domestic fishing operations, invigorated by export-friendly policies, an easing of criteria for loans and an encouragement of joint venture enterprises (Clark et al. 1988). Joint ventures and foreign charters were deemed necessary to build local capacity in the harvesting of offshore fisheries. Between 1967 and 1977, the domestic fleet expanded from 2,161 fishing vessels to 5,178, with the highest growth in vessel classes under 12 m (163 percent) and over 21 m (122 percent) in length (Connor 2001). Foreign vessels continued to dominate the harvesting of offshore fisheries. In 1977, for instance, 90 percent of the 476,000 tonnes of demersal finfish catch from the EEZ area was caught by foreign vessels mainly from Japan, Korea and the Soviet Union (Sharp 2008). The Ministry of Agriculture and Fisheries (MAF)[2] addressed this encroachment by the setting of TACs for deeper-water species, allocating these preferentially to the domestic industry, and only subsequently to foreign fleets under licence and government bilateral agreements. These policies offered foreign fleets less of the prime species and areas than those they had been fishing, resulting in a reduced total catch in the following years. By the early 1980s, due to increased local knowledge and changes to joint venture enticements, arrangements with foreign vessels moved towards the leasing out of New Zealand fishing quota to foreign vessels (Connor 2001). Such foreign vessel chartering has remained an important part of deep-water fishing in New Zealand.

Over-capacity, a largely policy-driven development, became linked to over-exploitation. The number of 24–33 m vessels and their total capacity increased by nearly 500 percent in the decade leading up to implementation of the quota system in 1986 (Connor 2001). The number of vessels over 33 m in length grew from 2 in the late 1970s to 12 in 1984 (Shotton 1999), reaching 62 by 1986 and 102 by 1987 (Clark et al. 1988). Some of these larger vessels, imported under government-enabled duty concessions to increase domestic participation in deep-water fisheries, had also been fishing inshore, increasing pressure on stocks. Correspondingly, it became progressively difficult for small-scale commercial fishermen, who were often part-time operators, to compete in the increasingly large and technologically sophisticated fishing industry. Moreover, as loans require collateral, they were often inaccessible to small-scale fishermen. By the late 1970s it had become obvious that over-exploitation was occurring and that many inshore stocks were under severe pressure and likely overfished (Hawkey 1994).

Economic inefficiencies were identified as equally problematic: 5 percent of the fleet was estimated to be taking two-thirds of the catch and the industry was perceived to have an overabundance of part-time operators. From a total of 5,184 licensed vessels in 1978, 2,492 are reported to have earned less than NZ$500 from fishing (NRAC 1980). In 1983 a discussion document published by the National Fisheries Management Advisory Council (NAFMAC) argued that poor, and in some cases negative, returns to larger vessels fishing inshore, provided further evidence in support of overfishing (Sharp 2008). The inshore fleet was said to be overcapitalised by about NZ$28 million. The surplus capacity was mainly concentrated on the north-east coast of the North Island, home to a significant number of Māori communities. Connor points out that the general economic conditions impacting larger vessels at the time 'may have made a substantial contribution to the crisis for the inshore, as vessels increased their effort to make businesses profitable' (2001: 225).

Both theory and practice at the time were conveniently compatible with the implementation of the ITQ regime. A persuasive global discourse in fisheries economics advocating the advantages of privatisation and, contrarily, the dire consequences of open access ownership, as state EEZs were then conceived (Mansfield 2004), provided a powerful local impetus behind the move to privatise fishing rights. This coincided with the development of scientific and managerial components of the existent management regime: the setting of TACs and Total Allowable Commercial Catches (TACCs; which was the responsibility of the government since the establishment of the EEZ). The activity of foreign vessels in offshore fisheries was also an impetus to privatise fishing rights. By 1979, 26 joint ventures existed, exploiting species not generally caught by New Zealand vessels. The motivation for domestic companies to enter into this relationship was enhanced by tax incentives. In 1982 these were removed and the government instead 'refocused on sustainability'. Notably, the introduction of ITQs was seen as a mechanism whereby the domestic industry could increase business opportunities and build capacity in the deep-water sector.[3] Importantly, though, it was the rapidly changing political-economic environment that stimulated the introduction of the new fisheries management system and ITQs in particular.

As property rights regimes for natural resources, quota systems provide a rich historical record of the outcome of struggle; a register of winners and losers; and a narrative of the social accommodation accompanying economic and political contentions over the national destiny. This struggle is illustrated in chapter 1, wherein I describe the initial opposition of Māori to the quota system; the process by which individual property in quota became aligned with Māori conceptions of common ownership and the repatriation of fishing rights through a major pan-Māori treaty settlement. Far from resolving Māori claims, the settlement set in train a new round of enclosures. I describe the resistance of a group of Māori fishers, who, through the concept of *koha* (gift exchange), attempted to reverse the 'fencing of the watery commons'. I also touch on contestations in Iceland and Ireland.

Chapter 2 addresses the role played by neoliberally conceived sustainability in the modelling of ITQs as the optimum economic *and* biological means through which to govern fisheries. This is reflected in (1) the configuration of biological sustainability through assessments of stock, the TAC and Maximum Sustainable Yields (MSY) and (2) the generation of social sustainability through the creation of (quasi) private property rights (ITQs) and markets. Rather than conceive of these as distinct spheres (nature and society), there may in fact be a crucial relationship between scientific assessments of the sustainability of natural ecosystems and economic theories about future wealth, derived explicitly through privatisation. I draw on two themes to help clarify the work of sustainability in ITQ fisheries: first, the quantifying and measuring of the environments of capitalism and, second, the exchange value of natural and human life under systems of enclosure.

Once privatised, quota has the propensity to become activated in markets. This tendency, captured in the T (transferability) of ITQs, is explored in chapter 3. Transferability has a powerful potency in market relationships. It is bound up with financialisation and crisis, and plays a decisive role in the emergent Blue Economy (Barbesgaard 2015). In many ways transferability is not about fish in the sea, it concerns, rather, the emergence of virtual fish and the attendant relegation of nature, and labour, as inconsequential in generating wealth. I discuss transferability in the context of the quota trading market and consider the implications of this for Māori fisheries assets. I also trace the financialisation of fishing rights in Icelandic fisheries and, finally, explore the link between ecosystem services and the Blue Economy.

Chapter 4 marks a departure from ITQ technologies. It explores the context of commercial and non-commercial fishing in contemporary Hawaii. A key objective is to explicate why, given US federal pressure and a mounting and powerful global consensus, there are no catch shares (ITQ) programmes in Hawaii. The anthropological juxtaposition of gifts and commodities provides an insight into the social forces at work.

Chapter 5 considers the potential for assuaging the neoliberal project in fisheries. I provide a general background to the fishing industry in Ireland in the context of EU reforms and the Irish state's attempts to accommodate the small-scale sector. I then describe, in more specific detail, fishing activities in two sites in Donegal, a county in the north-west of Ireland: Na Cealla Beaga (Killybegs), the largest fishing port in Ireland, and Árainn Mhór (Arranmore), a Gaeltacht (Irish-language speaking) island formerly famous for salmon fishing. The tension between nostalgia and precarity provides an overarching theme in this discussion.

1

Disciplining and Incorporating Dissent: Neoliberalism and Indigeneity

This chapter traces the effects of the individual transferable quota (ITQ) reorganisation of fisheries in Aotearoa/New Zealand, in particular, its impact on Māori fisheries. There is good reason why a book concerned with the relationship between neoliberalism and fisheries should start in New Zealand since it was the first country to apply ITQ governance as a national policy, and remains the country with the most comprehensive system in place. The quota management system (QMS) represents New Zealand's first attempt to manage the environment through market mechanisms and, unsuprisingly, it instigated dissent. There is a long history of Māori opposition to the loss of their property and resources, and this is particularly the case in terms of tribal fishing rights. A customary marine tenure system was in place pre-colonisation, one in which boundaries demarcated tribal *rohe moana* (seascape), and sophisticated *kaitiakitanga* (resource guardianship) practices existed. These included, for instance, the establishment of *rāhui*, that is, the placing of a *tapu* (taboo) on a seascape for conservational or political purposes, or following a death by drowning. *Kaimoana* (seafood) was variously shared or traded depending on kinship connections and the desire to create alliances with other tribes. Trade also occurred internationally; Māori were actively engaged in trading fish and agricultural produce both before and immediately after the signing of the Treaty of Waitangi in 1840, and owned boats capable of sailing to Australia on a frequent basis for commercial purposes. Cured fish was among the products exchanged (Waitangi Tribunal 1988: 44–66). The cultural significance of fishing also finds expression in Tangaroa, the god of the sea, and in numerous legends pertaining to ancestral activities in the seascape.

These ownership practices, which intertwine land and sea in the same property construct, are replicated across the Pacific (Clarke 1990; Hviding

1996; Johannes 1981). In New Zealand this linkage was inconsistent with colonial property ideologies whereby boundaries are drawn around where land meets the sea, the former being designated as susceptible to private property divisions and the latter subject to Crown ownership (Mulrennan and Scott 2000). The initial opposition of Māori to ITQs made explicit the irony of this most recent enclosure. It was couched in these terms: first, on colonisation, you denied that we had tribal property rights in the sea and claimed that it was public property, then you privatise it, exclude us from these rights and assume that we never had any commercial interests in fisheries. ITQs thus give to *pakeha* (New Zealand Europeans) the full, exclusive and undisturbed possession of the property right in fishing that the Crown has already guaranteed to Māori in the 1840 Treaty of Waitangi. This chapter describes how these disputes were eventually resolved or at least contained. While the major emphasis is on indigenous dissent in New Zealand, similar contestations are apparent in Iceland and Ireland; there are parallels in very different social settings to how people react to commoditisation and how they couch their objections: a moral economy is evoked, indigeneity is variously employed, and class and nationalist ideologies are utilised as discursive tools. These counter-movements, however, may have contradictory outcomes.

My initial interest in fisheries stemmed from two key series of court cases that occurred in New Zealand in the late 1990s. At the heart of these very different proceedings were disputes over the meaning of two crucial Māori concepts, *iwi* (tribe) and *koha* (gift exchange). Although at the time the cases were not linked in popular imagination or media representations, they were in fact deeply intertwined; both arose as a result of the introduction of ITQs and both were concerned with indigenous access to fishing rights. The proceedings were, however, very different events in terms of political and cultural legitimacy. The case concerning the contemporary meaning of *iwi* arose out of a 1992 pan-tribal settlement of Māori claims to commercial fisheries, and subsequent polemics around the appropriate kinship entity to which settlement assets should be distributed. It was cloaked in the aura associated with a High Court context, the weighty presence of elite lawyers and scholarly expert witnesses, including anthropologists, the authenticity of renowned Māori leaders and a throng of news reporters and photographers. The *koha* cases were much more low-key, played out in District Courts, and were shrouded in criminality. Both sets of cases, however, were definitive in establishing a legal basis for the transformation of Māori fisheries. Once reparations had been decided on, the key problem faced was the kinship entity to which assets from settlements should be transferred. The resolution to this was *iwi*, the strata of Māori society thought most likely to meet market criteria, though a particularly reified version of 'tribe' came to achieve precedence. Since neoliberalism promotes markets as the quintessential method of exchange, the need arose to delegitimise all forms of non-market exchange or redefine them as criminal. This, I argue, was the real issue determined in the *koha* cases. Before turning to these cases, however, I first describe the process by which individual ownership of quota as property became aligned with Māori conceptions of ownership. The implementation of the ITQ system in New Zealand articulated with indigeneity in such a way that it brought about a separation in Māori commercial and customary fishing practices; a radical development that aligns culture with ceremonial gatherings and a pure environmental ethos, and commercial rights with newly elevated kin constructs and the generation of future wealth.

Neoliberalism and the fisheries treaty settlement

ITQs became entrenched in New Zealand in the context of a package of radical economic, social and political 'reforms', and the emergence of a complementary ideology that came to dominate political discourse and the social functions of the state (Kelsey 2002). As early as 1938, at least a decade before Britain, New Zealand housed the first comprehensive social security system in the world. By the 1990s, this had been reversed and New Zealand led the transition to a new phenomenon: the post-welfare state. The 'neoliberal experiment' that took root in New Zealand in the 1980s is considered one of the most ambitious attempts at constructing the free market as a social institution (Gray 1998). The reorganisation was remarkable for the depth and speed of reforms, and, in particular, set in motion a shift of social responsibilities from the public sphere (government) to the private sphere (individuals, families and households) (Clarke 2004). Quiggan (1998) notes that accomplishing a change of this magnitude was facilitated by the fact that New Zealand is a unitary state with a unicameral government.

Neoliberalism's ability to reconcile itself with socially liberal identity politics is a striking feature of its rendition under capitalism. The New Zealand government's embracing of neoliberalism occurred concurrently with the implementation of polices aimed at addressing long-standing gay and feminist as well as indigenous concerns. A key development in the indigenous question occurred in 1985, when the mandate of the Waitangi Tribunal was backdated from 1975, the date of implementation, to 1840, the date when the Treaty of Waitangi was signed. The treaty, while subject to historical denial and counter reaffirmations, is a foundational document of colonial settlerism, contemporary identity and claims to nationhood. It is biculturally symbolic, and entitles *pakeha* settlement and governance while guaranteeing to Māori sovereignty and the ongoing possession of significant *taonga* (treasures), including fisheries. The decades leading up to the reassignment of the tribunal's jurisdiction are significant for the ferocity of Māori struggles, including protests, land marches, a Māori renaissance in *Te Reo* (Māori language), *tikanga* (Māori customs and traditions/law) and cultural practices, together with a new era of litigation. This was paralleled by an increase in the number of legal scholars and practitioners willing to argue for causes that would advance Māori rights. Raganui Walker, an eminent Māori scholar, activist and anthropologist, captured the emotions of the times by unapologetically writing of the *ka whawhai tonu matou* ('Struggle without end'; Walker 1990), and the pain of being a colonised people.

The Waitangi Tribunal was central to these struggles. As a commission of inquiry it is tasked with investigating Māori individual or group claims concerning alleged Crown breaches of the promises stipulated in the Treaty of Waitangi. The tribunal follows a relatively flexible para-legal process (Boast 1998) and has extremely limited adjudicative powers, though its findings and recommendations to the government of the time can carry a moral authority. It is structured as a bicultural, nation-building forum, being representative of the two peoples who are perceptibly seeking reconciliation in a postcolonial era (Rumbles 1999) and is composed of a chairperson and up to 20 members, Māori and *pakeha* being equally represented. It has become the primary arena whereby Māori document loss and hope, grievances, alienations, customary practices, property rights, kinship organisation and obligations, and so on (McCormack 2016). Following the hearings, the settlement processes mark a change in arenas from the tribunal to the government; from a pseudo-legal justice environment to an overtly political one.

Although inextricably embedded in the construction of histories and the political economy of postcolonial New Zealand society, contrary perceptions of the tribunal cloud political and civil society. Newly elected governments invariably bring about a shift in its financial fortunes, political and moral status, and predicted life span. The tribunal, in this regard, can be conceived of as a microcosm of the broader social struggles that characterise contemporary Māori society and the making of the tribunal retrospective to 1840 is, as noted above, significant for marking an articulation of neoliberalisation with an 'ever-emergent indigeneity' (Trigger and Dalley 2010). The 1992 settlement of Māori fisheries, prompted by a number of damning tribunal enquiries, may be seen as epitomising the constraining-enabling bent of this engagement, and is thus essential to understanding it; Māori treaty claims to fisheries both arose and were resolved within a particular ideological, social and economic framework, and the consequences flowing from this reparation can also be understood as rooted within this paradigm.

One of the striking ironies of the indigenous reparation process in New Zealand is that, although it is considered to have implemented some of the most progressive, sustained and successful policies for rendering reparative justice found anywhere in the developed world over the last few decades, this has had little effect on the comparative rate of Māori poverty (van Meijl 2013). A close examination of the settlement of Māori claims to fisheries provides a plausible reason for this paradox. In the mid-1980s Māori indigenous claims to fisheries accelerated to counteract the privatisation of commercial rights. Based on strong historical precedents, these confounded the government of the time and destabilised the introduction of ITQs. The implementation process had proceeded on the expectation that Māori interests would be undisturbed, given the assumed wholly traditional (read non-commercial) status of such rights. The objectives listed in a 1984 policy discussion document on ITQs, for instance, include stock conservation, economic efficiency, equitable allocation and, while it invisibilised Māori, contained an explicit reference to the protection of recreational fishing rights (Ministry of Agriculture and Fisheries 1984).

Throughout the late 19th and early 20th century, Māori mounted frequent challenges to the Crown's presumed ownership of the seascape and fisheries, and had, on many occasions, asserted their customary fishing or treaty rights against the Crown, especially when charged with criminal activity. The claims advanced were couched in terms of territorial use rights as well as the legitimacy of traditional fishing practices, including trade and exchange. Māori often found themselves before the courts for fishing in a manner that contravened the provisions of Fisheries Acts, particularly when these concerned the sale of fish, an activity from which Māori were unequally prohibited. This discriminatory construction of indigenous society is arguably still present today, albeit in a more insidious form.

Māori common property constructs in fisheries were recognised as aboriginal title rights for the first time in a seminal case (*Te Weehi*) in 1986.[1] This recognition correlated with two important reports issued by the Waitangi Tribunal following the Muriwhenua and Ngāi Tahu claims,[2] and claims lodged in the High Court challenging the ITQ system. Taken together these led to an unprecedented recognition of Māori property rights, in addition to evidencing an established pre-colonial trade in *kaimoana* (seafood). The Law Commission, in a review of the cases, commented:

> considered historically and conceptually, what the 1986 legislation[3] signifies is this. For more than a century the Crown consistently declined to recognize any exclusive right of the Māori in their sea fisheries. The ground was that the common right of everyone to fish below high water mark was a matter of basic legal doctrine and public policy, albeit subject to licensing and other regulatory regimes. On the Crown's initiative Parliament has now 'fenced the watery commons', established exclusive commercial fishing rights and given them to those operators who in the immediately preceding years had caught substantial quantities of fish. (1989: 11)

In 1987 a High Court injunction was granted against the further issuing of ITQs and the government was forced into a round of negotiations with the Māori litigants, as an alternative to further litigation. The liminality of this respite is striking. A real possibility had opened up to undermine the attempted 'fencing of the watery commons', and to imagine an alternative method to manage fisheries. The negotiations resulted in the Māori Fisheries Act 1989 (considered an interim settlement), significant for marking the moment when the Crown finally recognised that Māori have a commercial, and not just a cultural or ceremonial interest, in fisheries. Almost simultaneously, however, this recognition was undermined. This was achieved in the Act by making a legislative distinction between commercial and customary fishing rights, a distinction later formally incorporated into the Treaty of Waitangi (Fisheries Claims) Settlement Act 1992 – colloquially known as the Sealords deal – and the Fisheries (Kaimoana Customary Fishing) Regulations 1998. The latter set of regulations partnered Crown and Māori groups in a long and drawn out series of negotiations, whereas the former evoked internal struggles over the distribution of assets. Smith comments on the gravity of these developments: 'The state divided fishing up into commercial and traditional rights and this has cut across *rangatiratanga* (sovereignty)' (1998: 32). The dichotomy importantly revitalised the stalled extension of ITQs by divvying up Māori fisheries interests into capitalist and non-capitalist concerns, commercial and subsistence interests, and private or pseudo-communal property institutions. It also identified appropriate levels of Māori society to engage with each – *iwi* or *hapū* (sub-tribe), a division which had widespread backing. The Waitangi Tribunal, for instance, in a report written for the Minister of Māori Affairs in 1992, explicitly identified *iwi* as the body to which commercial settlements should flow, whereas customary rights, the non-commercial element, were to be allocated to *hapū*. Fundamental to the overall negotiations was the space opened by the creation of the new private property rights (ITQs), which could then be used as an instrument to resolve the claims.

The 1992 Settlement Act, considered as full and final, extinguished Māori claims to fisheries and blocked the development of aboriginal title thereafter. Māori interests became synthesised in the ITQ regime. Tipene O'Regan, chief Māori negotiator at the time, remarked:

> The [ITQ] model provided a forum in which Treaty of Waitangi rights could actually be transferred and given effect to … [T]he concept that there can be private property in fisheries is not a foreign idea to Māori but represents a component of *Rangatiratanga* or chiefly dominion. (1996)

This property equivalency arguably misconstrues the flexibility inherent in traditional ownership rights and an associated bundle of exchanges. Subsistence interests became a separate 'non-economic' domain, primarily concerned with conservation and marked by an arduous application process for permits to supply fish. Permits are granted on the occasion of ceremonial events, limited to *hui* (meetings) and *tangi* (funerals) – regulations which have become noteworthy for making illegal any material exchange. Customary Fisheries Regulations 1998 (discussed in more detail below), while allowing for the gathering of seafood for ceremonial purposes, as noted above, expressly prohibit the exchange, barter or sale of fish. The rendering of Māori *hapū* fishing rights as customary practices, understood in terms of non-commercial, conservational interests, is consistent with an ascription of eco-indigeneity, that is, the partnering of indigenous groups with contemporary environmental concerns. Although these interests may at times coincide, the association is often spurious and fraught with inherent tensions. At its most extreme eco-indigeneity is a primitivising interpretation, based on the supposed inherency of indigenous environmental knowledge and primordial attachment to place. It is a potentially constraining construct that sets up artificially limiting boundaries (Niezen 2002), particularly with regard to traditional resource extraction practices and the ability of indigenous groups to develop economically viable options for their communities.

For island fishermen in Árainn Mhór, Donegal, Ireland, discontent with the European Union (EU)-managed quota system is often articulated as a transgression of a traditional moral universe and an attempt to undermine nationalist ideologies. In more recent times this discourse has been married to an indigenous rights rhetoric which sets out to provide a critique of economic and cultural dispossession as well as providing leverage to envision an alternative future (see chapter 5). While enjoying some successes to date, substantial issues remain unresolved. This situation is likely to become increasingly fraught given the external pressure to designate the seascape surrounding the island a European protected site. Under Natura 2000 seascapes are envisioned as Marine Protected Areas, implying that a conservational ethos trumps indigenous fishing livelihoods.

Fisheries settlement and the iwi cases

Treaty settlement processes are inherently antagonistic. They are an arena in which kin groups compete for a recognition of their identity and alienated property rights, long reshaped by colonial processes, within a legal structure characterised by an unequal distribution of power. The consummation of fisheries claims, the point when negotiations between the Crown and Māori resulted in the identification of compensatory assets and repatriations, is materially represented in the following outcomes. The 1989 interim agreement, which augured the establishment of the Māori Fisheries Commission to which 10 percent of Crown-held fishing quota, shareholdings in fishing companies and NZ$50 million was transferred; the 1992 Settlement Act, which included 50 percent ownership of a major fisheries company, Sealords, 20 percent of all future ITQed species, more shares in fisheries companies and NZ$18 million in cash to enable Māori participation in the 'business of fishing'; and the pledge to develop customary legislation conjointly with Māori.

The fisheries settlement represents the first major treaty negotiation in New Zealand to encompass all Māori, though, like all restitutions under the Treaty of Waitangi, it is underpinned by the stipulation that it will be 'full and final'. The frictions initiated are, however, much more ephemeral, playing out in multiple guises across space and time. The wider grievances initiated by the settlement include the dubious legitimacy of incorporating over 500,000 Māori into an agreement signed by 43; the contested mandate of the 12 Crown-appointed Māori Fisheries Commission members, charged with decision making; the contradictory distributional goals outlined in the 1989 and 1992 Settlement Acts, namely, that while the former specifies that fisheries assets should be centrally held and managed for the benefit of all Māori, the latter favours devolution to tribal bodies; and the questionable morality of privatising a natural resource, a move considered by many to be culturally incommensurable and one that transformed the full breadth of a Māori *taonga* into a commodity to be traded in a capitalist marketplace. The depth of the discontent, which included a 1993 complaint to the United Nations over a settlement christened the 'tin of sardines deal', was displaced onto Māori. It was pursued in a series of legal challenges, including at the British Privy Council, and culminated in a High Court case tasked with resolving internal Māori politicking concerning the correct interpretation of *iwi*, such that the operationalisation of assets could proceed.

Briefly, the timeline of the legal proceedings can be summarised as follows: urban Māori authorities filed a case in the High Court in 1995 aimed at preventing Te Ohu Kai Moana (or TOKM, as the Māori Fisheries Commission was renamed in 1992) from allocating fisheries assets exclusively to *iwi*. The High Court avoided making a decision and turned the case over to the Court of Appeal. The Court of Appeal in 1996, under the authority of Robin Cooke of Thorndon, entered a radical decision. Cooke decreed that the original Deed of Settlement was not for the benefit of selected groups of tribal Māori, rather that it was pan-Māori in nature. His decision revolved around a meaning of *iwi* interpreted as 'the Queen's subjects already living on the land and others yet to come' (Lashley 2000: 41), thereby identifying *iwi* as a nation of people, not as a tribe. He considered the concept of *hapū* to be the correct Māori equivalent of both tribe and sub-tribe. Thus, the fisheries settlement should be for the benefit of all Māori, including urban Māori, even those without a coastline. This decision gave support to the idea that urban Māori groups, with no necessary inter-genealogical connections, could assume the status of *iwi*. The case was then taken to the Privy Council in London. In 1997 the Privy Council overturned the decision of the Court of Appeal on legal grounds, stating that its description of *iwi* was outside the bounds of the appeal it had considered. The case was referred back to the New Zealand High Court in 1998, where the judge was directed by the Privy Council to consider specific questions. These related to whether the distribution of fisheries assets should go exclusively to *iwi* and/or bodies representing *iwi* and, if so, whether *iwi* meant only a traditionally conceived Māori tribe (van Meijl 2006).

Although specifically concerned with establishing whether 'iwi' could encompass urban formations, based on residency and mutual support rather than genealogical connectedness and generational identification with land, much broader historical frictions underlay the proceedings. These included: the relative significance of Article 2 and/or Article 3 of the Treaty of Waitangi in the distribution of repatriated assets; the relationship of indigenous kin structures to colonial and postcolonial governance, and the nature of the entity created to manage devolved welfare policies and post-settlement assets.

In the 1840 Treaty of Waitangi, Article 2[4] speaks to property rights:

> Her Majesty the Queen of England confirms and guarantees to the Chiefs and Tribes of New Zealand and to the respective families and individuals thereof the full exclusive and undisturbed possession of their Lands and Estates, Forests, Fisheries and other properties which they may collectively or individually possess so long as it is their wish and desire to retain the same in their possession ...

Crown restitution through indigenous settlements thus implies the return of ill-gotten colonial property to tribes as they were conceived in the 19th century. Article 3 has relevance for contemporary ethnic inequalities and the Crown's ongoing role in administering social justice: 'Her Majesty the Queen of England extends to the Natives of New Zealand Her royal protection and imparts to them all the Rights and Privileges of British Subjects.'

The ethnic profile of contemporary Māori society is ambiguous, containing opposing tendencies of urban detribalisation and ethnic re-identification at the same time as a political reconstitution of tribes on a national level (van Meijl 2006). Some statistics will help clarify this point. In the 2013 national census, 14.9 percent of the total New Zealand population identified as Māori, a figure that had increased by 5.9 percent from 2006, and 40 percent from 1991. This figure refers to ethnic identification (either solely Māori or part Māori, that is, of mixed ethnic background) and is one of the two ways in which Māori are enumerated in national statistics. The other method used is to count the number of Māori through descent, that is, whether a person is a descendant of an *iwi* group. In 2013, 17.5 percent of the total New Zealand population were of Māori descent (so defined), a 3.8 percent increase from 2006, and an approximately 30 percent increase from 1991. In total numbers 598,605 identified with the Māori ethnic group and 668,724 identified themselves as of Māori descent. Of those claiming Māori descent, however, 16.6 percent did not know or chose not to identify the *iwi(s)* from which they were descended, and 66.6 percent of this group lived in urban centres.

Māori configure kinship ambilineally and organise by ambilateral affiliation. This flexibility is also apparent in the permeability between *whānau* (extended family), *hapū* (sub-tribe and tribe) and *iwi* (tribe) formations, and in the complication of achievement as a principle affecting that of primogeniture (usually, although not necessarily, male) in leadership. Van Meijl points out that, as a corollary of this openness, Māori have the option of changing their social position, either by affiliating to another kinship line or by improving their ranking within the political structure (2006: 186). These possibilities, while autochthonously embedded, have since colonisation both widened and become more constrictive. The restriction is tied up with the ebb and flow of 'iwi' organisations and their more recent articulation with neoliberal capital.

Since colonisation, *iwi* as social structures have followed a decidedly institutional trajectory. *Iwi* is the level of Māori society with which the Crown prefers to engage and through which the devolution of social welfare functions, participation in treaty settlement negotiations and the receipt of assets has been channelled. Superimposed on these kinship structures is the institution of *runanga* (tribal councils). As state-endorsed legal structures, *runanga* serve as a conduit for state-derived funding and services and, for administrative purposes, may be recognised as non-governmental organisations (NGOs). *Runanga* gained prominence with the Runanga Iwi Act in 1989, an outcome of the neoliberal reorganisation of society and the devolution of the central Department of Māori

Affairs to *iwi* authorities or tribal organisations. There is a certain irony in this elevation of tribal organisations. It occurred simultaneously with the increasingly pan-tribal nature of Māori society, a result at least partially of urbanisation since, especially, the 1950s. The Act essentialised *iwi* as having a set of identifiable sociological characteristics. These are listed below, with the assumptions inherent in the criteria explicated in the brackets:

1. descent from *tupuna* (ancestor, and the ability to trace this genealogically through *whakapapa*);
2. *hapū* (understood as sub-tribes subordinated to *iwi*);
3. *marae* (ceremonial meeting house complex associated with each *hapū*);
4. belonging historically to a *takiwā* (territory, bounded by *rohe* which neatly divide each *hapū* and which, when consolidated, define an *iwi*'s total territory);
5. an existence traditionally acknowledged by other *iwi* (the emphasis here is placed on intra-ethnic other-ascription).

The role and practices of *runanga* supposedly mimic the hierarchical and traditionally sanctioned relationship between *iwi* and *hapū*, however this is a contentious reconstruction. Ballara (1998), for instance, methodically documents the existence of politically independent *hapū* descent groups in the 18th century to whom *iwi* represented a wider conceptual grouping whose identity derived from a common ancestry. The subjugation of *hapū* to *iwi* was a pragmatic response to the need for an alternative, more centrally organised political structure through which to confront the contingencies of colonialism. This understanding of the historic centrality of *hapū* is largely uncontested by scholars of Māori society. It is also indisputable that *hapū* identities remain central to contemporary Māori society (Sissons 2010; Webster 1998). The merging of *runanga* and *iwi* concerns exacerbates existing kinship tensions. These often express themselves as an opposition between tribe (*iwi/runanga*) and *hapū* interests, where tribe (*iwi/runanga*) represents corporate, capitalist-oriented enterprise norms and disengagement, and *hapū* the lived experience of tribal members. Although the Runanga Iwi Act was repealed shortly after enactment following Māori protest, it left a lasting legacy of a strong centralised structure of tribal organisations (van Meijl 2006). Muru-Lanning (2011) points out that this restructuring has enabled ongoing state evaluations: *iwi* are required to compile membership lists and asset registers, conduct audits and produce reports on various tribal activities. The Runanga Iwi Act legacy is also apparent in mandated *iwi* organisations, the entities designed to manage fisheries settlement assets at a tribal level, and which recreate tribal *runanga* in a hyper-capitalist form.

Iwi, thus, are not the established traditional entities they are often presumed to be (Webster 2002) and their number has increased and decreased throughout colonial history (Ballara 1998). The more recent increases in those registering as descended from *iwi* is likely to be related to the promise of benefits deriving from the amplification of the role given to *iwi* in government policies as well as their centrality in managing settlement assets. Yet this tendency is counterbalanced by an increase in ethnicity, that is, a pan-tribal identification, and the percentage of those who cannot, or will not, acknowledge an ancestral *iwi*. The ambiguity underlying these trends, including that almost two-thirds of the latter groups live in urban centres, played out spectacularly in the *iwi* court cases.

The 1998 High Court case included at least nine diverse Māori organisations which coalesced around three distinguishable interest groups. The first was comprised of the urban groups, including representative organisations from New Zealand's major cities – Auckland, Wellington and Christchurch – whose primary argument was that *iwi* should be defined in the broad sense to mean people. Thus, the fisheries benefits ought to be distributed to all Māori in line with Article 3 of the Treaty and in recognition of the fact that 80 percent (now 84 percent) of Māori live in urban centres and do not necessarily engage with ancestral *iwi*. Crucial to this argument was the ITQ remodelling of the productive value of traditional fisheries as an abstract and exchangeable private property right. Indeed, the leader of Auckland's Te *Whānau* o Waipareira Trust had made it known that, 'The last thing urban Māori want to do is go fishing …' (*New Zealand News* 1996: 2525). The second and third groups included TOKM and a consortium of *iwi* associations. The groups differed, based on whether they favoured a distribution that emphasised tribal population or length of coastline. The common interpretation of *iwi* as tribe, what Webster (2002) terms the 'fundamentalist' stance, became a unifying factor. The primary contention, in line with Article 2 of the Treaty, was that the settlement was a restitution of alienated property and thus should be returned to the tribal bodies from which it was appropriated. Implicit in this contention is the entitlement to regain fishing rights, productively conceived.

TOKM revitalised the Runanga Iwi Act's criteria for identifying an *iwi* (listed above) in defence of their position. A list described as 'laconic' by

Webster (2002) and naïve by Metge (in Webster 2002). This time, however, the definition was not being unilaterally imposed by government but was the work of a group of Māori leaders commissioned by the government in the aftermath of the fisheries settlement. It is not coincidental that the definition of *iwi* utilised by TOKM has a strong anthropological flavour. It was influenced by the commentaries of Raymond Firth in the 1920s, whose own work was strongly swayed by the ethnographic descriptions collected by the salvage anthropologist, Elsden Best, at the end of the 19th century (van Meijl 2006). Further, many of the expert Māori witnesses called to outline their interpretation of the meaning of *iwi* had been trained in anthropology. Indeed, an observer commented that the case was in effect a gathering of Māori anthropologists (Pihama 1998). The endorsement given to this construct of *iwi*, in combination with the promise of capital benefits, instigated a scramble to identify such entities. Whereas in early 1998 there were about 55 named *iwi*, by later that year TOKM had acknowledged 78 (TOKM 1998). It also provoked a move, among some *iwi* organisations, to assert their influence over non-compliant *hapū* groups,[5] thereby redefining the structure of Māori authority and overriding historic rivalries between tribal segments (Webster 2002).

While the 1996 Appeal Court decision tended in favour of urban Māori, a ruling overturned in 1997 by the Privy Council, the 1998 High Court decision strengthened the position of the 'fundamentalist' camp. It decreed that Māori fisheries assets could only be allocated to *iwi*, traditionally conceived, or bodies representing such *iwi*. The final model for distribution, announced in 2003 by TOKM, after lengthy deliberations, was that inshore quota be allocated to *iwi* using a coastline formula, while all deep-sea quota be allocated through a formula that awarded 75 percent on the basis of *iwi* population and the remaining 25 percent on a formula based on the length of *iwi* coastline.

The interpretation of *iwi* on which the 'fundamentalist' arguments and the final decision were based was a curious amalgamation of early accounts of evolutionary anthropologists, the structural elevation of *iwi* groups in the neoliberal reorganisation and Māori epistemological accounts. Māori actively engage in ontological discussions about their culture, values and traditions, the contours of which are understood to change but also to remain the same over time. A real problem arises when key concepts become codified, are rendered static in law and then, when activated in society, constricted by broader political-economic ideologies. The evidence given by Māori witnesses in the 1998 High Court case, extracts from which are provided below, highlight the depth and complexity of Māori thinking on the question of 'What is an *iwi*?'

The origins [of *iwi*] are shared with other Polynesian Peoples of the Pacific World spreading from Easter Island to New Zealand, it means bones, it is a *koiwi Iwi*, the skeletal remains. It has spread to meaning people who have those bones and on to all people who have bones so it spreads from not only the individual but to every human being as part of the people of the world. I am proud to belong to Ngaphui Iwi [major North Island *iwi*] but also proud to belong to Te Mahurehure [urban-based *hapū*] and also *Te Iwi* Māori [the ethnic Māori population], I see no contradictions in having all defined by the term *iwi*. Referring to allocating the assets to *iwi* – I have gone back over the Deed of Settlement and it is quite clear that the assets go to all Māori so all *iwi* ... we are descended from the gods. (Pat Hopeha: Māori Studies, University of Auckland, Ngapuhi *iwi*)

Hoani Waititi whanau, and make no bones about it they are a *whānau* in every sense of the word and Waipareira [west Auckland urban Māori group] have Māori people who have settled in Auckland, some have retained strong links with home and *hapū* and some of us not knowing too much about those links, but all coming to live in west Auckland, we saw the need to cater for our cultural requirements, such as to mourn our dead, to plan to educate and to carry out our normal cultural life, hence we built a *marae*. We did it by going first to Ngati Whatua [major Auckland *iwi*] to ask for permission, then to *Whānau A Apanui* [East Cape iwi] for the name of Hoani Waititi and then by working together as a community to establish the necessary physical facilities. By the time we had completed this exercise we already had in place the spiritual and cultural aspects of being a *whanau, iwi, rōpū* [cultural group], whatever you want to call it. Now we feel an *iwi* or *hapū* in every sense of the sociological and spiritual and cultural description, even although we may not share a common ancestor linking the *waka* [canoe/founding ancestral canoe] together. (Pita Sharples: anthropologist, politician, founder of Hoani Waititi urban *marae*)

for us as Ngati Porou people no matter where we go, where we live outside the regions, we still have with us our Ngati Porou blood. I will not speak for other people ... but for me, for Ngati Porou, *iwi* means connected to an ancestor. (Apirana Mahuika: tribal leader of Ngati Porou, large East Cape Iwi) [referring to the term 'original' as way to describe which kin group had the right to receive settlement assets] That's an interesting term [original]. Can you tell me what you mean by original right? I don't understand what an original right is? ... There is only one thing I understand, all the rights that come to us as Māori, in the beginning it came from the great void, to Io Matua kore, through the times of night down to the times of Rangi and Papa, that is my understanding of the rights of Māori from way back. It began from that time. (Rima Edwards: Muriwhenua leader who mortgaged his home to fight the introduction of the ITQ system)

I am here today for the Tainui *hapū* of the Tainui tribes of the Waikato area, and our *tipuna* [ancestors] when they talked about Tainui talked about Tainui as being sourced from a common ancestor sharing a common boundary with Ngati Tahinga which stretches from the Waikato River down to south of the Kariori Mountain. Under that Tanui there are eleven *hapū*, or lesser *hapū*, but they shared the common land with no boundaries, as they shared the fishing grounds ... The words I've heard of Tainui here is what is commonly seen out there by people in the media, Tainui said this or that, that Tainui is the Tainui Māori Trust Board [that is, a different entity than that which she is representing], and we talk about *iwi*, who are they? [the Tainui Māori Trust Board, referring also to the associated Waikato-Tainui Iwi who received a major treaty settlement in 1995]. I know we are Tainui, we are *hapū*, *waka*. There is Tainui corporation and so forth [associated with Waikato-Tainui]. So what I am saying is, I'm here for Tainui *hapū* and Tainui people of the coastal area [that is, as Tainui *hapū* and coastal peoples we should receive the settlement benefits]. (Angeline Greensill: geographer, Tainui)

There are some permissible [interpretations of *iwi*] and some stretching imagination a bit I would think. Over emphasising the meaning of peoples is doing just that to me, taking the word *iwi* out to the margins and in many ways trivialising the word *iwi* as understood by most Māori people and I have some difficulties with that because I think its Māori people who should be making those decisions. We shouldn't really be here [in a *pakeha* court] arguing these matters. (Hirini Mead: professor of Māori Studies, anthropologist, and of Ngati Awa, Ngāti Tūwharetoa, Ngāi Tūhoe and Tūhourangi descent)

Disciplining dissent

Two reports published in 1985 and 1986 by the then Ministry of Agriculture and Fisheries (Fairgray 1985, 1986), a report commissioned by the Māori Economic Development Commission in 1985 (Habib 1985) and the Law Commission's review in 1989, predict in explicit detail the devastation that would be visited on Northland Māori as a result of the implementation of the ITQ system. Following the introductory 1983 Act the number of fishermen excluded in Northland was approximately 50 percent (see chapter 2). A large number of those excluded from both vessel and shore fishing were Māori, for whom fishing had been part of a mixed economy and a means of fulfilling subsistence, ceremonial and financial needs. At the time of implementation the annual per capita income over all sectors of Northland fishing towns was approximately NZ$11,000 (Fairgray 1985), slightly below the national average. By 1996 incomes had slipped to 15.9 percent below the national average (Martin 2000). Many fishermen living in small coastal communities were adversely affected and, in some cases, all catching for sale had to cease (Law Commission 1989). The effects did not stop there. Prior to the introduction of ITQs, the livelihoods of many people in coastal communities were directly or indirectly related to fishing and few alternative employment opportunities were available.

Writ large, the *koha* (gift exchange) cases, instigated by a group of Northland Māori fishermen, under the umbrella of the sovereignty protest movement, the Confederation of Māori Tribes of Aotearoa (the confederation), were an attempt to challenge the exclusions set in place by the ITQ system. The objective was to assert Māori livelihood and proprietary rights over an ancestral resource notwithstanding and irrespective of the existence of a settlement purportedly designed to address these very interests. The QMS, once imposed, progressively works to delegitimise practices that cannot be comprehended by the new regime. Paradoxically, the prohibitions bear most heavily on those practices that mimic the logic of market exchange.

Customary fishing and the koha cases

The Kaimoana Customary Fishing Regulations 1998 describe customary food gathering as:

> The traditional rights confirmed by the Treaty of Waitangi and the Treaty of Waitangi (Fisheries Claims) Settlement Act 1992, being the taking

of fish, aquatic life, or seaweed or managing of fisheries resources, for a purpose authorised by Tangata Kaitiaki/Tiaki, including koha, to the extent that such purpose is consistent with Tikanga Māori and is neither commercial in any way nor for any pecuniary gain.

The process by which the term '*koha*' was included in the description is intimately bound up with court cases during which Māori fishermen argued, first, for an expansive interpretation of customary rights and, second, asserted that the concept of *koha*, understood as gifting, incorporates the exchange of material items, including cash, a definition progressively rebutted by the Crown. These cases took place predominantly between the years 1992 and 1999 when Māori and Crown representatives were simultaneously locked in heated negotiations, in an era defined by ambiguities and one in which the rigid division of commercial and customary fisheries initiated by the settlement process was as yet incomplete. The negotiations were mandated to finalise an agreed upon set of customary regulations.

During this period there was a certain amount of flexibility at the legal level in the interpretation of customary fishing. A legislative 'void' existed, enabling an aboriginal or customary title argument to be used as a defence. The existent legislation (regulation 27 of the Fisheries [Amateur Fisheries] Regulations 1986), which exempted Māori who were catching fish for *hui* or *tangi* from full compliance with daily allowances and bag limits, provided they had a permit issued by a *runanga* or similar body, was variously, and sometimes progressively, interpreted in courts.

Around the end of March 1997, the last day of the scallop fishing season, John Hikuwai, a northern Māori fisherman from a Muriwhenua fishing *whānau* and a member of the confederation, was apprehended by fisheries officers with 1,200 kg of scallops on board his vessel. He had already landed 600 kg at a local wharf, the amount his daily fishing permit allowed. At issue, thus, was the fate of the on-board catch, which on a registered fishing vessel is 'deemed to be taken for purposes of sale'. John explained that while fishing he had received a cell phone call asking him to collect *kaimoana* for two upcoming ceremonies, a *tangi* and an unveiling,[6] and that the on-board scallop were harvested to meet those requests. The fact that he did not have a *runanga*-issued permit became the pivotal theme in a case brought before a District Court in September of that year.[7] In the hearing John argued passionately for recognition of Māori aboriginal rights, the contextual relevance of a fisherman's knowledge in relation to a land-dweller's and referenced the inequities arising from the absence of livelihood opportunities resulting from the fisheries settlement. He argued, for instance: that his *mana* (prestige/power) and *whakapapa* (genealogy) gave him the right to decide where to take fish under customary rights; that as an experienced Muriwhenua fisherman and as a descendant of a fishing family, he had the responsibility to provide seafood for his local community; that the control and usage of customary resources rested with the harvester, and that, like many Māori, he did not recognise the government established mandate of *runanga* as no actual custom existed which gave them the authority to issue permits. Further, he reasoned that the future implementation of customary regulations would remove the *mana* and traditional authority from fishermen and, as attested to by his lawyer, the negotiations surrounding the 1992 fisheries settlement included the assertion by Māori that 'they would need to access their commercial fishing resources at times for customary purposes outside of the quota system'.

In his decision the presiding judge referred to the 'legislative void', accepted that regulation 27 was differently interpreted by 'local Māori in tribal areas', that 'rules differed from area to area and were objected to by some on the grounds of custom'. Although decreeing that certain actions of the defendant 'raised suspicion', on balancing the probabilities, Hikuwai did not, he felt, 'intend to commit the offence'. Dover Samuels, the Labour Māori Affairs spokesman at the time, also of Muriwhenua descent, condemned the decision. He accused the judge of 'cultural naivety', stating that 'Pakeha judges were too scared to punish Māori fishers who abuse customary fishing rights' (*The Press* 1997).

Later that year a fisherman from the east coast of the North Island argued in court for his entitlement to take and distribute seafood in accordance with Māori custom. He had set up a table in a flea market for the sale of *kina* (sea urchin) and *kahawai* (*Arripis trutta*) in pottles, labelled with the words 'Koha Nga Hinerupe' rather than a price tag. Hinerupe was the name of a *marae* for which he was raising rebuilding funds. A Māori witness in the case described *koha* as being similar to a European barter system. The judge disagreed and convicted the fisherman, reasoning that:

The activity was clearly in the commercial arena. He was seeking money for the fish in a public setting in a public market. There is no legislative basis for Mr Reedy's claim to be entitled to sell fish under a customary fishing right ... This ability for Maori to exercise a customary fishing right to obtain money for fish even where this may be for fundraising purposes, has been closed by the 1992 Settlement Act ...[8]

In July 1998, another member of the confederation, Eru Manukau, was also unsuccessful when he invoked aboriginal rights in his case against the Ministry of Fisheries.[9] In court Eru, representing confederation members, claimed damages totalling NZ$2.4 million, including NZ$1.25 million for injury to *mana*, deep embarrassment and loss of dignity for actions taken by the Ministry of Fisheries in curtailing the confederation's fishing system. Two years previously the ministry had instigated an investigation, resulting in the seizure of documents and the confiscation of a truck and a fishing boat. In court Eru questioned the legitimacy of these actions and argued that the confederation derived their fishing rights directly from Article 2 of the Treaty of Waitangi and for this reason any subsequent legislation was irrelevant.

The confederation had set up an alternative market based on exchanging fish through *marae*, the meeting house complexes associated with *hapū*. They issued certificates to register fishing vessels, and by 1998 six were registered to the confederation. They had also issued fishing permits to fishers and licences to fish receivers – 'Māori Licensed Cooperatives fish receivers' – so that fishers could sell their catch to the receivers who would then resell through *marae*. The system was set up so that a percentage accrued to the *marae*, a percentage to the fisher and a percentage to the confederation. Fish were typically purchased from fishermen for NZ$4 per kilo, though different species attracted different amounts, and were sold from *marae* for around NZ$8 per kilo, significantly cheaper than in the formal economy. The confederation named the scheme the 'Marae-based *koha* system'. In many ways the exchange system the confederation had established had simply brought into the open the 'black market' regime that had prevailed up to this point, and argued for the legitimacy of this arrangement on the basis of cultural rights and indigenous livelihoods. A confederation member explained: 'Up north, my cousins go out and get fish with the blessing of the local *kaumātua* (elders) ... soon my cousins could make their living with some dignity instead of having to sneak around at night selling their fish on Auckland's black market so they could survive.' John Hikuwai commented 'some of my relations are saying, "why don't you do it in the dark and run up the beach with it?" Well, that's being a criminal and if we did that nothing would change for our children. It's time to come out in the open.'

Eru claimed in court that the operation was a non-profit one, that some of the fish were given away, and that both the payment of NZ$4 per kg to fishermen and the money received by *marae* from selling the produce, was a *koha* or gift. The judge rejected this, disagreed with the findings in the 1997 Hikuwai case and refused to accept the suggestion that fishing rights were derived from Article 2 of the Treaty as this had been replaced by the full and final 1992 settlement. The judge contended that the '*koha* system', under which the fish was distributed, was a commercial operation; that the evidence showed a payment to fishermen for fish produced (NZ$4/kg), the issuing of invoices, and a price list for different species, all of which clearly identified a commercial enterprise. Crucially, the judge argued, that the existence of a set of arrangements indicating a certain sum of money per kilogram of fish was inconsistent with the definition of koha *as a present or gift*. Over the following years this interpretation became increasingly concretised.

In December 1997 John Hikuwai landed about 7 tonnes of snapper from his boat, the *James O'Brien*, at Whangaroa harbour. Most of the fish had been caught by another fishing vessel in excess of its quota allowance and was passed to John. At the time he held a fishing permit issued by the confederation and his vessel was registered to the confederation. The snapper were unloaded by a Māori Licensed Cooperatives fish receiver, Toby's Seafood, and distributed to approximately 40 *marae* from Auckland to the far north and were destined to be consumed during Christmas and New Year celebrations. Some of the fish, which were no longer fresh, were sold to a bi-products company. In January 1998 the Ministry of Fisheries seized the *James O'Brien* in an action that Hikuwai described as 'piracy and high treason'. The following day the government announced interim rules to 'crack down' on customary fisheries. Consequently, regulation 27 was changed to stipulate that fish could not be caught 'where the taking is commercial in any way or is for pecuniary gain or trade'.

In 1999 John Hikuwai faced two charges in the Auckland District Court under the Fisheries Act 1983.[10] The use of this Act, as opposed to regulation 27 of the amateur regulations, where a defence of customary usage and the koha argument might feasibly have been accepted, permitted no interpretation other than that the *marae* snapper distribution was a crime against the QMS. Hikuwai was charged with being an unauthorised person in possession of fish, namely snapper, taken in New Zealand waters for the purposes of sale. In his defence he advanced a critique of the legislation governing customary fishing, and pointed out that *koha*, in some instances, involved a legally sanctioned exchange of money: 'just very recently I attended a two day *hui* at Otara at Ngati Otara *marae* ... and I saw numerous envelopes passed across to the *kaumātua* that held cash that came in for *koha*'. The judge, in convicting Hikuwai, described the confederation's fishing activities in para-legal terms:

> it is apparent from his [Hikuwai's] evidence and the evidence of various Fisheries Officers that the Confederation of United Tribes of Aotearoa was an organization outside both the provision for amateur fishing ... and the regime set out in the Settlement Act 1992 ... the Confederation of the United Tribes of Aotearoa has taken upon itself the operation of a fishing regime outside the Fisheries Act, the Settlement Act and the various regulations ... The Confederation [and Mr Hikuwai] were clearly involved in the setting up of a separate system outside the laws enacted by the New Zealand Parliament. In doing so they were setting up a system which relied as much on the exchange of goods for monies worth as much as does the fishing regime controlled by legislation.

She also set out her deliberations on the meaning of *koha*:

> It appears to this Court that the word *koha* has a number of meanings attributed to it ranging from an unsolicited gift given from the heart to an exchange for money ... It would be inappropriate for this Court to endeavour to define or redefine the word *koha*. What is important is the nature of the transaction and whether or not it falls within the definition of sale set out in the relevant legislation. The fact that the expression *koha* may be used for the transaction does not itself invest that transaction with some form of magic which exempts it from the legislation. From the evidence, there was to be an exchange for money or monies worth in at least some of the situations, to pay for the running of the boat and the wages. This clearly fell within the definition of sale.

The confederation, having achieved a level of notoriety, declared its ongoing commitment to gathering seafood under a customary entitlement without commercial fishing quota and to continue to distribute this to *marae* as *koha*. Media coverage exploded. As was the case a few years later when Māori questioned the Crown-presumed ownership of the foreshore and seabed, the snapper case was portrayed as instigating a racial divide. In this depiction one section of New Zealand society, that is Māori, were 'abusing liberal cultural rights to secure economic gains at the expense of non-Māori'. Treaty settlements are often interpreted as unfairly rewarding Māori 'culture'. The confederation was accused of jeopardising 'sustainability and conservation' and of 'plundering fish resources'.[11] *Pakeha* fishermen were particularly incensed and warned, in print, of a backlash.[12] Some Māori Members of Parliament were equally vocal, questioning the mandate of the confederation and pointing to the illegality of its fishing operation. Strong support for the confederation was voiced by others, including the Māori Council and Northland *kaumātua*, one of whom declared 'the only mandate there is is that one sees the *whānau* is hungry and wants the food, then they go and get it'.[13] Five major northern *iwi* groups, in a letter to the Minister of Fisheries questioning the reduction of customary fisheries to tribal *hui*, wrote: 'we strongly advocate that all Māori within their *rohe* have customary rights to gather for their own use'.[14] The Minister of Fisheries, however, termed the snapper case an abuse of customary rights and promised that regulations would shortly be in place, with or without Māori agreement.[15] The Māori–Crown joint working group developing the customary regulations had broken down at the end of 1997. Margaret Mutu, a Māori member of the consortium, believes that the John Hikuwai case provided a convenient smoke screen, that many other Māori fishermen throughout the country were carrying out similar, though less transparent, operations and could equally have been scapegoated. The Hikuwai case, Mutu told me, cloaked the intended introduction of much contested, government-defined Customary Fisheries Regulations.

In another confederation case in 1998,[16] the court was again confronted with *koha* fishing and a challenge to the reduction of customary fishing to discrete practices. It was claimed by the defendant, John Ututaonga, that 'a customary right is not just for a *hui*, it's for survival everyday.' John and a friend had parked a trailer packed with ice buckets and fish in bins at a Northland *marae* with an advertisement on the side announcing 'koha priced fish'. At issue in court was whether or not the fish was sold, that is, whether the sale under a *koha* system fell within the definition of 'sale'. The judge reasoned that it did if any benefit was received and that 'sale' could also cover bartering arrangements or the exchange of goods such as vegetables or fruit for fish: 'thus you can say that the *koha* system as I understand it operating on the day 20 January fell within that very method of disposition for valuable consideration, the valuable consideration being that Mr Ututaonga would be reimbursed for his petrol money.' He went on to state:

> a *koha* in the sense of the word for a gift taken from the Williams Maori Dictionary [1st edition published in 1844] does not involve money. It seems that things may have developed since the time that the Reverend Williams wrote his dictionary, in that *koha* has taken upon meaning other than a mere gift. Although it is not entirely clear, it is not for me to say how Māori people define concepts and terms which they use.

Yet the judge, through his decision, went on to interpret *koha* as a gift requiring no reciprocation, not even for *kumara* (sweet potato) or oranges.

The crucial issue in these cases is not the amount of fish caught, nor whether the fishing was unsustainable, but whether the *koha* fishing challenged the legitimacy of the QMS to incorporate all market transactions in fisheries. In an interview the then Minister of Fisheries stated that if, for instance, Hikuwai's snapper had been distributed to *tangi* without any money being exchanged, this would have been acceptable. 'All rights to take fish under the guise of customary take have been extinguished for commercial use, for pecuniary gain or trade. That is in the 1992 Act ... and that's part of the law of the country.'[17] He defined *koha* as a 'one-way transfer'.[18] Paradoxically, the restrictive definition of *koha* applied in fisheries determinations is not replicated in other government departments. A 1998 pamphlet issued by the Inland Revenue department, titled 'Payments and Gifts in the Māori Community', describes situations where *koha* is taxable and where it is not. The former includes where 'it is a payment for services' and the latter, where 'it is an unconditional gift [and] ...gives no direct benefit to the givers' (Inland Revenue 1998). In both situations *koha* may involve the exchange of money.

Property struggles: coastal communities and commoditisation

Property is a nexus of struggles reflected at all levels of social organisation. Recent anthropological attempts to reconceptualise property have provided a nuanced picture of the complexities and contradictions involved in ownership and exchange that challenge the grand paradigms of private/communal and market/moral (see Hann 1998; Humphrey and Verdery 2004; Strathern and Hirsch 2004). Helgason and Pálsson (1997) suggest that, in terms of economic life, a crucial characteristic of all exchange is the resultant movement of things between individuals and groups. Further, that a moral environment, constituted and sustained by members of the same group, both signals and constricts this movement. The advantage of this perspective is that it moves beyond the dualism of gift and commodity exchange, embedded and disembedded economies and, I suggest, individual and common property. Property is seen as fluid and multifunctional, encompassing cultural, political, legal and economic dimensions (von Benda Beckman et al. 2006). This expanded understanding helps to explicate ongoing global economic transformations in which property becomes a site of social struggle, acting, for example, as a potential brokering tool in indigenous claims forums.

In Iceland, the ITQ propertisation of fish (initiated in 1984 and cemented into place in 1990) is at variance with the constitutional vesting of Icelandic fish stock in the common ownership of the Icelandic people, a contradiction Icelandic fishermen, like Māori, brought to the attention of lawmakers through deliberate acts of contravention. Níels Einarsson describes one such incident:

> In September 2001, the fishing vessel Sveinn Sveinsson from the Icelandic West fjord coastal village of Patreksfjörður sailed several times to fishing grounds to catch fish. What was unusual about these trips was that the owners and crew of the boat were publicly defying a fisheries management system that they saw as immoral and unjust, and which in their opinion denied them the right by birth to harvest local resources that were indeed defined as common property of the Icelandic nation. However, they were soon stopped in their fishing activities, their boat and catch confiscated, and the two men brought before the courts. There they were sentenced and found guilty of breaking the laws of the Icelandic Fisheries Management Act (FMA) of 1990, the same law they referred to in order to justify their actions ... They were acting on the culturally and historically ingrained assumption among Icelanders that the fisheries could not belong to anyone as individual property and that their actions thus were ethically justifiable and in defence of equal rights to access the commons. (2011: 111)

The fishermen, Erlingur Sveinn Haraldsson and Örn Snævar Sveinsson, labelled the 1990 Act as unethical, and argued that it undermined their own livelihoods and the social economic viability of communities around

Iceland. They were convicted in 2002, fined 1 million Icelandic krona each, or three months in prison, and required to pay the costs of the trial; a decision, which was upheld by the Supreme Court. This resulted in desperate financial consequences for the men and their families, including bankruptcy and the loss of their boats. The fishermen, however, continued their case extra-locally through the United Nations Human Rights Committee, claiming to be victims of a violation of Article 26 of the International Covenant on Civil and Political Rights (Einarsson 2011: 111–13).

In 2008 the Human Rights Committee came to the conclusion, though there were dissenters, that the Icelandic state had indeed violated the human rights of the fishermen and that the two men were victims of discrimination. Such rulings, while not legally binding, nevertheless may carry moral weight. While there was much local dissension, the perception was that the decision by the Human Rights Committee – the first substantive challenge given to Iceland, a Western democracy – had ethical weight. This ethical consideration was further bolstered by the Icelandic financial collapse in the same year and the connection made, by many commentators, between this traumatic social and political event and the financialisation of quota (see chapter 3). Indeed, the coalition government formed by the Social Democratic Alliance and Left-Green Movement that came to power in April 2009 campaigned on the need for fundamental change in the governance of Icelandic fisheries (Einarsson 2011: 114–15). That this electoral promise has remained largely unfulfilled will be discussed in chapter 3.

Helgason and Pálsson (1997: 455) liken the Icelandic ITQ system to a process of commoditisation whereby fish have become 'fictitious commodities'. This recreation of what were formerly common goods, a disembedding in Polanyian terms, evokes a local discourse loaded with feudal descriptors of quota owners as having lordships over the sea, or being sealords, whose fief is the sea and whose tenants are fishermen. This counter-response draws heavily on a moral economy in which boat owners are labelled as immoral profiteers. It is the profit-oriented monetary exchange characteristic of ITQs that is particularly condemned. The process of commoditisation, the authors argue, the movement of social things to a more central position, seems to engender particular discontent when commodities are fictitious, when they have been removed from a radically different construct of ownership.

In Ireland, as noted, the discourse of morality and tradition is employed to counter the quota system and there has been a recent mobilisation of indigeneity as a means to confront enclosures. Fishermen are similarly involved in subterfuge, fishing 'illegally' in order to highlight the inequities of fisheries policies. Property struggles are commonly expressed in terms of class and nationalist ideologies. In Ireland, for instance, the inshore sector (boats less than 12 meters fishing within 6 nautical miles [nm] of the shore) which comprises 80 percent of the Irish fleet, is pitted against the large-scale sector as poverty is to wealth: 'there is a quota for the rich and a quota for the poor', is a way a fisherman from Árainn Mhór island expressed it. The Scottish, Spanish and French fleets are thought to over-fish in what are perceived to be Irish waters, and 'control by Europe' of fisheries is identified as a threat to Irish sovereignty: 'Michael Collins[19] must be turning in his grave at what we have done to an independent Ireland', the same fisherman commented.

Conclusion

In Māori fisheries, ITQs and the bundle of rights encoded in customary regulations evidently represent the opposite poles in the private versus communal property spectrum. Legally, they serve different ends: ITQs are created to underwrite a commercial enterprise and customary regulations are put in place to maintain a traditional sociocultural system. However, a restricted model of property rights and relations is present in the constitution of both systems. Ideologically, these arrangements suggest an essentialist representation of private and common property, market and moral exchange, a binary much endorsed by policy makers and legislators. Thus, Māori commercial fisheries conceived of as 'non-customary', and customary fisheries identified as 'non-commercial', are reflections of this dichotomy. This crude opposition, however, is not easy to maintain in practice, as people do not operate in multiple divorced worlds discretely compartmentalised as 'economics' and 'culture', 'public' and 'private', 'individual' and 'communal', and so on. A lived reality, crystallised in the *marae*-based *koha* fishing ventures, still operates. Māori 'non-commercial' fishers continue to harvest fish, to distribute catch to family and community members, to exchange fish for other 'things', including cash, and to draw on customary rights in their defence. Alternatively, Māori 'commercial' fishers at times fish for customary occasions. Yet while these local and diverse systems of ownership and exchange undoubtedly exist it is important to remember that they do so in the shadow of the constraints inherent in exogenously conceived dominant structures and institutions (legal systems, markets, property tenure regimes, political systems and so on).

The contradictions that inhere in ITQs and Customary Fisheries Regulations can be usefully understood within a global framework of indigenous claims to reparation for resource alienation, destruction or depletion, where the authority for such calls arises from a conception of indigenous as the premise for a special sort of claim. At this point, myriad and competing conceptions of value enter the equation, both between the claimants and the dominant group and within the indigenous group itself. An example is provided by the differing perceptions of value attached to ITQs that are articulated by the Māori settlement negotiators in 1992 and the *koha* fishing participants, referred to above. In indigenous claims forums, complex relations of value may be reduced to those that can be accommodated more readily to markets, and thereby lead to resource commodification. Or, the opposite may occur: acts of compensation may emphasise an idealised indigenous cultural or 'traditional' value system which, in its prioritising of the primordial, excludes any other, including commercial, relationships of value (as in the Customary Fisheries Regulations). These differences, apparent also in the context of Donegal islands, hinge on competing, though also overlapping, discourses of value; the enclosures implicated in conserving nature and a shifting of wealth generation to future markets in ITQ systems are not disconnected phenomena. Both involve a manipulation of value creation, align with a 'greening of the economy', and are at odds with community understandings of human–nature relationships and the perpetuation of historical livelihoods.

The proclaimed 'settlement' of Māori fisheries is something of a misnomer, irrespective of the massive mobilisation of state machinery remitted to advance the settlement, including the Waitangi Tribunal, the judiciary at home and abroad, and TOKM. The assumed bicultural-ity of treaty proceedings, the symbolic reworking of the historic colonial/indigenous relationship through the hearings and subsequent repa-triations, in the final instance merely misdirects the responsibility of historic inequalities, the sheer messiness of imposing a capitalist market, on to those most discriminated against by these processes. This results in the creation of new winners and losers and the emergence of a set of grievances for which no one is perceived to be accountable and for which no treaty avenues for resolution are available.

While property rights have implications for modes of exchange, they do not determine them. In this regard, Melanesian ethnographers have long argued for an expanded view of individualism (see Errington and Gewertz 1995; Harrison 2000). Robbins (2007), drawing in particular on conceptions of possessive individualism, suggests that individuals are not only participants in the market but also combine this involvement with an alternative model for the structuring of their social life. It is this agency of the 'possessive individual' –the ability to move successfully between ostensibly discrete ideologies (individual and communal) and practices (market and reciprocal exchanges) and integrate these into multiple contemporary social contexts – that I suggest is constrained by the enclosing of common fishing rights as ITQs.

Neoliberalising the environment can, however, only be an impure process. Its philosophy, programme and practice is everywhere moderated by local biophysical environments as well as the economies, communities and social systems with which these engage. In New Zealand this hybridity is apparent in growing tensions between *iwi* quota-leasing activities and the fishing and livelihood rights of coastal *hapū* (see chapter 3). In Iceland, it is apparent in recent attempts to step back from the more extreme alienations of the ITQ system by attaching quota to communities and setting aside some quota for summer coastal handline fishing (see chapter 3). In Ireland, this struggle is expressed in the ongoing resistance of the inshore sector, and the reluctance of the Irish government to implement transferable fishing concessions, the nomenclature used for ITQs in the EU (see chapter 5).

In New Zealand, and also Iceland, a central objective of implementing the QMS was to promote conservation and reverse stock decline. In the next chapter I look at the sustainability claim of ITQs and consider how not just social systems, but also nature, is reconstructed.

2

Sustainability: A Malleable Concept

In popular imagination New Zealand fisheries represent a globally recognised story of a successful sustainable management regime, an indicator of national ingenuity and a 'clean green' environmental ethos. This local sentiment is borne out by international recognition: New Zealand's fisheries have been twice ranked as the most sustainable in the world. This accolade is perceived to be based on its early and wholehearted adoption of a quota management system (QMS) as a way, ostensibly, to conserve major fish stocks and inspire economic efficiency. On a comparative global scale, New Zealand has made the most comprehensive commitment to its QMS (Townsend 2008). All major fisheries are incorporated, that is, some 100 fish species designated as 638 fish stocks, each of which has a catch limit (Ministry for Primary Industries 2014): this represents an expansive and growing incorporation considering that seven offshore species were introduced in 1983, followed by 26 inshore species three years later. By 1999 quota was available for 180 fish stocks and by 2014 the QMS encompassed 638 stocks, representing 95 percent of all commercial fish catch.

Sustainability is the theme of our time (Wu et al. 2014). Its florescence in global and local agendas following the United Nations (UN) Brundtland report in 1987 and the later Rio declaration of 1992 is a striking example of a paradigm shift. The acclaimed interpretation of sustainable development in the *Our Common Future* paper (WCED 1987), *to meet the needs of the present without compromising the needs of future generations to meet their own*, although horribly opaque, is nonetheless visionary in its interlinking of temporal and spatial aspects: the present and the future; and the economic, social and environmental spheres. While mindful of the vast amount of good work accomplished under the rubric of sustainability, the sheer malleability of the concept has meant that, over time, it has come to be a blanket descriptor. Showing opportunistic-like features, the notion of sustainability now adds a moral valence to a vast range of interests often pursuing contradictory agendas (Raco 2005). Consumer choices in shopping, eating and travelling can all be acclaimed as sustainable or criticised as unsustainable. Similar judgements can be applied to the cross-sectoral policies and practices of educational institutions, neighbourhoods, schools, cities, councils, community gardens and buildings. Claiming the sustainability tag adds a competitive advantage to a spectrum of business enterprises, from the small and local to transnational conglomerates and global banks and financial institutions.

Rather than reject the term as devoid of any substantial meaning, it remains a critical analytical task to examine how 'sustainability' has come to be endowed with an inherent morality; a morality which works to misdirect attention from the operation of sustainability in particular social spheres and ethnographic contexts. A protagonist for this discussion is provided by a field observation. In Hawaii fishermen and their kin sell fish from stalls at the side of the road, to the local Big Island supermarket chain, KTA, to the fish shop and former fish market, Suisan, and door to door. Shortly after I left Hawaii to return to New Zealand in 2012 a regional newspaper, *The Waikato Times*, ran a front page picture: a blurry image of a customer caught on camera holding a fish in a fish shop. The story, in journalistic hype, recounted the outrage of the retailer at the criminal intent of the customer, whose transgression was not that he was attempting to steal fish, but that he was offering fish for sale. The ethical reprehensibility of his action being that he was threatening the sustainability of New Zealand's fisheries. Unpacking this event, and the increasing morality of the discourse construing such activities as 'illegal', 'poaching', 'black market', 'criminal' and 'risking sustainability', deeds which are apprehended by Ministry of Primary Industries (MPI)[1] compliance officers who conduct 'undercover operations', 'execute search warrants', 'close in', 'swoop on', 'shut down' and 'protect our fisheries', means tracing the co-evolution of sustainability with the normalisation of market approaches in rights-based fisheries. It also implies conceptualising sustainability as an ideological legitimation of neoliberalisation.

Medovoi (2010) provides a provocative account of the lexical history of sustainability, one that offers a basis through which to untangle the power of neoliberalisation to embrace other, seemingly contradictory, frameworks. The *Oxford English Dictionary* dates the sentiment expressed in the Brundtland definition to the 1980s. However, the verb 'sustain', the pre-nominalised version from which a singular understanding of sustainability emerged, can be traced back to Old English. Medovoi writes that several meanings of this ancestral form have contemporary analytical relevance, with 'cause to continue in a certain state' being the most obvious. Three others are of particular interest here. First, 'sustain' in the sense of sustaining a judicial argument, for instance, is aligned with 'uphold the validity or rightfulness of; to support as valid, sound, correct, true or just'. The moral orientation of this cluster is striking, and, the probable origin of present-day survivals. Sustaining that which is humanly valued, such as clean air, fish stocks, ecosystems, even generalised nature, is clearly embedded in today's sustainability discourse. It is also apparent in sustaining communities, traditions, material environments, languages, wealth and economies. The ethical claim to 'rightness' this understanding elicits prevents its application to that which we do not value, such as disease, hunger, unemployment, greed, exploitation, inequality and racism. In the case of fisheries management, sustainability is a means through which present and future society–environment relations are valorised. It is also a means through which past relations are evaluated, an added temporality which has real consequences for the perceived 'rightness' of the traditions and practices of generational and indigenous fishermen.

This morality claim is associated with another meaning of 'sustain', which is 'to furnish with the necessaries of life', that is, sustainability as sustenance. Medovoi points out, 'in alluding to a notion of nourishment, "sustainability" thus evokes an ethics of "provision"' (2010: 130). The apparent neutrality in sustaining something at current levels is underwritten by a moral universe where calls for a reflection on what is worth sustaining is rooted in conceptions of a nourished life where the balance between food production, the needs of humans, and their natural and social environment, is paramount. Conversely, sustainability, in its association with provisioning and nourishment, arguably rests on the assumption that nature – being radically different from society – exists primarily to serve the material needs of humans. This opposition between humans and nature has been the subject of critique from the radical 'dark green' end of the environmentalist spectrum, but also from scholars of the environment and landscape (Bender 2002; Ingold 2000). The separation, it is proposed, recreates nature as multiple, objective, quantifiable, spaces.

A third cluster of meanings reveals this darker side. To sustain something can also mean to endure or withstand it – according to the *Oxford English Dictionary* (2012), 'to undergo, experience, have to submit to (evil, hardship, or damage; now chiefly with injury, loss as objective, formerly also sorrow and death). As Medovoi indicates, 'This is a striking definition precisely because it inverts the valence of the others. Instead of suggesting the support of life, it signifies instead a suffering unto the edge of death' (2010:131). To speak of sustainability, in this regard, is to contemplate how much pain, injury and suffering can be endured. It is suggestive of a damage that is not so much eliminated, or even mitigated, as merely survived. Similarly, sustainer can mean 'a person who sustains or suffers an injury or endures an affliction'. An example of this cluster, dating from 1640, is: 'The griefe of the sustainer is doubled by the indignity of the Afflictor' (*Oxford English Dictionary* 2012). Associated with this is another meaning of 'sustain', stretching back to 1406, as 'to bear (a burden or charge, esp. a cost)' and the exemplars all refer to a monetary charge or cost (*Oxford English Dictionary* 2012). These darker semantics clearly resonate with the discourse surrounding payment for ecosystem services. Our fisheries, atmosphere, water and soils have to suffer the damage of human exploitation. Yet, their very ontology enables the calculation of a monetary exchange value in order to conserve their services. Such sustainable management practices enable a moral mitigation of the indignity of human afflicters.

A link between sustainability and neoliberalism has been asserted in social science studies on the 'green economy', 'green capitalism' and the 'neoliberalisation of nature' (Büscher et al. 2012; Castree 2010a; Prudham 2009; Sullivan 2013; Wanner 2015). Although many authors call for a recapturing of the concept to better reflect issues of social justice (Redclift 2005; Manderscheid 2012), there is a strong consensus in this work that sustainability is primarily concerned with economic systems and that it has increasingly been wedded to neoliberal orthodoxy. This alignment is apparent in the translation of environmental choices into market preferences (Redclift 2005); the framing of environmental degradation as an impediment to economic development (Raco 2005); and the valuation of environmental protection in terms of markets and prices. This also, and importantly, has implications for how sustainability is assessed. Davidson (2011) points out that the dominance of neoliberal discourse has implications for what is actually measured by sustainability monitoring systems. Further, he argues that evaluations invariably fail to address the interrelationships between social, economic and environmental contexts.

There is now a solid corpus of literature linking individual transferable quotas (ITQs) with broader neoliberalisations (Einarsson 2011; Mansfield 2004; McCormack 2010, 2012; Pinkerton and Davis 2015). Much of this work critiques the assumption that private ownership of resources motivates stewardship and that ITQ holders are therefore natural custodians. Pinkerton (2014), for instance, challenges the link between the claim to stewardship and assertions that ITQs enhance biological sustainability. Problems arise, for example, from tradability. Control over resources may be shifted to an inaccessible investor who may have no long-term incentive to protect the resource. Private owners, unattached to a particular seascape, are more likely to be motivated by interests other than those pertaining to the local environment (Pinkerton 2014). In fact, the very market logic that invigorates ITQs also claims as rational the liquidation of the resource if interest rates and profit make this a more logical option than sustainable harvesting. Pinkerton also points out that, in British Colombia at least, the claims to stewardship (which remain unsubstantiated) emerged *after* the initial justification of ITQs on economic grounds. In New Zealand and also Iceland, however, a central objective of implementing QMSs was to promote conservation and reverse stock decline.

There is little scholarship, however, that addresses the role played by neoliberally conceived sustainability in the modelling of ITQs as the optimum economic *and* biological means through which to govern fisheries. In this vein, it can be argued that ITQ fisheries take two separate approaches to sustainability. These are structured to reflect a nature/society distinction, each sphere with its attendant disciplinary boundaries, expert practitioners and subjects of analyses. These divisions are reflected in (1) the configuration of biological sustainability through assessments of stock, the total allowable catch (TAC) and maximum sustainable yields (MSY) – the work of fisheries biologists, and (2) the generation of social sustainability through the creation of (quasi) private property rights (ITQs) and markets – the work of fisheries economists and the subsequent field site of social scientists. Yet rather than conceive of these as distinct spheres – each with its subject area (nature or society) and disciplinary paradigms – it may be more useful to consider the linkages. There may in fact be a crucial relationship between scientific assessments of the sustainability of natural ecosystems and economic theories about future wealth, derived explicitly through privatisation. The objective of this chapter, then, is not to point to instances where QMSs have failed to enhance biological sustainability or reverse stock depletion. Rather, its intention is to examine the overarching paradigm informing the generation of biological and economic sustainability. In what follows, I draw on two themes to help clarify the work of sustainability in rights-based fisheries: first, quantifying and measuring the environments of capitalism and, second, the exchange value of natural and human life under systems of enclosure.

Quantifying and measuring the environments of capitalism

Sustainable fisheries management is a highly politicised process, one in which, as suggested by Mansfield (2011), a culturally particular vision of nature is imposed along with a prescription for human participants: who should control it, how it should be used and who should benefit. Nevertheless, it is popularly framed as a closed, seemingly depoliticised, bureaucratic regime concerned with technical issues surrounding biomass levels and stock assessments (Thornton and Hebert 2015). These procedures prescribe a bounded space within which scientific assessments of fish productivity are held to reflect the reality of nature, the assumption being that knowledge and resources are adequate to reveal limits and to exploit resources safely up to that level. This resultant reductionist account of a dynamic ecosystem as a single-species productivity model is illustrated in the transformation of fish *species* into fish *stock* for the purpose of assessing abundance, the latter of which recreates species to better 'describe[s] characteristics of semi-discrete groups of fish with some definable attributes which are of interest to fishery managers' (Begg and Waldman 1999:39). The certainty with which measurements are projected to sustain current and to enhance future fish stocks is technically expressed through conceptualisations of MSYs (and various derivatives such as BMSY, the B referring to biomass),[2] TACs and quota management areas (QMAs) adding to the soup of acronymic discourse. Having developed out of a combination of administrative concerns with establishing clearly defined regional entities that can then be compared with each other, and scientific assessments of species boundaries and species productivity, the concepts now signify a powerful management instrument and a definitive point of intervention.

MSY[3] is a foundation of both the 1982 Convention on the Law of the Sea and the 1995 Food and Agriculture Organization (FAO) Code of Conduct for Responsible Fisheries.[4] Put succinctly, MSY implies that no stock may be reduced beyond the point at which it cannot be renewed, hence, a sufficient spawning biomass must be conserved to maintain the stocks' capacity to reproduce. MSY incorporates a tension between a theoretical recognition of multiple species in a dynamic ecosystem, the practice of constructing assessments based on a singular stock and economic projections of future wealth. The accountancy includes the rate at which intra-species competition is reduced, fishing mortality rates are lessened, all of which are calculated in order to optimise the harvesting of commercially valuable fish stocks (Thornton and Herbert 2015). Finley and Oreskes, in a historic review of the MSY measurement in the United States, comment: 'Once MSY had been adopted, it became necessary to develop techniques to try to calculate the parameters it required: the number of spawners, the maximum yield from each cohort, and the maximum total harvest for each year' (2013: 248). The question of whether this was the right framework to begin with remained unasked.

Ascertaining the biological characteristics is the work of scientists who uncover the facts of nature through methods such as trawler and catch surveys, acoustics, tagging and, more commonly, modelling or simulations, data which is then inputted into the stock assessment model framework – seemingly autonomous undertakings which provide the foundations for managerial projections of sustainability. A stock status of below 20 percent unfished biomass is generally considered to be depleted or overfished. Degrees of hierarchy can be added to this statistic. For instance, in New Zealand MSY incorporates soft limits, whereby a fish stock requires a rebuilding plan, and a hard limit, which may trigger a fisheries closure. In order to set harvest levels at MSY two prerequisites are necessary: fish need to be individuated into singular, unitary fish stocks and management areas for each stock need to be identified. Both processes involve slippage between scientific and managerial paradigms, belying the supposed isolated neutrality of the scientific endeavour from the messy realm of the social (Holm 2003). Roepstorff, in his work on the halibut fishery in Greenland, makes visible this relationship: 'One simply has to determine the species, or subsets of it, that move around within more or less spatial-temporal borders, ideally without mixing with neighbouring subsets, and voilà, one has identified a stock' (Roepstorff 2000: 171). Maguire points out that nature is not nearly so compliant in practice: 'genetic mixing tends to take place in fisheries more so than in other biological habitats because of a high degree of larval drift due to constant current flows and temperature changes' (2015: 124). There is no single distinctive biological marker by which an individual fish can genetically be allocated to a stock and different scientists define stocks in dissimilar ways (Pawson and Jennings 1996). Given the degree of complexity and variation in the process, the definitive manner in which fish species in any given management system are allocated to one stock and not another misrepresents what is inherently a contested process. This political dimension is more visibly expressed in the definition of stock boundaries (QMAs) and the setting of catch limits (TAC).

The spatial aspect of stock ontology is expressed through QMAs. In the New Zealand case each of the 100 species or species groups in the quota system is subdivided into 638 separate fish stocks. Stocks are identified with approximately ten independent spatial locations, known as QMAs. Each stock can subsequently be identified by name and area, for instance, snapper in QMA1, becomes SNA1. The starting point for QMA determinations underlines the scientific-administrative hybridisation that characterises fisheries knowledge production (see Holm 2003): the generation of biological knowledge concerning fish stocks is prescribed by existing administrative regimes, that is, the ten Fisheries Management Areas which make up New Zealand's Exclusive Economic Zone (EEZ). In New Zealand the Kuhnian nature of scientific knowledge regarding fish stock identification has been recognised in legislation which enables the redefinition, and expansion, of QMAs (note the 'approximately' ten QMAs referred to above).[5] QMAs have, however, been altered only once to date, a situation that speaks more to broader political concerns regarding the importance of certainty in markets and the rights of quota property holders, rather than any development of scientific knowledge or changes in the ecosystem. This confluence of QMAs with the rights of quota holders, suggests that the designation of so-called natural boundaries around fish stocks is, in reality, a prefiguration of the enclosures embedded in individualised quota.

The recreation of fish species as stock whose reproductive rates can be measured (MSY) and habitat quantified (QMA) is combined with assessments of catch limits to produce an environment-in-waiting for capital infusion. A TAC, being rooted in assessments of MSY, is the instrument used to set an overall ceiling on catch per fish stock. At this larger scale the anthropogenic interests, particularly concerning economic growth, become explicit: a duality expressed in the FAO's qualification of 'environmental *and economic factors*' as the criteria for sustainable use.[6] My concern here is to emphasise not the inclusion of economic factors per se, as these arguably fit with the social aspirations of the sustainability paradigm, but that the type of economic factors deemed incorporable are pre-aligned with the efficiency perceived to be flowing from the individualisation of fishing rights.

In New Zealand the job of setting catch levels sits yearly with the Minister of Primary Industries.[7] The knowledge which informs this decision arises from plenary reports produced by scientific working groups which detail biological and stock data, quantitative information regarding the total harvest of commercial, recreational and Māori customary catch, environmental effects of fishing and risk assessments. Before setting the TAC, consultations must occur with the commercial fishing industry and other interested parties. The minister, thus, must balance the 'net marginal benefits' between commercial and non-commercial allocations, MSYs and maximum economic yields (Sharp 2008: 21).

Once calculated, the TAC is then divided among designated user groups: in each quota management area a certain quantity of fish stock is set aside for Māori customary take, recreational users and commercial operators. The latter is called the total allowable commercial catch (TACC) and is set in tonnage. The distribution of catch under ITQ systems is, according to Anthony Scott, 'the least demanding function', requiring merely the 'dividing of total allowable catch (TAC) to obviate the need for fishermen racing and capital stuffing' (1993: 188). Three points can be made here. First, TACs are not synonymous with ITQs and exist in many fisheries where fishing rights have not been privatised. However, where ITQs exist they require TACs as a means through which to allocate rights, and it is this circumstance to which Scott is likely referring. Second, TACs themselves do not prevent overcapitalisation or a race for fish. British Columbia, which had TACs and limited entry long before ITQs, experienced both racing and overcapitalisation.[8] The notion that fishermen race is much more complicated than typically suggested, and is highly unlikely to be a natural attribute of fishermen's behaviour (Finley and Oreskes 2013). Finally, the function of TACs in ITQ regimes suggests a linkage between the construction of property in nature and the emergence of individualised fishing rights. That is, the tools used to ascertain biological sustainability, to a certain extent, delineate natural territories (QMAs) to which fish species are assigned as stock, which can then be converted through TAC assessments into the individual property rights of quota holders.

Notably, the allocation of TACs between commercial, customary and recreational users is a contested process in New Zealand. TAC increases are routinely granted to ITQ shareholders. In the event of a TAC reduction, preference is given to maintain current proportional allocation among user groups. A reduction, however, in the allocation of TACCs, is perceived to threaten the property rights of quota holders and results, often, in litigation. On at least five occasions a case has been brought challenging TACC reduction under section 13 of the Fisheries Act 1996. The 2008/9 proposed reduction in TAC for *kahawai* (dubbed 'the people's fish') is the most high profile to date, pitting recreational interests against commercial ones and leading to a change in legislation. Boyd outlines the implications of this change: when scientific data concerning sustainability is not available, the minister may still limit or increase the TAC; since research is now devolved to the industry there is an incentive 'to do the least research possible'; and the 2008/9 decision benefited 'the big boys', that is, the small number of consolidated quota holders, by providing them with 'considerable certainty' (Boyd 2010: 785). This certainty is a corollary of the political construction of ITQs as analogous to individual property rights and the weighting given to this construct of ownership.

Concerning biological sustainability, some of the critiques that are directed against ITQ fisheries include: (1) it is a single-species approach to a complex ecosystem (Gibbs 2008) and does not address ecosystem protection (Degnabol et al. 2006); (2) it is based on a data-hungry approach with associated costs; (3) similar to other TAC managed fisheries, there is an over-reliance on modelling fish stock and best estimates that do not mimic the real world but instead reflect what the modeller believes are the most important functions for a particular species of fish (de Freitas and Perry 2012); (4) there is little evidence of rebuilding in ITQed fish stocks. New Zealand, for instance, was overfishing 21.4 percent of stocks of known status in 2011. The proportion of stocks being overfished, however, is argued to be declining and scientific evidence purports that the status of many stocks has improved since the inception of the QMS (Mace 2012); (5) there is no reward for sustainable fishing practices (Bromley 2008); (6) TACs change relatively infrequently: most are not changed in response to overcatch or undercatch situations (a consequence of budgetary concerns and political pressure from quota holders) but remain constant from year to year (Sanchirico et al. 2006). ITQs make the monitoring of biological impacts much more costly (Pinkerton 2013); (7) there is uncertain and incomplete scientific evidence on which to base decisions. For instance, in New Zealand as of 2010 there was sufficient information to characterise stock status for 119 out of the then 633 stocks (Ministry for the Environment 2010). Scientists generally qualify but do not entirely refute these critiques. They largely assert, however, that, although not perfect, the QMS is better at achieving sustainability than alternative regimes (Sissenwine and Mace 2003; Shotton 1999).

ITQ systems are, however, acknowledged to encourage high-grading, dumping, poaching and misreporting. In a recently released working paper detailing New Zealand catch reconstructions from 1950 to 2010, Simmons et al. 'conservatively' estimate commercial catches were roughly 2.9 times the amount officially reported, and 2.2 times the amount since the introduction of the QMS in 1986. The authors claim that this is due, primarily, to 'deliberate, widespread and systematic under-reporting' (Simmons et al. 2015). The introduction of the MPI onboard observers programme in 1986, though, strengthened compliance monitoring and contributed to a decline in invisible catch. However, such monitoring is limited, for instance to 20–25 percent of the deep-water fleet and only recently has been introduced in inshore fisheries. Further, the observers programme is primarily geared towards collecting scientific data for stock assessments rather than compliance per se. Dumping is also implicated in under-reporting, an activity Simmons et al. (2015) claim to have long been normalised. The QMS, however, has added additional incentives to this practice. While the perceived low economic value of a fish encourages dumping, this is now combined with factors such as quota being unavailable to cover the catch, and the prospect of a high deemed value fee (see below) (Simmons et al. 2015). How scientific research is solicited is also a factor in determining sustainable outcomes. Mace et al. (2014) point to a connection in New Zealand between the method by which research is tendered, budgetary restrictions and the fact that most species have received little, if any, research attention for many years. Fisheries research is fully contestable and, while the research budget has remained largely static, the number of species and stocks in the QMS has increased 3.5 times. The actual purchasing power of the budget is calculated to have decreased to 50 percent of the level in the early 1990s (Mace et al. 2014).

My interest here is not to evaluate the effective biological sustainability of ITQ fisheries vis-à-vis other fisheries management regimes, a task complicated by the absence of a common methodology for assessing sustainability (Gibbs 2008: 28). Nor is it to demonise or reify the science being practised. Rather my concern is to unravel the type of knowledge production that is embedded in this operation of sustainability and the mutability of this in relation to a particular type of economic system. MSY and TAC are stipulated by law in New Zealand. As instruments they demand a distinct type of data and create a path for the type of data requested, effectively excluding other types of management tools (Degnbol et al. 2006). Thornton and Hebert (2015), in their work on herring, a highly mobile, schooling fish, in south-east Alaska, point out that the spatial and temporal (production boundaries and historic baselines) data paths required to produce MSY are aligned with the interests of a privatised commercial fishery.

Regardless of the seeming autonomy with which the science of fish stocks proceeds, and the claimed empirical neutrality upon which management decisions are based, biological fisheries science in ITQ systems is intimately wedded to management; and management is structured to increase economic efficiency, not to achieve broader ecological goals (Gibbs 2008). Pamela Mace, principal adviser of fisheries science for the New Zealand MPI, comments on this union:

> If it is desirable to maintain TACs at constant levels over long periods of time (e.g. because ITQs are denoted as absolute tonnages, because the fishing industry requires stability in catches, or because there is insufficient research or monitoring to change TACs very often), it is essential to recognise the trade-off in long-term average catches … and in the risk to stock sustainability. (2012: 3)

Fisheries scientists point out that the perception that the science has been compromised has led to growing controversies over the objectivity of their assessments and advice (Mace and Sissenwine 2002). Although Mace and Sissenwine refute suggestions that concessions have been made, they propose that the separation of scientific institutions from management is needed to address the mounting challenges from environmental groups, the commercial fishing industry and recreational fishing groups. Yet while this boundary making may alleviate concerns regarding a purely scientific operational space, it does little to address broader issues of social injustice. For instance, the fact that this sustainability knowledge production (whether tainted or not by its association with management) prevails and prefigures the individualisation of fishing rights and that indigenous and local knowledge is rarely considered viable data.

Since the late 1980s there have been endeavours to include indigenous knowledge, or traditional ecological knowledge, in sustainable development programmes (Soini and Birkeland 2014). This progression is not mirrored in the sustainability projects in rights-based fisheries. Where culture, particularly indigenous culture, is recognised in ITQ systems it seems to be in terms of negotiating access to fishing rights, that is, property (typically in terms of a community development quota), not in the acceptance of local and traditional knowledge as a valid basis for management decisions, nor in accommodating a differently conceived interpretation of sustainability. In New Zealand, for instance, while Māori indigenous knowledge of fisheries is recognised in non-commercial customary regulations, largely in terms of conservational features, it plays no part in fisheries sustainability outside of this sphere (McCormack 2010). Mccarthy et al. (2014) highlight the disparity between New Zealand's internationally acclaimed fisheries management strategy and the concerns of local, in particular Māori, stakeholders. In their interviews with over 100 seaside inhabitants they found very different assessments concerning the health of stocks from those reported by fisheries scientists and the commercial industry. They comment: 'The locals also draw attention to a much wider suite of social and cultural consequences from unsustainable fishing than just the economic consequences emphasized by commercial interests that dominate Ministry of Primary Industry research and policy' (2014: 385).

Similarly, the knowledge accumulated by generational fishermen in Ireland is omitted from management decisions, an exclusion which has profound consequences for the reproduction of identity. Meanwhile, Thornton and Hebert (2015) show that in the south-east Alaskan herring fishery, MSY calculations and the biomass framing of biologists do not take into account indigenous and locally based knowledge. This results in policies based on generational amnesia, strategic scale framing and fallacious notions of steady states. The Sitka tribe, for instance, configure space and time much more broadly than the imperial notions characteristic of MSY calculations. They maintain that a healthy spawning population is characterised by its broad distribution in time (duration of spawning) and space (areas associated with spawning over generations), and argue that the MSY regime is sustaining herring at a depleted rate, that it ignores 'the web of life' that is dependent upon herring as foundation forage fish, and that it has undermined a critical subsistence food. Since 2007 the Sitka herring fishery in Alaska has been variously subjected to quota cuts and enclosures.

Sustainability is likely to be differently conceived by indigenous peoples. Rikarangi Gage, *rangatira* (tribal leader) of East Cape *iwi* Te Whanau a Apanui, explained his tribal 'worldview' to me through a story: the son of *tipuna* (ancestor) Poumatangatanga followed him down to the beach and drowned. Looking for his son, the *tipuna* asked the *kahawai* fish if he had seen him, then asked Tangaroa, the parent of all fish, but Tangaroa said, 'No, though I'll come to your son's *tangi* [funeral] and we'll weep together' and Poumatangatanga knew his son had drowned and that Tangaroa had him. Gage explained that the story reinforced a reciprocal relationship, or *utu*, between Te Whanau a Apanaui, fish and Tangaroa – 'we kill his children, and sometimes Tangaroa takes from us' – and that such stories 'help our mental apparatus adjust to things like death at sea'.

> There's a deed of agreement between us and these *atuas* [ancestors/ gods] … social or cultural contracts with the *atua* and we're saying that that's the world we want preserved, kept sacrosanct … because that's the world that informs or should inform the way in which we behave, you take that world, or take the basis away, and what you have is legal behaviour, and we want Māori Whanau Apanui behaviour based on our worldview. (Personal communication 2008)

Sustainability, in this view, is embodied in rights in ancestors, includes a spiritual basis, accountability to future generations and the integrity of the relationship between ancestors, spiritual base and future generations. This exclusion of indigenous and local knowledge in the management of a resource is perhaps surprising given the growing popularisation in policy and academic circles of traditional and local ecological knowledge. It raises the question as to why the scientific basis on which ITQ systems function, and in particular the claimed enhancement of sustainability, is considered to be incompatible with indigenous and locally based knowledge?

The exchange value of natural and human life

The quantification and measurement of environments of capitalism in the construction of sustainability, as illustrated by the recreation of fish species as stock and the intervention of MSY, QMA and TAC instruments, seems to separate nature and society in order that the latter can fully exploit the former. Thus, the damage that sustainability asks that we endure appears to be primarily environmental. Yet, while this may hold true in the industrialised, expansionist era of fisheries, the suffering-nature/exploitative-human dichotomy does not capture the context today, if indeed it ever did. Sustainability, having its origins in sustainable growth and development movements, has always explicitly referenced economic systems, more particularly the system of capital accumulation (Medovoi 2010: 132). In its neoliberal incarnation sustainability does not so much instigate a separation of nature and society, rather it proposes a subjugation of both human and non-human environments to capital accumulation, and it asks that we tolerate the damage done to both. In order to achieve this subjugation two conditions are required: first, the intrinsic value of human and natural worlds needs to be reconfigured as an exchange value and, second, mediation needs to be accomplished through the medium of money.

Sustainability in ITQ fisheries allows for substitution between natural and human capital (Pearce and Atkinson 1992). Thus fish stock may be reduced through harvesting and replaced by a corresponding increase in other forms of capital of at least equal value (Garcia and Staples 2000). This claim to equivalence assumes the existence of a common attribute that makes it possible to reduce these very different phenomena to a common denominator, namely capital, so that a loss in one can be counterbalanced by a gain in the other. Medovoi points out the flaws in this argument:

> Natural and social phenomena, such as the fish in the sea, the knowledge in my head, initially belong to other kinds of systems, that is, ecological systems and systems of knowledge. They can also be considered forms of human wealth in that they are of use to us and they can be made indispensable in the production process. However, it is only when they are enclosed, turned into private property so as to become saleable inputs in a capitalist production process, that they interact for the first time with capital. They are themselves not intrinsically capital as they are in no sense self-expanding forms of value. While fish may breed more fish, outside of a production process they play no part in the accumulation of capital. Thus to suggest that they are capital is to engage in an obfuscating metaphor. It is the case that capital is accumulated through production processes that rely on natural and social elements, however, those elements are not themselves capital; they must be mixed with capital in order to breed more capital. (Medovoi 2010: 135–36)

The necessary precondition to accomplish this equivalence is privatisation. Natural and social phenomena must be enclosed.

Enclosing the seas

As a property rights regime for natural resources, quota systems are popularly rooted in the belief system informing Hardin's tragedy of the commons thesis. This, for decades, has influenced the management of fisheries and marine ecosystems (Longo et al. 2015) and is now implicated in directing the pathway for conceptualisations of the standard MSY, TAC and QMA instruments. Hardin's paradigm, while initially modelled on the maximising behaviours of commons herdsmen which, he asserts, inevitably lead to tragedy as each adds 'one more animal' to his herd, found its most axiomatic expression in fishermen chasing too few fish. Indeed, Hardin's 'tragedy' was pre-dated by the work of fisheries economists Howard Gordon (1954), Anthony Scott (1955) and Jens Warming (1911). Thus, the over-exploitation of fisheries, which, on a global scale was obvious by the 1980s, could simply be resolved by privatising and enclosing ocean fisheries.

A concern with property rights is perhaps a peculiar feature of fisheries; property struggles and transformations have historically dominated the work of managers and fisheries-interested scholars across academic disciplines. This work is centred on property, the commons and the use of privatisation to create markets for governing access to and use of ocean resources, and a variety of critiques of these propositions. Mansfield (2004) points out that this property-centred history of environmental regulation in fisheries influenced the development of a particular dynamism in neoliberal approaches to ocean governance.

Neoclassical economic analysis took hold in fisheries in the 1950s. This was largely propelled by Gordon's (1954) paper and Scott's (1955) response, whose analysis not only pre-dated Hardin's argument, but also critiqued the *über* focus on biological issues and the lack of theoretical economic research in fisheries at the time. Gordon argued that fisheries management is as much about the economic actions and decisions of people as it is about fish; that the economic decision making of fishermen should be seen as endogenous to fisheries systems, and that although this fact was recognised by some biologists who, he conceded, had been 'forced to extend the scope of their own thought into the economic sphere ... virtually no specific research into the economics of fishery resource utilization has been undertaken' (1954: 89–90). Gordon's central preoccupation was the lack of private property in sea fisheries, which, he claimed, was at the time a common property resource. The solution to overfishing, in his view, was to focus on economic efficiency and to reform the property regime to harness individual decision making to both economic and ecological realities.

Mansfield describes the gradual population of fisheries research from the 1950s onwards by economists and traces the development of their ideas concerning the inherently problematic nature of common property. She outlines their objection to the creation of economic inefficiencies through, for instance, limitations on gear, which they saw as a fallacious way of solving problems in fisheries (2004: 316). A heavily canvassed solution was the creation of mechanisms for limiting entry to individual fisheries as a way to progress property rights. Economists promoting this agenda soon gained access to international forums, such as the UN FAO, which, in 1956, convened a roundtable discussion on the 'economics of fishing'. Mansfield points out that identifying the commons with market failure was the central tenet of the increasingly powerful field of fisheries economics. From this alleged failure it was deduced that an absence of specified property rights leads rational individuals to 'race for fish', resulting in economic and environmental failure.

The era, marked by the ascent of fisheries economists (albeit in ongoing competition with biologists) also coincided with wider political and geographic concerns about what some observers perceived as the unsettling phenomena of a propertyless sea space. This perceived vacuum was the context to conflicts over mineral rights, maritime and military transportation, and, importantly, global tensions over fish resources, their exploitation and conservation, the epitome of which were the Icelandic cod wars. Over the three decades from 1950 to 1980 nation states sought to expand the areas of sea under their territorial control, generally from 3 nautical miles (nm) from the shore, to 12 nm and, eventually to 200 nm. These 200 nm EEZs became customary international law in the 1980s and thus enclosed what was a substantial body of open access waters. Mansfield writes that while these state-derived jurisdictions may seem anachronistic to the privatisation and the 'rolling back' of state control which is the hallmark of neoliberalisation, the very creation of this new expanse set the stage for the next round of privatisations. Notably, fisheries economists generally supported the move towards expanded political jurisdiction in the oceans as it had the redeeming feature that the space could be subjected to further enclosures through limited licences or other privatisation schemes (Christy and Scott 1965; Scheiber and Carr 1998).

The 1980s also saw the emergence of scholarship in anthropology, insti-tutional economics, and other disciplines challenging the assumption that 'common property' was the crux of fisheries problems. Mansfield, however, critiques the interchangeability of much of this multidisciplinary work with the tragedy of the commons paradigm. In her words:

> what all these seemingly different perspectives on the commons share is that they link forms of property, economic rationality, and environmen-tal outcomes. Once common property theorists replaced the 'tragedy of the commons' with the 'tragedy of open access' the differences between what seemed like quite opposed positions are no longer so great. (2004: 319)

Thus property regimes, whether private or common, are essential for constraining rational human behaviour which inherently leads to a race for fish, overcapitalisation and environmental exploitation. What might be termed a generalisation of property regimes and relations has, I have suggested, tended to narrow if not collapse the differences between radically different property regimes and in doing so obfuscated important social, political and economic distinctions. For instance, it sanctioned the alignment by Māori negotiators of traditional common ownership regimes with the abstracted, future-oriented construct of individual quota. In this process complex natural and social arrangements are both transformed into capital.

New Zealand claims to the seascape

New Zealand began to formalise its claims to the seascape in the mid-1960s establishing a 12 nm territorial zone in 1965, expanding it in 1977 to the present 200 nm EEZ. As directed by the UN Law of the Sea, the newly established EEZ included the obligation to set TACs and TACCs. Notwithstanding this scene setting, and the pervasiveness of theories propounded by fisheries economists, further propertisation was a haphazard business involving an amalgamation of privatisation measures (such as limited licences) and efforts to grow the business of fishing (such as tax incentives, export-friendly policies, an easing of criteria for loans and the encouragement of joint venture agreements with foreign vessels). The 1970s witnessed a rapid growth in fishing operations, an expansion that exponentially threatened the fishing practices of the small-scale sector (see Introduction for more detail).

By the early 1980s it was increasingly obvious that over-exploitation was occurring, many inshore stocks were under severe pressure, and the industry was overcapitalised. The effort to expand the domestic fisheries in New Zealand following the declaration of the EEZ is not unique, and indeed at a global level many state management efforts followed a similar trajectory. The emergent problems occasioned by this policy triggered a new round of critical economic commentary and abstract theorising. However, the new issue, as identified by fisheries economists, was not the specific type of regulations, programmes or government incentives that were in place, rather the problem was that state property now functioned as a type of common property. Thus the extended jurisdiction heralded by the introduction of EEZs was used as an illustration of the abject failure of 'common property' to curtail economic inefficiency and resource degradation. The 1980s, of course, also punctuates environmental history as the point at which fisheries economists adopted a fully neoliberal approach. In 1982 the New Zealand government removed incentives from the fishing industry and announced its intention to refocus on 'sustainability'.

The 1983 Fisheries Act, the first major legislative change since 1908, introduced the quota system for offshore fisheries. Section 89(g) of the Act provided for regulation to be promulgated which stipulated TACs and authorised the minister to allocate quota in a discretionary manner to any specified commercial fishers. A TAC was set for seven offshore species, the domestic allocation of which was converted to quota and allocated to nine commercial companies (the seven largest companies and two consortia of smaller companies fishing for them). A further amount of quota was to be fished by owner-operator 'others' as a competitive TAC.[9] The 1983 Act also, and notably, changed the criteria for commercial fishing licences. Applicants henceforth needed to satisfy the Ministry of Agriculture and Fisheries (MAF) that their annual income relied wholly or substantially (80 percent or NZ$10,000 per annum) on fishing activities, or that they had made or intended to make an appreciable investment in the industry. Some 1,500 to 1,800 part-time fishermen were permanently excluded from renewing their licences. These criteria, although clearly directed at part-timers, impacted Māori fishermen disproportionately (see chapter 1). This 'rationalisation of fishing capacity' was an intended consequence as the problem was constructed in the classical idiom of too many fishers chasing too few fish. However, although the 1983 legislation instigated a sharp reduction in the number of small boats, larger vessels more than compensated for this loss, filling the gap as small boats exited (Connor 2001). Hence, despite the drastic restructuring of the industry the total catch was reduced by a mere 5 percent (Law Commission 1989). In 1986 an amendment to the Act put the QMS into place for New Zealand's inshore fisheries (26 fish species) and established ITQs. Only those who had held licences in the preceding 12 months were entitled to quota. This was then freely gifted to qualifying operators.

This transition explicitly linked environmental and economic crises and trumpeted the QMS as the new panacea. Privatising fishing rights was considered the means through which to increase the profitability of what was deemed a hyper-regulated, overly capitalised, somewhat chaotic and underdeveloped market, particularly in terms of its export potential, and to simultaneously conserve fish stocks by allocating rights to the most 'efficient' users. Sustainability, having been popularised in international agendas, became the unifying theme.

Concretising the property right: New Zealand

Fishing quotas are subsets of the TAC and are typically specified by tonnage and broken down by species. They have the propensity to become individualised and made transferable; as in the cases of New Zealand's ITQs and Iceland's individual fishing quota (IFQ). The purest version of private property rights has, however, been attained in New Zealand. This achievement requires continuous innovative tinkering given the somewhat intangible nature of the 'thing' subject to commodification: the future right to catch a certain quantity of fish species from a certain geo-graphically defined stock.

Following the establishment of quota for seven offshore fisheries in the 1983 Fisheries Act and the attendant redefinition of commercial fishing, the 1986 Fisheries Amendment Act augured the introduction of a full-blown quota system. In the first few years, however, the strength of the actual property right was uncertain. During this period government intervened in the quota market, buying or selling quota when it wanted to alter the TAC. Additionally, ITQs were not readily accepted by banks as loan collateral, hence the status of ITQs as financial assets was insecure. This was despite the governing legislation equating quota rights with registerable interests in 'real property', provisions for which were simply lifted from the New Zealand Land Transfers Act 1952. There was, thus, no legal impediment to the use of ITQ as security for bank loans, but the Ministry of Fisheries at the time did not make explicit provision for the registration of liens or caveats against the title to ownership. This perception of insecurity altered as government 'interference' in the market diminished. In 1990 there was a significant change in approach to the effect that henceforth ITQs were denominated as a percentage of the TAC rather than a specific tonnage. This meant that adjustments to quota no longer necessitated government intervention, simply the automatic pro rata adjustment of all ITQ holdings at the beginning of each season to match the TAC (Yandle 2008). As noted above, changes in TAC occur very seldom in practice.

Three other developments were crucial in solidifying this property right. First, the use of ITQs in 1992 to fully and finally settle Māori Treaty claims to commercial fisheries, a repatriation which had major symbolic and economic implications and accelerated the growing perception of quota as a tangible thing of value. Second, in 1994 and again in 1996 and 1999, aspects of management were devolved from government to quota owners, now relabelled stakeholder groups, a strategy associated with strengthening the perception of quota holders as owners as opposed to resource renters. Third, in 2001, under the auspices of the 1996 administrative reforms geared towards encouraging loan financing, Annual Catch Entitlements (ACE) were introduced. ACE refers to the tonnage of fish that the quota owner is able to harvest in the year. In terms of strengthening the property aspect of quota, it provided a clear distinction between short-term harvesting rights, and rights concerned with the perpetual ownership of the resource.

Although marketisation will be discussed in greater detail in chapter three, it is important at this point to emphasise the link between privatisation in quota fisheries and the generation of markets. The introduction of ACE, for instance, enabled the creation of a second market in fisheries quota. There is thus a market in which ITQs can be bought, sold and inherited – what is traded in the exchange is the right to receive ACE in perpetuity. There is, in addition, a market in trading individual ACEs – this is the market in which the quota holder leases out yearly fishing rights to generate income. The ACE trading market has grown, particularly in the inshore fisheries, as quota has been aggregated, via market trading, into fewer and fewer 'more efficient' user hands, whose preference is to rent out yearly fishing rights. This upsurge of ACE leasing is also linked to the distribution of quota to Māori iwi starting in 2004. The market value of quota has risen considerably so that it is much more profitable to trade virtual fish (quota) than land actual fish.

'Deemed values', a catch balancing system, symbolises the uneasy relationship between sustainability, privatisation and markets in quota fisheries and is championed as an 'answer' to problems in all three. Deemed values were introduced in 2001 as part of the broader ACE reform policies and are, simply, financial penalties fishermen must pay if they do not have enough ACE to cover their landed catch. Fees are set for each species in each management area at a level that theoretically discourages dumping fish, encourages landing and thus promotes 'sustainable' practices. Fish dumping arises when a fisher does not have enough catch rights, that is ACE, to land the fish that they have caught. Both deemed values and ACE are aimed at reducing 'transaction costs' for the fishing industry and government, that is, the costs incurred in making a market exchange (Walker and Townsend 2008). Deemed values reduce such costs by deflecting this payment onto the fishermen whose leased ACE is less than their landed catch. They further reduce transaction costs by directing the deemed value fee paid by the ACE-leasing fishermen to the quota holders. This might be considered a rather innovative way to tax the lessee. Deemed values are also implicated in stimulating the ACE trading market as fishermen engage in frantic arbitrage trading, trying to lease enough ACE to cover their fish rather than pay the higher interim or end-of-year deemed value fee. In practice, there may have been over-optimism regarding the sustainability aspiration residing in deemed values. Deemed value fees are perceived as fines and have reduced the willingness of fishers to report or land all of their catch; such misreporting is of noteworthy magnitude (Simmons et al. 2015).

Property as quota in Ireland

The process of individualising quota is at different stages of development in quota fisheries globally. Fisheries in the European Union (EU), for instance, show a patchwork of approaches, though the general trend seems to be towards individualisation and transferability. In terms of the configuration of property, there is a major distinction between the Irish quota system and its New Zealand and Icelandic counterparts. In Ireland quota is neither formally privatised nor is it transferable. Quota 'ownership' is filtered through a hierarchy of levels – from the EU, to the national government, to vessel owners. These differences have implications for the perceived character of the property as well as for marketisation.

The Common Fisheries Policy (CFP) originated in the 1970s, when the EU extended its EEZ from 12 nm to 200 nm offshore. Under the CFP each of Europe's 49 designated fishing areas is assigned a TAC on an annual basis. The TAC is then divided between the member states according to formulae determined by socioeconomic criteria. Member states are then allocated quotas for each commercial species (see chapter 5 for more detail). The water to be fished includes the entirety of the EU's member states' 200 nm limit, except in specified waters. While the TAC has been the primary 'tool of conservation' employed by the EU there is a coexisting directive aimed at curtailing overcapitalisation, that is the perception that 'too many boats are chasing too few fish'. A plethora of policies have been aimed at reducing the size of fleets.

EU member states have responsibility for policing national waters and for internal quota allocation policies (for example, through licences, limited entry or IFQ). In Ireland, quota is attached to fishing vessels. This method of allocation, however, is perceived to favour larger operators (as noted in chapter 1). In the Celtic sea herring fishery, for instance, 89 percent of quota is allocated to boats over 15 meters in length (Le Floc'h et al. 2015).

It is the Irish state which quintessentially 'owns' the quota. Yet this is a tenuous claim given the centralised European management structure; the historic propensity towards TAC – and thus national quota – reductions (which ironically increases the value of quota) and the perceived political biases in the European annual TAC setting process. While at a state level, Ireland supports the TAC and quota system, it remains 'deeply aggrieved at the discrepancy between the volume of fish which Ireland contributed to the CFP (through its large and productive 200 mile exclusive economic zone) and the share of fish stocks it has received through the CFP' (Bord Iascaigh Mhara n.d.: 13). I was told by fishermen that this discrepancy, which is keenly felt, was the result of a number of factors, including perceived power and cultural norms. Thus, for instance, it is thought that an historic stereotype of the Irish peasantry was adopted by politicians who, in the initial quota distribution rounds in 1983, went cap in hand to the EU grateful for any crumbs; another factor was the particular characteristics of the Irish informal economy where it is historically valued to display enough cunning and intelligence to avoid hierarchically imposed fees, fines and other charges – a value that can be contextualised in reference to the colonial era. Prior to the introduction of the quota system, under-reporting of catch was a means by which individuals could avoid fees. On a national level, this meant that when quota was distributed to member states, based partially on catches between 1973 and 1978, the Irish catch, on paper, was substantially lower than it was in reality. A principal criterion in quota distribution is historic levels of catch.

There is a tenacious momentum in European CFP regulations to expand the privatisation and marketisation characteristics of fishing quota: Transferable Fishing Concessions (TFCs), essentially an ITQ, although rejected in the most recent EU Common Fisheries reforms, are increasingly naturalised as the way to do sustainable fisheries management. Albeit supported by, in particular, large-scale, pelagic fishermen producer organisations in Ireland, TFCs are strongly contested by inshore fishermen organisations and the conservative Irish government:

> Ireland strongly opposes any attempt to introduce an ITQ management system at European level and will not support any arrangement that leads – either directly or indirectly – to privatisation of national 'public resource' fish quotas ... Ireland states clearly that an enforced ITQ or similar system will result in the concentration of resources into the hands of large corporations which will have no link with the coastal communities' dependant on fishing. (Bord Iascaigh Mhara n.d.: 13).

Conclusion

Sustainability is a morally persuasive concept, an effective label for a plethora of human activities ostensibly engaged in the pursuit of 'good' environmental and social causes. The type of sustainability operating in QMSs, however, challenges this normative discourse. Referring to older lexicons suggests a more germane vernacular, for instance 'sustain' interpreted as to suffer, endure or withstand or bear a burden or monetary cost of. These semantics imply that the burden is imposed not only on the environment but also on human society.

In its neoliberal incarnation, sustainability manifests particular characteristics. Redclift (2005) traces how a previous focus on needs, inherent in the Brundtland interpretation, shifted in the 1980s to one centred on rights alongside an attempt to translate environmental choices into market preferences. This trend towards marketisation connects with a longer history of economic theorising in fisheries centred on the crucial role of private property in harnessing 'rational' behaviour. The enclosure of the oceans, in this view, is necessary not only for curtailing the 'race for fish', but importantly for fostering exchangeability between natural and human capital. Natural capital (such as fish stock) may be reduced through harvesting and replaced by a corresponding increase in other forms of capital. Thus if fish stocks have been reduced to a small fraction of virgin unfished biomass, this is acceptable as long as the natural capital extracted from the fish stocks have more than been compensated by an increase in economic and/or social capital (Gibbs 2008:31). Through this reasoning the very ontology of natural resources (now rendered as ecosystem services) is recreated through interventions of TAC, MSY and QMA instruments, and made interchangeable with wealth generation in society; a wealth generation which is far from equally distributed.

Rather than consider the biological sustainability practised in ITQ fisheries as a separate ontological sphere from the social sustainability as enacted in quota systems, each with its attendant disciplinary methodologies and paradigms, I suggest that there is in fact a frightful symmetry. A fixation with future wealth is present in both models: the assessment of fish stocks, MSYs and TACs is undertaken to enhance future yields of commercial fish stocks; ITQs are a virtual property regime granting a right to catch a certain quantity of fish species from a certain geographically defined stock. Sophisticated markets have emerged to trade in the future value of this commodity. Both models also institute enclosures, QMAs are the spatial counterpart of the property structure vested in ITQs and each regime finds its meaning only in relation to the other.

ITQs also have an expansive power. Although in theory the rights have no explicit spatial component, in reality this spatial component is implicit and has the potential to hinder the establishment of, for example, new marine spaces for alternative uses. As argued, there is a spatial component reflected in QMAs. This expansive power is also expressed through the extension of rights associated with accumulation, for instance, the receipt of fishermen's deemed value fees and an increase in state monitoring and protection of these private property rights. In 2012 New Zealand was recognised as the leading country (among 41 surveyed) for the quality of its fisheries monitoring and surveillance work. This accolade cannot be divorced from the international sustainability acknowledgements, and a

2010 endorsement from the World Bank decreeing the lack of subsidies in New Zealand's QMS as a goal to be emulated.[10]

Since the late 1990s, much of the emphasis of fisheries management staff has been placed on consulting with stakeholders, that is quota holders, and there has been a deliberate policy of centralisation. There is an intricate relationship between attempts to privatise fishing rights and the devolution of managerial, administration, research and market responsibilities to quota-owning stakeholders. This devolution of regulatory and market responsibilities to private entities has reconstructed the government's role to that of policing and compliance, the ultimate guardian of private fishing rights. The work of fisheries officers employed by the Ministry for Primary Industries is primarily land-based and is geared towards the surveillance, detection and investigation of quota fraud, 'poaching' and 'black market' activities, in effect, protecting the income streams of private quota investors. This labour force is bolstered by a Memorandum of Understanding with the New Zealand Police which enables its members to take on the role of a fishery officer.

To return to my original field observation: the fisherman selling fish in a fish shop is criminalised not because of any real impact he may have on the life cycles of fish in the sea, but because he is a threat to the rights so carefully constructed as ITQs. Like the *koha* fishers in chapter 1, his major violation is not an ecological one, irrespective of the obfuscation provided by the sustainability discourse, rather it is a crime against property. He highlights the precariousness, and indeed absurdity, of designing rights to generate wealth from fish that have not yet been born. Quota fisheries tell a particularly poignant story of the practice of neoliberal sustainability in general environmental governance, one that involves a complex mix of abstract economic theorising, the selective use of science, and one that instigates enclosures in both human and natural worlds. Once privatised, quota has the propensity to become activated in markets and while there is no logical relationship between quota as property rights and free market trading, there is an assumed innate trajectory. This tendency, captured in the T (transferability) of ITQs, will be explored in the next chapter.

3
Transferability and Markets

This chapter builds on the ideas laid out in the introduction concerning the marketisation of the environment and the key role that ecosystem services play in reconstructing human–environment relations. While, as Moore (2000) suggests, every phase of capitalism emerges from a restructuring of nature–society relations, the present era may be, as argued by Eriksen (2016), an accentuation or an acceleration of this process. This speeding up is evidenced in a proliferation of commoditisations and dispossessions, but also in the growth of international alliances between seemingly antagonistic global actors. For instance in 2015 in New York, an executive roundtable discussion championing investment in the 'Blue Economy' included as participants, the Nature Conservancy, Goldman Sachs, Lockheed Martin and the World Bank (Barbesgaard 2015: 1). The theme of this discussion, as a briefing paper explained, 'examines how money can be made from a growing ocean economy in a context where environmental considerations and principles of sustainable natural resource management could shape the investment environment' (The Economist Intelligence Unit 2015: 6–7). The participation of Goldman Sachs is significant. Kalb and Visser identify this bank, and J.P. Morgan, as the two dominant financial corporations which are the 'actual engines of financialized and globalized late capitalism' (2012: 80). Over the last few decades Goldman Sachs has profited from oligopolistic tendencies in investment banking, strategically positioned itself in the internal boardrooms of the US state and achieved renown as an innovative market-maker worldwide. The Blue Economy, undoubtedly, signifies a qualitatively different era of enclosures.

Marx's description of 'primitive accumulation' captures a process that continues unabated today, though in perhaps more insidious forms than his portrayal of it as a history written in 'letters of blood and fire' (Büscher 2009). This analysis, like Harvey's (2005) more recent conception of 'accumulation by dispossession', refers to how enclosures, which mark a separation of producers from the means of production, create a pliant and abundant proletariat and the conditions necessary for the development of capitalism. In this way nature is imported into production and opened up to the logic of capitalism. Neoliberalisation, however, extends the reach of classical primitive accumulation in contradictory ways. While privatisation implies the transference of resources and property from state to private ownership, for instance in fisheries, from 'the public' to quota holders, the process may not end at this point. In the context of natural resources there may also be a provision to secure rights for the poor, as for example the community development quota assigned to indigenous groups in New Zealand, Western Alaska and, more recently, fishing communities in Iceland. However, as Harvey (2005) notes, this opens the door for subsequent appropriations. This can happen through outright violent dispossession, a delegitimisation of the new resource owners through legislation, and critically, '"through the market" whereby those who have valuable assets, but are earning incomes too low to permit social reproduction, inevitably have to sell them' (Fairhead et al. 2012: 243). Alternatively, as is the case with Māori-owned quota, the assets may be leased, a dispossession not of property per se, but of productive rights.

Harvey (2003, 2005) identifies four key dimensions in neoliberalism that facilitate accumulation by dispossession, namely, privatisation, financialisation, the management and manipulation of crisis, and state redistribution. All of these promote accumulation but accomplish this in different ways. Crucial to all four dimensions in the context of interventions in nature, is the presumption that 'once property rights are established and transaction costs are minimized, voluntary trade in environmental goods and bads will produce optimal, least-cost outcomes with little or no need for state involvement' (McAfee 2012: 109). As noted in chapter 2, the privatisation and marketisation of fishing rights is a highly constructed political process; there is no necessary connection between property creation and marketisation, though the establishment of this relationship has far-reaching social consequences. Importantly, it is a never fully realised relationship and requires continuous state intervention.

The most distinctive feature of the current nature–society reorganisation is the centrality of the market, the logic of which mediates and reconstitutes humans and the environment. As Fairhead et al. comment, this 'involves novel forms of valuation, commodification and markets for pieces and aspects of nature' (2012: 237). The marketisation of marine environments, for instance, deconstructs nature by slicing up fishing rights into competing units of transferable property. It also differently positions value. Locating value in the marketplace draws attention away from productive activities, holistically conceived: from catching fish in nearby waters, and the transformation of the labour and knowledge tied up in small-scale harvesting; from the spatial and temporal dislocation of fish; from the fact that, in New Zealand, 60 percent of the offshore quota is caught by foreign chartered vessels and much of it is processed in China and then onward exported or shipped back to New Zealand for sale (Pinkerton 2014). Placing value in the market also draws attention away from consumption; contrary to popular sentiment it is highly unlikely that fish purchased from a quintessential fish-and-chip shop in New Zealand's coastal communities will have been caught by local fishermen, or that it will have been landed and processed nearby. It also obscures a critical assessment of the principles that govern the distribution of wages, profit and rent, and it incurs the emergence of future value. Büscher et al. (2012) observe that the marketisation of nature is accompanied by an intense focus on the future and a rejection of historical context and awareness. This future fetish is apparent in the increasing saliency given to virtual fish, those that come alive in exchanges and in electronic marketplaces, and upon which extraordinary sums of money can be made (Maguire 2014).

My focus in this chapter is on the marketisation of individual transferable quota (ITQ), with a particular stress on transferability, one of the key characteristics of the system. Transferability has a powerful potency in market relationships; is inextricably bound up with financialisation and crisis; and plays a decisive role in the emergent Blue Economy. Thus, in many ways transferability is in essence not about fish in the sea, rather, it concerns the emergence of virtual fish and the attendant relegation of nature, and labour, as inconsequential in generating wealth. I first discuss transferability in the context of the quota trading market and then consider the implications of this for Māori fisheries assets. The third section traces the financialistion of fishing rights in Icelandic fisheries and the fourth links ecosystem services and the Blue Economy.

Transferability

In ecosystem services, transferability describes one of a bundle of rights that accompany the creation of private property rights, that is, the right to transfer goods from one entity or asset holder to another and, the regulation of this right through a market-based instrument. This right directly facilitates an economistic valuation of 'natural capital'. Quota management systems (QMS) are largely measured by the aggregate value of quota share prices, that is, success is measured by increases in share prices. Value, proponents assert, arises out of transferability. When quota are freely tradable it is deemed possible to calculate the commercial value of the fish resource from the market price of quota, where the price of quota reflects the commercial value of the fish stock in conjunction with the resource rent.

In ITQ fisheries, a distinction can be made between quota holders, that is, those who have the right to fish and/or to lease this right to others, and fishers who do the actual harvesting. In Iceland and New Zealand, where quota is individualised and freely tradable, more wealth can be generated from trading activities than chasing fish in the seas. This is true not only of activities in the quota trading market (buying and selling quota) but is also reflected in the rewards that accrue to owners who lease their quota as distinct from fishing it. An illustration of the latter is provided in the case of fishing for snapper. SNA1 refers to snapper off the east coast of the North Island in Quota Management Area One (QMA1), and is New Zealand's most valuable inshore finfish fishery. Over the last few years the Total Allowable Catch (TAC) in SNA1 has been set at 7,550 tonnes. Of this, 4,950 is allocated to the commercial take (TACC – total allowable commercial catch) and about 2,550 to non-commercial catch. Of the latter, about 50 tonnes is harvested as customary take[1] while the remainder is recreational catch.[2] The quota asset value of snapper in SNA1 in 2009 was NZ$186 million, making SNA1 the fifth most valuable stock by quota asset value in the QMS (Ministry for Primary Industries 2013: 18). To use a different metric, in the 2014/15 season, data[3] indicates that the average quota price per kilo for SNA1 was NZ$72 per kilo. This is the asset value which can then be used as collateral in banks. The average annual catch entitlement (ACE) value (the earnings quota owners receive when selling their annual catch rights) was NZ$3.92 per kilo. The average port price (the price that fishers receive) was NZ$5.85 per kilo; thus, after paying for the trading arrangement, fishermen receive NZ$1.93 for their effort per kilo of fish sold.

The ratio of the price of quota to the price of fish is approximately 12:1 (NZ$72: NZ$5.85). The differential evaluation of ownership and labour is illustrated by the inequality in outcomes: in this example the owner obtains two times as much from leasing quota for one year (NZ$3.92) than the fisher gets from harvesting (NZ$1.93). However, this under-estimates the degree of inequality since the accountancy conceals the totality of links between property rights, marketisation and new ways of accumulating value under ecosystem services. For instance, the crew, vessel, maintenance and compliance costs that the skipper has to meet are obscured, as is the fact that quota owners are also likely to be Licensed Fish Receivers (LFRs) that is, fishermen likely lease ACE from the same body that they sell their fish to.

Another example: about 1,200 tonnes of *pāua* (abalone) are caught commercially in New Zealand each year, the majority of which is exported and export earnings are about NZ$60 million a year. The value of *pāua* quota has risen considerably over time. The average price of quota increased by 63.5 percent in the first six months of trading – from NZ$11 to NZ$17.99 per kilo. By 2003 the average price reached NZ$300 per kilo, 27 times the price at the start of *pāua* quota trading in 1988. Figures for the 2014/15 year put the dollar per kilo price of quota at NZ$338. The average ACE value is NZ$15.50 per year whereas the port price is NZ$16.50 per kilo, thus, after paying for the leasing arrangement non-quota-owning harvesters receive NZ$1 per kilo of *pāua* sold. The ratio of the value of quota to the price of fish is approximately 23:1 (383:16.5) and the owner obtains fifteen and a half times as much from leasing quota for one year (NZ$15.50) as the fisher gets from harvesting (NZ$1). Unsurprisingly, *pāua* quota holders describe their right as akin to having won the lottery.

The tension between labour and ownership in these statistics is reflected in the distinction between production and quota trading. Production, including the vertical integration of companies and the sale of fish, is a historic process. It is arguably a real, or at least visible market, whether free or feudal. The quota trading system is a virtual market in which the participants buy and sell 'fish' without ever having any need to have fish to sell (sellers) or ever wishing to own fish (buyers). Fish in this instance may be considered an example of Polanyian fictitious commodity production. Quota trading, however, may be a radically different type of fiction: while there is a physical limit to the amount of fish that can be harvested, quota trading does not appear to be constrained by any obvious boundaries.

Transferability encompasses a much broader social field than that allocated to it by the narrow economistic interpretation of market valuation. For instance, it is associated with market power, the emergence of new types of labour, and the conversion of fishing rights into financial assets. The tendency of quota systems to consolidate quota shares embeds a political structure that limits substantive participation in management decisions to those who hold quota. Thus, for instance, 'stakeholder groups', a conglomeration of quota holders, gradually silence the voices of more and more groups of people who consider themselves participants in fisheries – fishermen who lease fishing rights, fish processors, fishing families, boat builders, net makers, pot makers and so on. Such a silencing has structural implications – the rendering of livelihoods and communities as obsolete and/or the movement of people into even more exploitative relationships with capital. In Iceland this process is linked to the initial gifting of quota to vessel owners in 1984 (dependent on a three-year catch history) and, crucially, transferability, a mechanism used to unleash market trading from 1990, encouraging a flurry of mergers and acquisitions. Many fishing communities suffered a dramatic reduction in, or even the total loss of, their fishing rights as ITQs passed into the hands of non-local vessel owners (Eythórsson 2000). Between 2003 and 2007, 428 fishing companies ceased to exist through 282 mergers (Benediktsson and Karlsdóttir 2011). Fishing-dependent jobs also disappeared from some communities as processing at sea displaced land-based labour, a loss amounting to three out of every five such jobs in the two decades after 1990, undermining the economy of villages while simultaneously consolidating power in the hands of vessel owners (Karlsdóttir 2008). These losses occurred despite seemingly strong provisions favouring local preference. There is a stipulation, for instance, that each vessel be allocated a home port in one of eight regions, and that when quota shares attached to vessels (ACE)[4] are transferred outside of a community, the community itself in which the seller is located has the right to buy at the negotiated price. Thus, the transfer of annual catch shares between geographic regions is subject to revision by fishers' unions and local authorities (Arnason 1993). The latter provision, as Matthiasson and Agnarsson (2010: 302) note, has seldom been utilised as municipalities have not had the funds or the political will to intervene in the quota market. For this reason, few inter-regional transfers have been blocked in practice (Arnason 1993).

Transferability has created new forms of labour to work in the emergent facilities required to service the system. In New Zealand these include services surrounding quota and ACE maintenance, the management of share registers, the registration of ACE transfers, the registration of caveats and mortgages over quota shares, the recording of catch effort returns and vessel registration. Such services, among other statutory requirements, are undertaken by FishServe, a privately owned company.[5] Quota trading takes place through brokers and also through bilateral trading agreements. Most small and medium sized quota holders execute their transactions through brokers, whereas larger companies often employ specialist personnel to engage in bilateral trading with other large companies (Lock and Leslie 2007). Various online systems have emerged in conjunction with these exchanges. Among the many instances are FishStock, which provides an online auction system for dealing with the buying and selling of ACE; FishTech Ltd, which offers an ACE 'balancing service' which purports to optimise the value of ACE distribution; and FinestKind, a company which sells seafood, sources quota and acts as a broker.

Transferability and consolidation

The contradictory spaces opened for indigenous people under neoliberal governance are apparent in Māori fisheries. The settlement of fisheries claims in 1992 has resulted in a marked indigenous presence in the New Zealand industry; some 50 percent of fishing quota is ostensibly 'owned' by Māori, a significant asset given that the commercial fish resource is valued at roughly NZ$4 billion. Fisheries are New Zealand's fifth largest export, 90 percent of fish by value are exported and the yearly earnings from this activity are about NZ$1.4 billion.

ITQ enclosures, however, have opened the door to subsequent dispossessions in Māori fisheries. These dispossessions include: the expropriation of small-scale and part-time fishers, a development held to be a necessary condition to increase the economic efficiency of the fleet; the delegitimisation of the new resource owners through legislation pertaining to, for instance, the mandated construction of corporate entities to receive and manage quota; and the removal of exchange from Customary Fishing Regulations. They also include, critically, the consequences flowing from transferability, whereby those who hold the valuable assets are, via the logic of the system, incentivised to trade them. In addition, transferability implies consolidation, a key thematic in ITQ restructuring. In Iceland, for instance, consolidation is seen as one of the most reprehensible aspects of the quota system, not least because of the regional repercussions, which are perceived to have favoured the capital Reykjavik and the city of Akureyri at the expense of other locations, the Western Region in particular. In Iceland there is a specified maximum to the amount of shares that fishing firms can amass, a provision that suggests there is a definite limit to the aggregation of quota. The practice is outlined by Agnarsson et al.:

[in the regular quota system] The combined quota shares of fishing vessels held by individual parties in each fishery may not exceed a certain maximum, which is 12% of the total quota shares in the case of cod, but 20% for haddock, saithe, Greenland halibut, herring capelin and deep-water shrimp, and 35% for redfish. Maximum holdings are much smaller for vessels with hook-and-line quotas ... Quotas of different species may be added together in tons or kg. using cod equivalents ... for vessels operating under the regular quota system, the combined share in all fisheries may not exceed 12% in cod equivalents, but the corresponding maximum for hook-and-line boats is 5%. (2016: 264)

Matthiasson et al. comment, 'if the aim of restricting the share of a single firm in quota holdings was to prevent excessive concentration it can hardly be characterized as effective' (2015: 2). Two quota systems exist in Iceland: the 'regular' quota for boats larger than 6GRT (Gross Registered Tonnage) and, since 2001, the hook-and-line quota, restricted to smaller boats using handline and longline methods. While quota is freely transferable within both systems, transfers from the larger to the smaller sector are permitted while the reverse is not (Agnarsson et al. 2016). Despite the apparent separation of the two quota systems and the attempt to accommodate small-scale livelihoods, consolidation occurs in both sectors. In the regular quota system (bigger vessels) the ten largest fishing firms' command of quota rose from a fifth of all quotas in 1984 to more than half (56 percent) in 2015. Similarly, in the hook-and-line-quota (smaller vessels) system, the largest firm tripled its share over a 15-year period (Matthíasson et al. 2015: 2). There is also an established link between consolidation and the capture of processing wealth. Pálsson and Helgason note the early emergence in Iceland of 'fishing for others'. In this practice the first actor is the supplier of ITQs (who has aggressively aggregated quota) and the second actor is the fisherman who does the actual harvesting. The first actor, the supplier of ITQs, is a large vertically integrated, typically non-fishing company, controlling two or more companies and a processing plant. Between the two actors:

a contract is arranged, whereby the large ITQ holder transfers ITQs [sic; actually ACE] to the small operator's boat. The latter then fishes the ITQs [sic; ACE] and delivers the catch to the supplier's processing plant. In return the smaller operator receives payment, which usually amounts to about 50%–60% of the market value of the catch. (2000: n.p.)

Meanwhile, Bodwitch identifies an early development in New Zealand concerning the rationale motivating strategically positioned, vertically integrated fish processors who, 'wanted quota to ensure their access to fish would not be restricted by control of quota in the hands of fishers' (2017: 90).

In New Zealand quota consolidation is advanced. About 80 percent of catch is supplied by five companies, three of which are Māori owned.[6] The largest of those, Aotearoa Fisheries Limited (AFL),[7] emerged out of the interim fisheries settlement in 1989. It is the commercial arm of Te Ohu Kai Moana (formerly the Māori Fisheries Commission) and is tasked with operationalising quota. AFL adopted an early policy of leasing out quota and using the accrued profits to purchase more quota as well as fishing companies. Currently, it owns seven companies whose interests include fishing, processing, marketing, aquaculture and *pāua* (abalone), and it holds the Māori shares in the Sealords fishing company. In 2008 AFL had a net profit of NZ$19 million and in 2009 it began paying an annual dividend (40 percent of net profits) to qualifying *iwi*. By 2014 profits had risen to NZ$21.9 million. AFL outlines its objectives as follows: 'Our vision is to be the key investment vehicle of choice for *iwi* in the fishing industry, to maximize the value of Māori fisheries assets and to ensure that we are a strong seafood business delivering growth in shareholder wealth' (Aotearoa Fisheries Limited n.d.). Investment here translates as catch rights. Currently 14 *iwi* lease catch rights to AFL under long-term leasing arrangements, and other *iwi* do so on a year-by-year basis. *Iwi* are collectively the major suppliers of leasing rights to AFL. Through these agreements, and other acquisitions, AFL manages commercial seafood assets of over NZ$530 million. AFL, as a market participant, vies with other companies in the highly competitive quota trading market.

Transferability and Māori Treaty assets

The devolution of quota to *iwi*, which began in 2004 with the implementation of the Māori Fisheries Act, is, as noted, implicated in an upsurge in trade. The Act set out the legislative basis for a pan-*iwi* distribution of fisheries settlement assets, that is the capital and quota centrally held by Te Ohu Kai Moana up to that point. In order to qualify for fishing assets *iwi* must set up a mandated *iwi* organisation (MIO) and one or more asset-holding companies. There are currently 57 recognised MIOs, inclusive of four collective groupings of *iwi*. MIO entities blend a corporate structure with a charitable trust fund complex: the new bodies can sell quota, or lease or fish their rights to generate tribal wealth which then must be distributed for the benefit of *iwi* members. Very few *iwi* actually fish their quota and there is a conspicuous absence of Māori fishers at all levels in the industry.

To illustrate the activities involved in the marketisation of fishing rights I will draw on the post-settlement history of one *iwi*, and although other *iwi* will have different stories to tell, there is, nonetheless a general commonality of experience. Waikato-Tainui has an extensive tribal estate, a membership of approximately 60,000 individuals (67 percent live in the tribal area, 28 percent elsewhere in New Zealand and 5 percent overseas) and comprises 33 *hapū* and 68 *marae*[8] (meeting house complexes). Since an emotionally charged historical land alienation settlement in the mid-1990s (see Hopa 1999; van Meijl 2013), the *iwi* has emerged as a significant economic force in the region, with net assets amounting to approximately NZ$921.4 million in 2016 (Waikato-Tainui 2016). Tainui Group Holdings (TGH) and Waikato-Tainui Fisheries are the commercial entities of the tribe and in 2015 had a combined net operating profit of NZ$35.6 million (Waikato-Tainui 2015). The self-proclaimed objective of these bodies is wealth creation, 'to deliver commercial returns on assets for the Waikato-Tainui people' (TGH and Waikato-Tainui Fisheries Ltd 2011: 2). Wealth generation is kept distinct from wealth redistribution, which is handled by a separate body, Waikato-Tainui Te Kauhanganui Inc. The latter received a dividend to the value of NZ$13.9 million in 2015, NZ$1.9 million of which came from the activities of Waikato-Tainui Fisheries (Waikato-Tainui 2015). The combined debt of the commercial entities is approximately 26 percent of the total assets and this is managed through a financial instrument designed to hedge interest rate risks.

In terms of fisheries, wealth is generated 'by investments in fishing managed funds and equities' (TGH and Waikato-Tainui Fisheries Ltd 2011: 26). TGH is the asset-holding company of quota and other assets allocated under the 2004 Māori Fisheries Act. The company has entered into an alliance with two other MIOs through which they lease out the aggregated quota held by all three. None of these *iwi* actually fish their quota. Wealth is also generated through income shares held in AFL, of which TGH holds 5.5 percent. The market in fishing quota has recently been supplemented by the Emissions Trading Scheme, a carbon market with opportunities for global trade, in which TGH has been granted units for the quota held in fisheries.

The wealth generated from TGH investments, including that created from quota leasing activities, is distributed to beneficiaries in the form of dividends to *marae* for upkeep, tertiary scholarships and so on. Yet, the general impact on individual Māori is virtually non-existent. Ngapare Hopa (1999) contends that in the case of Waikato-Tainui (of which she is a member) this is a result of the capture of wealth by an elite. This expropriation, she suggests was enabled by an articulated manipulation of Māori kinship organisation by both the Crown and Māori Treaty negotiators; treaty settlements in Waikato-Tainui elevated the status of *iwi* and disempowered *hapū* and *whānau* (extended family), resulting in a centralised and corporatised control over communal resources and wealth (Hopa 1999). In Waikato-Tainui this is further complicated by the existence of a kingly lineage to which wealth and power gravitates. Meanwhile, Angeline Greensill (Tainui Iwi and member of a non-beneficiary coastal *marae*) argues, first, that the disenfranchisement of *hapū* is exacerbated by the fact that treaty settlement dividends are allocated to *marae* rather than *hapū*, and, second, that representation on central decision-making forums is determined by *marae* rather than *hapū* membership (Greensill 2010).

A new hierarchy, confluent with the fisheries settlement, is emergent in Māori society, though the contours of this are complex and far from complete. At one end of the ladder sit the tribal bodies obligated to generate wealth through quota investments. At the other end are coastal *hapū* and *iwi* groups whose fishing practices and livelihoods have been radically transformed and whose compensation for this is a trickle-down distribution flowing from quota-leasing activities. Given the disparity in wealth within Māori society, a number of commentators argue that treaty settlements are themselves facilitating a gradual transformation of tribal hierarchies into class distinctions. Rata (2011), for instance, points to the emergence of a corporate, alienated, resource-capturing indigenous elite and a new and exclusive form of biculturalism. This bicultural exclusivity, she argues, marks a shift in the interpretation of treaty settlements from one concerned with the reparative settlement of historical alienations to one based on the promotion of a political partnership between tribes and the government. This discourse, suggests Rata, developed to justify the political and economic claims of the neo-tribal elite to public resources and services. Rata asserts that the rapid rise to success of this elite is interlinked with the production by its intellectual members of an indigenous ideology of two peoples, which while capturing 'the rhetoric of biculturalism's reparative and redistributive ideals ... redirects it in ways that serve the interests of the small tribal elite' (2011: 361). Focusing attention on the confluence of treaty settlements with the emergence of tribal elites, as well as the convergence of indigenous and non-indigenous entrepreneurial enterprises, Rata suggests that new forms of class alliances in New Zealand have an effective smokescreen through appeals to indigeneity. This analysis, arguably, does not take adequate account of both the contingency and the messiness of 'culture'. Consequently, her conclusion that New Zealand's democracy is threatened by 'tribalism' and indigeneity which is incompatible with 'a unified nation with a constituted government accountable to its equal citizens' (Rata 2013) is potentially deeply reactionary. Rata's promotion of the notion of a 'universal human being', while much lauded by socially conservative, free-market political parties, ultimately implies a New Zealand with no Māori, no treaty and no history (McCormack 2016).

The new class relations and consciousness that have emerged in Māori society, I suggest, are ambiguous, incomplete and intersect with culture in often unpredictable ways so that we are just as likely to see instances of retribalisation as neo-tribalisation. One of the noted distributional effects following the introduction of a market-based fisheries regime is the development of a new class structure (Pinkerton and Edwards 2009). Yet rather than the alienated elite imagined by Rata, Māori tribal leaders simultaneously interact in Māori communities as kin and perform reciprocal obligations that are themselves rooted in 'tradition'. This dual practice of leaders, at once striving for entrepreneurship *and* communality, challenges the telos that is assumed to be the trajectory of neoliberalism (Ganti 2014). There are, however, structural constraints to such agency.

While not disagreeing with the observation that new indigenous hierarchies have arisen, and that these may articulate with the appropriation and control of material resources by a select few, I root the source of these new relations within a broader political-economic framework. The settlement of Māori fisheries rights coincided with the marketisation of fisheries, a process that has increasingly influenced the production and exchange of fish, to an important degree coerced the behaviour of actors within the sector, elevated the status of traders and brokers while devaluing the knowledge associated with harvesting, the result being the transformation of nature into a financial derivative. Quota trading works through a radical disembedding, in this instance disembedding the economic issue from the historical question of how to manage fisheries in a way that sustains coastal communities and the ecosystems on which they depend. This issue has a particular resonance for indigenous fishers.

These extensive social shifts are further illustrated through a consideration of foreign charter vessels (FCVs), a phenomenon recently brought to the attention of the New Zealand public following the deaths of a number of crew members and subsequent accusations of inhumane labour conditions on board these vessels (Simmons and Stringer 2014). Of the 43.3 million tonnes of fish currently caught in New Zealand waters each year, approximately 34 percent is harvested by foreign flagged fishing vessels (Simmons et al. 2015). FCVs make up 50 percent of the deep-water fleet and are hired by New Zealand-based companies to catch their quota. Te Ohu Kai Moana estimate that iwi lease a maximum of 17 percent of the catch of such vessels (Innes 2013).

There are a number reasons why iwi are likely to lease catch rights (ACE) to FCVs. First, given the regulatory requirement that the sale of iwi settlement quota be supported by 75 percent of adult iwi members, leasing rather than selling may be the least controversial option. Second, while for some iwi Māori settlement quota is owned as part of a more diversified set of asset holdings, for many iwi fishing quota is their only significant asset. For the latter, reducing risks and reaping the highest profit from the least amount of capital input may appear to be the only rational economic choice. Third, many iwi groups do not have the technology, the capital (boats and equipment) or the knowledge to harvest, in particular, deep-sea fish. No iwi operates their own deep-water fishing boat.[9] Fourth, the tonnage of quota held for a particular species is often too small to sustain a local fishing venture, hence quota is leased to companies which then aggregate it. Fifth, iwi-owned quota packages contain a disproportionate amount of high volume species on the lower end of the commercially valuable spectrum; thus, in order to be economically viable it is necessary to lease rights rather than incur the cost of harvesting. Finally, the use of FCVs may be invisible as ACE leasing arrangements go through a maze of brokers – ACE is channelled (or solicited) through traders who then lease either to FCVs or New Zealand vessels. This 'quota maze' is part of an international commodity chain: FCVs typically process fish at sea, pass it on to a New Zealand Licensed Fish Receiver, which exports it for secondary processing to China, Thailand or Vietnam, before the fish is marketed internationally by leading firms that buy fish.

FCV leasing highlights the irony inherent in ITQ systems. The saliency of recapturing fishing activities in New Zealand waters from foreign vessels, the impetus behind claiming the Exclusive Economic Zone (EEZ) as state property, appears to have been counteracted by these new trading arrangements. Significantly, the trading of catch rights in general may point to a radical change in the role of property. This change is institutionalised through the slicing up of fishing rights into short-term harvesting rights (ACE) and the granting of ownership rights in perpetuity (quota). In his analysis of Māori settlements, van Meijl (2013) contends that in modern economies the idea of exchanging property in markets, a defining feature in capitalist economies, is now becoming an anachronism. Although property continues to exist it is much less likely to be exchanged, which in turn forces owners to hold on to their property and to seek different ways to generate income from their assets. ACE provides an ideal solution to this conundrum. It also goes some way towards explicating the disparity between the large amount of Māori 'business interest' in the industry and the disproportionate level of Māori unemployment.

Commercial fishing for most Māori, at least at the *hapū* level, is largely synonymous with receiving annual dividends from quota investments. These dividends flow to *marae* rather than individuals, and only to those *marae* whose members have agreed to the terms of the settlement. For many Māori fishers, whose expertise is generationally validated and whose identification with a particular seascape is ancestral, there is a profound sense of exclusion. This disaffection is ongoing, influences livelihood and identity practices and manifests itself in the outmigration of young people from coastal communities. It also affects the ability to fulfil cultural obligations surrounding the supply of *kaimoana* to kin and guests.

In New Zealand commercial fishing is increasingly part of a global system of trade. Since 2000, the post-harvest processing of fish has been largely transferred to China, where the potential to maximise financial returns through the utilisation of low labour costs means that it has become the option of choice for most of New Zealand's largest seafood processing companies (Stringer et al. 2011). These trends, which can be conceived of as financialisation, are bound up with a concentration of fishing rights and quota ownership, and a decrease in new entrants, and signify the new ways in which fishing firms pursue returns on their investments. They also account for the decline in the processing of fish in New Zealand's coastal communities and a decrease in the number of locally based commercial fishers. The financialisation of ITQ fisheries is fundamental to the activities surrounding quota transference, the remodelling of quota (through ACE) to better facilitate trading, the growth of markets and businesses around quota trading, the increasing offshoring of the industry, and the elite control of these financial activities. In 2016, of the top twelve richest people in New Zealand, two had amassed their fortunes through fisheries.

The magic of finance

Smith (2007) intimates that something new is afoot, namely, that emerging environmental markets accomplish the capitalisation of nature more profoundly than either extractive resource capitalism or agricultural capital. This is so because in the process they transform nature into a thing that can be fully abstracted into exchange value and financialised. Thus, fish have not just been redesignated under quota systems as resource commodities but are now entirely reconstructed as financial commodities. This potential for ecosystem services to incorporate the functions of nature as exchange value is not a recent event. Gallagher and DiNovelli-Lang (2014) persuasively trace the origins of this movement to the evolution of the academic discipline of ecology during the 20th century and its ongoing relation to classical and later neoclassical economics. Neither is financialisation a new phenomenon, rather it should be understood as a recurrent phase in capitalist development (Arrighi 1994). What perhaps is new, however, is the entanglement of neoliberalism, ecosystem services and financialisation.

Following Epstein (2002), I take financialisation to refer to the increasing importance of financial markets, financial motives and financial elites in the operation of the economy and its governing institutions, both at the national and international levels. Kotz (2010) argues that the immediate cause of the financialisation process of recent decades is to be found in the neoliberal restructuring in the 1970s and 1980s. This restructuring of the institutional arrangements of capitalism, from a previously regulated era, set the stage for the expansionary role of finance in economic activity, and the classification of more and more social and natural domains as 'economic'. As a key instrument in corporate capitalism, financialisation preceded neoliberalism. However, under previous socioeconomic regimes, it was more or less constrained by the specific institutional arrangements capitalism assumed at different points in its history. Neoliberalism essentially opened the floodgates. Kotz

(2010) contends that the financial sector displays specific qualities under neoliberalism. In the current era, the financial sector does not stand in a relation of dominance vis-à-vis the non-financial sector (as it did in the 1920s, before the 1929 economic collapse), rather, the financial sector is independent of it. It is this apparent independence that helps explicate the discontinuities between quota holders, leasing arrangements and fishers.

Transferability makes possible the transformation of fishing rights into financial assets. Finance is distinct from traditional banking in that traditional banks sell money in their possession whereas financial firms sell something they do not have. This virtual quality underlies the thrust in the financial sector to be innovative. It is in the context of this requisite hyper-creativity that Sassen conceives of finance as a capability, 'though one with variable valence' (2014: 118), one which first creates an economy and then seeks to expand to a point where it securitises just about everything in it. Securitisation involves the relocation of a good, a building or a debt, into a financial circuit where it becomes mobile and can be bought and sold over and over in local and global markets. In the past few decades the financial sector, which has long been peopled by mathematically trained physicists, has invented very complex instruments to securitise arcane instances of familiar items – for example, used car loans and fishing rights. Once an input is securitised, financial engineering can keep on building long chains of increasingly speculative instruments that all rest on the alleged stability of that first step. In this sense Sassen warns: 'The power of finance, and what makes it dangerous, is its capacity to build up its own value even as households, economies and governments lose value' (2014: 118). It is precisely this magical aspect of finance that underpinned the Icelandic financial crash of 2008, an event linked to the evolution of transferable fishing rights as financial assets (Benediktsson and Karlsdóttir 2011; Einarsson 2011; Flaaten 2010).

By recreating fishing rights as transferable property a spectacular investment frontier was opened. This was bolstered by two other key components of ITQs, first, the division of property into short-term harvesting rights (ACE) and permanent TAC shares (quota) and, second, the existence of an invented currency, the cod equivalent. Cod equivalents for each quota year are determined on the basis of the average unit value of the landings of each species the year before, and provide a measure of the relative value of individual species compared to cod. Thus cod equivalents enable the conversion of different species of fish into the standardised currency of cod (Helgason and Pálsson 1997: 452–53), work undertaken somewhat similarly by the deemed value system in New Zealand. These mechanisms form a complex and oblique system which functions primarily to empower finance to disembed value from nature and labour and resituate it in an unencumbered, utopian future.

Fishing rights were the foundation of the pre-crash Icelandic economic renaissance, an era in which the country was transformed from one of modest means to one of the world's wealthiest nations. The new, modern Iceland threw off the shackles of a colonial past, witnessed a revitalisation of Viking imagery and celebrated the arrival of fearless, adventure seeking, business entrepreneurs (Loftsdóttir 2010). In 1990, when quota was made transferable and thus alienable, new conditions of accumulation by dispossession were created and fortunes were made by a handful of increasingly consolidated quota holders. In 1997, when it became legal to use quota as collateral for loans, fishing firms began to accumulate enormous debts through the mortgage of fishing rights. This marked the point at which the rift between work and future value creation became substantiated: wealth could be attained simply by owning and exchanging quota and no longer required direct engagement in fishing.

In the late 1990s, the three main Icelandic banks began a process of privatisation, a development that coincided with a growth in investment companies. A number of large quota holders became owners of the newly privatised banks, a move alleged to have involved corruption and partisanship (Benediktsson and Karlsdóttir 2011). The new owners of privatised banks and investment companies engaged in frenetic, speculative, overseas investment adventures (football teams, pension funds and so on), much of which rested on the presumed stability of quota as the first step. In this way quota became activated capital and was financialised to create credit expansion and its corollary, indebtedness. Icelandic economist Ragnar Arnason enthused: 'ITQ wealth is living capital ... with the help of the financial system, ITQs have been used to generate financial capital to be used in other industries' (2008: 32). The level of indebtedness, which doubled between 1997 and 2007, is here seen as a sign of the virility of the system. The historic hierarchy of the expansive power of credit and the restrictive capacity of debt is in this instance challenged: it is debt that becomes the crucial constituent of financial markets, a phenomenon that suggests that debt itself has productive qualities (see Roitman 2005).

The new dispensation to use fishing rights as collateral meant that the market price of firms, and the prices of stocks and number of commodity markets escalated rapidly. This collateral also enabled banks to convince foreign investors that they had strong assets and equity and therefore their credibility was assured. The market price of fishing rights (that is, quota) became increasingly inflated. In 2000 the price of cod equivalent was 800 Icelandic krona per kilo – a figure far higher than any fisherman could consider as a reasonable investment given a disparity between the price of actual fish landed and the price of quota. By 2008 the price of cod equivalent was 4,400 krona per kilo, creating a brick wall for new entrants. The profit to be made from the sale of virtual fish, at this stage, amounted to approximately 80 years of fishing revenues (Maguire 2014). The total value of quota in 2008 reached an astronomical 2,000 billion Icelandic krona, 50 times the entire annual profit of the fishing industry (Einarsson 2011), a disparity which is reflective of the capacity of finance to innovate, to securitise and to alienate what was once perceived of as a common and constitutional right to a natural resource. It also indicates how great fortunes and escalating inequality are generated in a process that is only tangentially related to the production of physical commodities.

Quota debt spread to the small-scale sector, with devastating consequences. As large quota holders with newly acquired wealth abandoned coastal villages for the pull of Reykjavik and a perceived modernity, small-scale fishers and smaller firms, with the encouragement of banks, took out loans to purchase the quota before it disappeared entirely from the local fishery. It is important to consider the way in which the debt/credit relationship may be thrust on debtors by zealous creditors. Strathern (1992) notes that debtors are not necessarily needy, rather, new needs are created which in turn necessitates the taking on of new debts. In this context, Icelandic banks merely serviced the needs already created by the introduction of transferable property in fishing rights. Banks, keen to optimise quota transactions, began to offer what at the time seemed to be generous loans for investments in quota shares, some of which were denominated in foreign currency. The ensuing increase in transactions resulted in raising the price of quota, together with the collateral equity and the virtual fish asset base in the balance sheet of the banks (Einarsson 2011: 147). After the financial crash, the quota-cum-collateral, or virtual fish, was in the control of the banks (newly salvaged by state funds) and their foreign creditors. The costs of servicing these quota debts escalated, especially those denominated in foreign currencies, due to the collapse in the value of the Icelandic krona. For many small-scale operators discharging these debts is extremely difficult, if not an unachievable fantasy. After the 2008 collapse the fishing industry owed about 465 billion krona, roughly twelve times the industry's annual profits. Ragnar Arnason's celebration of the natural ability of living capital to stimulate the economy is now considered an exercise in speculative gambling; an amoral venture in risk-taking that mortgaged the entire industry, including future generations of fishermen, without any significant improvements in boats, processing facilities or fishing technologies (Maguire 2014).

It is interesting to note the link between the impact of ITQ and debates over the morality/immorality/amorality of the credit/debt dyad itself (see Peebles 2010). Debt is conceived of as both destructive and productive, as creator and dissolver of social borders and hierarchies. This dual capacity is contingent not only on how people strategically position themselves, but also, and in particular, on the entrenchment of pre-existing inequalities during the financial crisis. As a result of the crisis, small-scale, quota-holding fishermen frequently became trapped in a vicious cycle of debt, whereas large firms and corporate quota holders were able to deflect their supposed obligations (Einarsson 2011: 147). Verdery's (2003) work concerning the socialisation of debt is helpful here – she points to the tragic ways in which collective debt is foisted onto individuals while corporations accrue previously collective credit onto themselves.

Fisheries are crucial in Iceland, which, with a population of 300,000, is among the largest seafood nations in the world, both in terms of volume of catch as well as value. Since the 1990s fishing and processing have represented about 10 percent of gross domestic product (GDP). The export of fish, mostly to the European Union (EU) though in particular to the UK, accounts for over half of the value of exported goods (Christensen et al. 2009). The fisheries sector is thus central to the overall economy. Iceland has not applied for membership of the EU largely because of concerns about the Common Fisheries Policy – CFP) and historic disputes over access of foreign fishing vessels to Icelandic waters. Given the fishing-dependent nature of the economy, and the strong and generational identification of Icelandic people with fisheries, it is unsurprising that there has been passionate debate on issues surrounding the ITQ system for over 30 years. This debate is especially concerned with the fate of the small-scale sector. Some concessions have been made, in particular, the establishment of two parallel quota systems (discussed above), the implementation of catch fees, the allocation of community development quota to villages and the reintroduction of a derby-style fishery[10] in 2009. Compromises such as these can be viewed as a corporate attempt to 'humanise' the economy, a moral neoliberalism that softens the market variety (Muehlebach 2012).

Yet, the type of opportunities assumed to be engendered rests ultimately on the market as a distributor of equality, the results of which are likely to be ambiguous at best.

In 2002 the Icelandic Parliament revised the Fishery Management Act to include a catch fee (*veidigjald*) payable by quota-holding vessel owners. This concession was aimed at appeasing the public disquiet caused by the free assignment of quotas, an injustice considered inequitable if not unconstitutional (Matthiasson 2008). The catch fee, in this regard, can be thought of as an attempt to recapture the commons quality of Icelandic fisheries and an associated morality. It is levied yearly as a given amount (to reach 9.5 percent of estimated resource rent) per cod-equivalent kilo. The formula used in the calculation is decreed in law, though as Matthiasson (2008) points out, explicit references in the formula to prevailing economic theory indicate that catch fees can be opportunistically lowered if the economy is perceived to be in need of bolstering. Other ambiguities are also apparent: the introduction of the catch fee occurred simultaneously with the discontinuation of some fishing levies which previously accrued to the public purse. The new income thus merely compensates for money lost; the catch fee has so far been in the range of 0.6–1.6 percent of the rental price of quotas, where the rental price is seen by many as a proxy for the resource rent, and it has not significantly reduced the tension caused by the free assignment of quotas.

The community development quota system (*byggðakvóti*), was introduced in 2003 in an attempt to mitigate the impact of transfers of quota from small and vulnerable communities (Kokorsch et al. 2015). Each year the Ministry of Industry and Innovation allocates quota directly to fishermen who undertake to land fish in particular communities according to regulations specific to that community. The quota is not exclusive, overlaps with the small-boat ITQ sector and can also be given to large-boat ITQ holders. Comprehensive surveys and qualitative research conducted by Icelandic scholars point to a high level of dissatisfaction with the community development quota system as a means to assuage the exigencies of the ITQ system in general, and transferability in particular (Chambers and Carothers 2016; Korkorsch et. al 2015).

In 2009, in response to concerns about new entrants and the inequity of the ITQ system, the post-economic crash government instituted a new coastal fishery, the *strandveiðar*, a summer inshore handline/jigging fishery. This in effect was an attempt to reverse enclosures, prompted partly by the United Nations Humans Rights Committee (UNHRC) report on the social injustice occasioned by the privatisation of fisheries. The *strandveiðar* operates as follows: all registered boats, including those holding quotas, may join the fishery, which runs during May, June, July and August. The fishing grounds off Iceland are divided into four areas and a pre-determined cod-cap is set per month in each of the areas. It is an open-access fishery and fishing in each month and area is suspended once the cap is reached. Fishers are further curtailed by technology, time and harvest; only handline technology can be used, fishing is restricted to 14 hours per day from Monday to Thursday, and the catch limit is 650 kg in cod equivalents of demersal fish (Agnarsson et al. 2016). Chambers and Carothers (2016), in a survey of Icelandic small-boat fishermen, find scant optimism among their respondents. For instance, it does little to enable new entrants; the average age of fishers in 2013 was 60 and time spent working in the fishing industry was 30 years. The cost of boats, jig machines, bait, captain licences, fuel and compliance with safety regulations prohibits access by newcomers. Further, the fishery does not support a full-time livelihood; rather, it is perceived to benefit those already engaged in quota fishing or those for whom fishing is an enjoyable pastime (Chamber and Carothers 2016: 9). Crucially, the *strandveiðar* does not operate in a vacuum, irrespective of the non-ITQ nomenclature used to describe it; the mechanisms of privatisation influence the operation and success of this fishery.

The pelagic mackerel has emerged as a critical new rejuvenator in the post-crisis Icelandic seascape, generating a revitalisation of fortunes and around which old and new contestations are being played out. Such conflicts are rooted in ecological as well as political and economic origins. Rising ocean temperatures are implicated in the boom in mackerel stocks in Icelandic waters in 2008; a northern translocation that instigated an international dispute between Iceland, Norway, the Faroe Islands and the EU over the constitution of a sustainable mackerel quota. An uneasy truce was reached in 2010 granting 640,000 tonnes of mackerel quota to Iceland, a development that especially concerns Irish fishers (see chapter 5). In Iceland a new bill, dubbed the mackerel quota, is before parliament, which, while vesting 5 percent of the quota to small-boat owners contentiously allocates all mackerel quota for a period of six years. The bill is deemed to contravene the annual setting of TACs, the method through which quota is allocated as ITQs and through which a semblance of state ownership is maintained. It is also seen as problematic as individual members of the ruling Progressive Party, themselves heavily involved in the quota market, are poised to benefit unduly. An online petition challenging the bill had attracted 20 percent of the Icelandic electorate by April 2016. Andri Sigurðsson, a democracy advocate, member of the Pirate Party and one of the petition's organisers explains:

> This new law needs to be scrapped and re-written. Our fisheries' policies need to use open market solutions where Icelanders are guaranteed their share of the famous pie everyone loves talking about. Because right now, the gluttonous bastards who hold the fishing rights want to have the whole pie for themselves, crumbs and all. (in Fontaine 2015)

A sentiment that aligns with the long-standing use of feudal metaphors to critique Iceland's ITQ system and which proffers the open market as a more equitable alternative.

Ecosystem services, the Blue Economy and ocean grabbing

The rise of the Blue Economy has its roots in an acceptance of the ecosystem services model in the marine environment. The advocates for this model stress the untapped wealth-generating potential of the earth's ecosystems; that it is inequitable that the goods and services provided by nature to sustain the economy are essentially free. Since the 1990s environmental economists have pointed to the absence of a monetary value on the cycling of nutrients for the production of renewable resources (such as fish and forest products), the pollination of flowering plants, and the regulation of the environment (Pearce 1998). In response to this 'concern' a group of scientists, ecologists and economists spearheaded an effort to assess the value in US dollars of the earth's ecosystem services and estimated the entire value of the biosphere to be US$33 trillion per year in 1995 (Costanza et al. 1997) revised to US$125–45 trillion in 2011 (Costanza et. al 2014). Since, there has been a proliferation of efforts to place a monetary value on ecosystems, in other words, to audit nature. This furore, which ostensibly provides a platform for unifying environmental and economic interests, is explicit in the Blue Economy.

The concept of the Blue Economy, while less popularised than its Green Economy sibling, emerged out of the Rio+20 conference in 2012. The United Nations (UN) Food and Agricultural Organization (FAO) solidified the idea with the launching of its Blue Growth Initiative (BGI) in 2013, wherein blue growth is defined as 'the sustainable growth and development emanating from economic activities in the oceans, wetlands and coastal zones, that minimize environmental degradation, biodiversity loss and unsustainable use of living aquatic resources, and maximize economic and social benefits' (FAO 2015: 8). The initiative addresses four key components: capture fisheries, aquaculture, livelihood and food systems (that is, access to markets and value chains), and *economic growth from ecosystem services.*

Maria Bargh, a Māori political scientist, argues that the Blue Economy framework, (as promoted by 'serial entrepreneur' Gunter Pauli [Pauli 2010]) operates from a particular 'cultural genealogy' which 'places a focus on individual entrepreneurs and innovations rather than collectives and communal-owned operations per se' (2014: 467). An overt future orientation displaces historical practices and traditional knowledge. Meanwhile Barbesgaard (2015) points out that the ideology informing the proposal is clearly aligned with the extension of market mechanisms in environmental governance:

Each of the four [BGI] components stress the catalyzing role of market-based mechanisms in ensuring ecosystem stewardship [in addition to prioritising] the need for partnerships among industry, governments and communities and how especially the private sector and public–private partnerships play a fundamental role in this process. (2015: 6)

Clearly big picture stuff. Arguably the Blue Economy accentuates the centuries-long process of enclosures in the world's fisheries by identifying a new wave of 'growth opportunities' in marine and coastal ecosystems.

Although not initially framed as a market-based mechanism to achieve environmental goals, privatisation policies in fisheries, such as ITQs, have been rebranded to meet these new priorities. In the context of the Blue Economy, ITQs have been incorporated as an exemplary ecosystem tool, showcasing the opportunities such conversions enable. This inclusion ties ITQs into an emergent meta-ideology and implies not only a 'greening' of inherent conflicts but also a newly invigorated drive to extend their global reach (see Longo et al. 2015). The Coastal Fisheries Initiative, for instance, a partnership of six organisations[11] aimed at reforming fisheries in six countries in three continents,[12] promotes secure tenure rights as a vital step in catalysing private sector involvement (Barbesgaard 2015: 7).

Meanwhile, under the umbrella of the Blue Economy and the EU Directive on Maritime Spatial Planning, Ireland is implementing an initiative entitled 'Harnessing our Ocean Wealth', promoted as key to stimulating economic recovery. Crucial to the initiative is blue growth, private sector participation and 'strike[ing] a balance between protecting our marine ecosystems and maximising the use of its resources as a source of economic growth' (Irish Marine Development Office 2012: 4). Such strategies not only imply propertisation but also a massive speculation-driven trade through newly created markets and the incentivisation of entrepreneurial actors not formerly predisposed to engage with the wealth potential of fisheries.

In the next chapter I depart from an investigation of ITQ technologies. Drawing on the anthropological tradition of the gift I illustrate how this framework pervades fishing activities in contemporary Hawaii.

4

Gifts and Commodities: Hawaiian Fisheries

The thesis advanced by the Tongan scholar Epeli Hau'ofa (1994) on the deep intertwining of Pacific peoples' identity with the Pacific Ocean, however generalised and romantic, resonates in the social landscape of Hawaii where the sea is a ubiquitous presence in everyday existence. Fishing is an expression of this identification. For Native Hawaiians to be an esteemed fisher is culturally valued; it indicates an ability to provide food from the seascape; it signifies the *'ohana* (extended family) values complex in its capacity to feed kin and fulfil reciprocal and ceremonial obligations as distinct from the perceived *haole* (non-Polynesian/ white/ outsider) value of individualism, and it references a profound environmental knowledge. I was emphatically told by a young Hawaiian student from Molokai island that 'to be a fisherman is to be Hawaiian', and a Hawaiian *kupuna* (elder), from Keaukaha (a Hawaiian homestead community on the Big Island) characterised fishing, along with taro growing and hunting, as 'real culture', opposing it – somewhat dismissively – to hula dancing and other creative arts. In Hawaii fishing is embedded in a gift economy: the social and kin obligations this entails, the claims to ownership and livelihoods it references, and the politicking that enlivens it. Gifting fish also maintains significant aspects of personalisation. Recipients, for instance, may have personal ties to the fisher and often also to the family of the fisher. Stories are recounted concerning the donor's fishing exploits and prowess and when gifted seafood is dried or processed as *poke*,[1] distinct tastes also become associated with particular fishers. Fish is also frequently sold by those classified by the state as non-commercial fishermen.

This chapter explores the gift as it permeates contemporary Hawaii. The concept of the gift is used here not in the sense of a nostalgic return to a venerable social theory, nor does it flow from a perspective of a moral injunction that we ought to bring the gift back into our own society. Rather, the theory of the gift allows for a nuanced language that mediates between abstract conceptualisation and empirical analysis; and it does so in ways that highlight the quotidian, the daily work of navigating social relations, of maintaining a sense of collective identity, and the emergence of often small and unremarkable forms of resistance that, writ large, become powerful obstructions to neoliberalisation. Importantly, the theory of the gift best captures the discourse Hawaiians themselves employ to engage with their fisheries. At a more general level, while commoditisation, the subjection of goods to market exchange, appears antithetical to gifting, threaded throughout this chapter is the argument that fish, as products of social labour, can be concurrently both commodity and gift; that this possibility is embedded in local economies and property regimes and does not signify a schism in either social or economic spheres.

The activities of fishermen in commodity exchanges do not imply inauthenticity, or a move away from a gift economy. This point is also made by James Carrier (1995) in his discussion of Melanesian ethnography where he comments on the Occidentalism produced when societies are envisioned as either purely commodity or gift driven. Margaret Jolly (2015) has raised the possibility that the binary between commodities and gifts may be eclipsed, at least in the case of Oceanic *braed praes* (bride price), by considering the exchange as simultaneously both. This transactional permeability is key to understanding how Pacific peoples balance an engagement with capitalism with the richness associated with their traditional ways of life (McCormack and Barclay 2013). I contend, further, that neoliberalisation, as epitomised by the rolling out of individual transferable quota (ITQ) regimes, works to rigidify the distinction between gifts and commodities, transforming both phenomena into extreme and alienated versions of their original selves. Yet this dichotomisation is never stable, as Tsing suggests: 'Despite all the apparatus of private property, markets, commodity fetishism and more, taking the gift out of the commodity is never easy. It is work that has to be repeated over and over' (2013: 21).

This chapter begins by detailing the contours of commercial and non-commercial fishing divisions in Hawaii, followed by a description of fieldwork carried out with the latter category of fishers on Hawaii Island (the Big Island) over a period of two years (2010–12). It then reports on more recent research (2015) with commercial fishermen and fishery policy makers in Honolulu, Oahu. Here the main objective can be summarised as discovering, 'why, given federal pressure and a mounting and powerful global consensus, are there no catch shares [ITQ] programmes in Hawaii'?

In the final section, I compare the organisation of fisheries in Hawaii with that of ITQ regimes, using the anthropological juxtaposition of commodities and gifts. The analysis is particularly mindful of the commensurability between Māori and Hawaiian fisheries. This comparison is apposite: both are Pacific islands with substantial coastal resources and both have been settled by Polynesian peoples with an extensive maritime history and for whom fish is a crucial material and cultural food source. Seascape was owned and managed in a sophisticated way by coastal *hapū* (sub-tribes) in New Zealand through tribal *rohe moana* (customary marine tenure) and in Hawaii through the *ahupua'a* system; each island was divided into several *moku*, which were then subdivided into *ahupua'a*, a wedge-shaped land section that ran from the mountain to some distance out at sea. Over the years colonisation, privatisation, the process of capital accumulation and modern fisheries management regimes have ridden roughshod over these claims to ownership. In Hawaii, however, there has been no privatisation of fishing rights. Since Hawaii was annexed in 1898 (see Kaiser and Roumasset 2004) policy decisions have created an open access regime out of what was, in effect, a commonly owned resource.

Commercial and non-commercial sectors: permeability

As is almost universally the case in fisheries management, Hawaiian fisheries are categorised into two distinct sectors, commercial and non-commercial. The line between them is, however, decidedly fluid. The Hawaii Division of Aquatic Resources (HDAR) requires that those who fish for 'commercial purposes' hold a Commercial Marine Licence. Commercial purpose is defined as:

> The taking of marine life for profit or gain, or as a means of livelihood, when the marine life is taken in or outside of the State, and when the marine life is sold, offered for sale, landed, or transported for sale anywhere in the state. (HDAR n.d.)

The licence fee of US$50 per year or US$200 for non-residents (markedly cheap compared with other US states) is renewable annually. For monitoring, assessment and policy-making purposes, holders are required to submit a monthly report with respect to effort and marine life taken, and gear and bait used.

The non-commercial sector is generally not subjected to a licensing system, however fishers are required to abide by various regulations governing size, take and seasonal gear restrictions. The sector is made up of 'recreational' and 'subsistence' fishers, with neither category being formally defined by the HDAR. Recreational fishing, however, is popularly understood to mean fishing that is undertaken primarily for enjoyment or sport rather than for food or monetary gain. Hawaii has the most developed recreational fishing infrastructure in the US Pacific, an activity which contributes substantially to the revenues of the state.[2] The sector includes charter boat fishing and fishing tournaments, both of which are an integral part of the tourist market. Charter boats, though, are required to carry commercial licences and report their catch, and local commercial fishers also fish in fishing tournaments.

This blurring of the distinction between commercial and non-commercial fishing is apparent in the practice of those loosely categorised as subsistence fishermen. Many subsistence fishers sell fish although they do not consider themselves to be commercial fishers and may overlook or ignore the HDAR requirement to possess a commercial licence, or they may sell fish under another person's licence (Hospital et al. 2011; Zeller et al. 2007). On any particular fishing trip fishermen may, based on a multitude of factors, decide to sell their fish, or alternatively gift it, only after the fish has been harvested. Although the non-possession of a licence somewhat restricts the sale of fish to shops or restaurants, there is an abundance of alternative sites for exchanging fish for cash; for instance, stalls at the side of the road (often manned by the fisherman's kin), through established social networks, to passers-by, to fish brokers or buyers and, on one occasion I witnessed, an exchange took place in a dentist's waiting room. Geslani et al. comment, 'while non-commercial catch is intended for household consumption, it is, nevertheless, interesting to assess its level of contribution (supply flow) to the retail sector' (2012: 16). From observation, such fishermen are unlikely to be accused of threatening the sustainability of Hawaiian fisheries (see chapter 2).

Recent critiques of subsistence as a mode of production point to the racial and evolutionary underpinnings of the mode of production typology (see Moss 2010). Subsistence producers as a category are, for instance, classically distinguished from peasants by the ability of the former to subsist without dependence on a cash economy and the latter's predominant powerlessness. Tsing (2003) alerts us to the danger of romanticism when we identify tribal/subsistence peoples with nature and peasantries with national futures and occasional revolutionary potential. Sahlins's classic, *Stone Age Economics* (1974), and the vast anthropological literature on exchange makes the point that production is not always, or evenly mostly, for consumption but may be for transactional purposes and thus has social and political dimensions.

In the social science literature two distinct types of transactional activities are identified in subsistence fishing – economic subsistence production and sociocultural production (Berkes 1988; Brown et al. 1998; Eversole 2003; Feige 1990; Freeman 1993). These diverse conceptualisations are variously associated with different academic schools and their accompanying conceptual paradigms, global regions and ethnic groups. Economic subsistence fishers, for instance, are typically identified with the global north and are analysed as part of the informal economy, whereas sociocultural subsistence fishers are identified with the global south, or with indigenous groups within the global north, and such fishers are assumed to engage in 'cultural exchange' and a gift economy (Akroyd and Walshe 2000). This again mirrors the assumed incompatibility between gifts and (petty) commodity exchanges and accounts for this on ethnic and spatial grounds. As an ethnographic descriptor, the distinction between market and gift exchange is likely to be inadequate since it introduces a rigid barrier which is arguably spurious. Rather, what is likely to be more pertinent is the elastic nature of the relationship between the two.

At the policy level, three developments point to the emergence of a distinctive understanding of subsistence fishing in Hawaii. First, in Hawaii 'barter' is considered to be an important characteristic of subsistence practices in contrast to federal law where it is described as a commercial activity (the Magnuson-Stevens Fishery Conservation and Management Act). Second, there is a growing awareness of the importance of non-commercial catch in terms of food security and cultural identity. Fish consumption in Hawaii has been historically high relative to other American states and has increased over time. From 2000 to 2009 the average annual consumption is estimated to be 1.8 times that of the USA as a whole (Geslani et al. 2012). Approximately 51 percent of the seafood eaten in Hawaii is produced in Hawaii and non-commercial catch contributes to approximately 39 percent of local harvesting (Geslani et al. 2012). Approximately a third of households fish non-commercially (Hamnett et al. 2004). Third, in Hawaiian fisheries management circles there is a burgeoning interest in 'customary exchange', understood as a particular type of 'fish flow' which operates to maintain social ties and culture, a non-market activity that differs from barter, trade or sale, even though cash can be involved (Severance 2010). Severance explains: 'It's not just a commercial-like transaction, it's a gesture of social status and social generosity, and it contributes materially to communities' (Severance, personal conversation 2015).

While there is no formal definition of subsistence fishing in Hawaii, there is an emergent fluidity in its interpretation which postulates that the distinction between 'economic' and 'sociocultural' subsistence fishing is arbitrary (see, for instance, Friedlander and Parrish 1997; Glazier 2009; Severance et al. 2013). A 2008 draft paper prepared for the Western Pacific Regional Fishery Management Council on subsistence fishing points out that customary exchange, barter and trade are all components of the subsistence fisheries complex (NOAA n.d.). Given the anthropological nuances implicit in this formulation, it is unsurprising to note that at least two anthropologists hold key research positions within Hawaii fisheries management. It might thus be suggested that subsistence fishers are motivated not solely by consumption, nor by economic survival, accumulation or (Maussian) interestedness on the one hand, nor on the other hand are they purely concerned with cultural obligations or disinterestedness.

Fish flow: the social movement of fish

The following discussion draws on fieldwork, informal interviews and small surveys on the Big Island of Hawaii. The ethnographic research was predominantly based in a Hawaiian homestead community and its surrounds on the eastern (Hilo) side of the island, supplemented by research in a small Hawaiian fishing community on the western side, south Kona. The surveys tracked the distribution of fish by six fishermen over a period of five months. All of the respondents are either Native Hawaiian or ethnically 'local',[3] that is, a mixture of predominantly Hawaiian, Filipino, Japanese, Pacific Islander, haole and Portuguese heritages, whose language of choice is Hawaiian Creole English (pidgin). Two of the fishers were unemployed, one earned US$50,000 per annum, while the other three earned between US$8,000 and US$28,000 all in non-fishing related jobs.

Generally, unless specifically requested to supply fish for an event such as a lū'au (traditional feast/party), fishers decide on how the catch is to be distributed after the fishing trip. This seeming spontaneity relates to the uncertain nature of fishing and the fact that fishers respond to various opportunities as they arise; gifting fish to a nearby fisher who has had less luck, selling catch to people on request and even occasionally buying fish from another fisher when their own trip had been unsuccessful. Yet fishers also act in accordance with the reciprocal obligations and social networks in which they are enmeshed, and in this sense, since these concerns pre-date each fishing trip, they may be the principal motive for harvesting.

Fishermen gift fish to people who 'help them out', to whom they 'owe things' and to people in return for 'favours'. Such reciprocation is for both material gifts (for instance other food items or beer) and for services (for example, help with car repairs and lifts to other parts of the island). Fish is typically gifted to close kin, older community members, friends and sometimes workmates. While fishermen explained their gift in terms of a discourse which emphasised sharing, cultural values and the traditional distributional obligations inherent in the fisherman's role, they also stopped gifting seafood to people they perceived to be 'not appreciative', or 'who don't deserve it' or who 'treat me wrong', or if potential recipients are able to catch their own fish but are 'too lazy' to do so.

The transactional flexibility of fish distribution is illustrated in post-landing practices which are both commodity-like and gift. After a diving trip in which a fisher had caught an *uku* (grey snapper), a *moana kali* (blue goatfish) and an *uhu* (parrotfish), the first was gifted to his boss, the second sold to the restaurant in which his girlfriend worked, and the third gifted to a close friend. A second fisher, who caught eight fish on a particular trip, sold a large *omilu* (bluefin trevally), a *kala* (unicorn fish) and two *uhu* to people who approached him on shore, and gifted two *menpachi* (soldierfish) and two *moana kali* to his grandmother's household. Fish is also frozen for future use, sold to raise money for specific events, for instance, Christmas presents, a trip overseas or to provide the means for a child to attend a sports tournament on another island. The sale of fish may be merely to offset fishing costs but it can also be an important source of cash, particularly in periods of unemployment or for those in low-wage employment. An older Hawaiian/Filipino fisherman, recognised for his expertise, sold reef fish and *he'e* (octopus) during a year of unemployment, most often door-to-door in a known Filipino neighbourhood, while also processing fish as *poke*, a delicacy he gifted to relatives in an old people's home.

Fish as both commodity and gift has precedents. A homestead *kupuna* who fished with his grandfather (later his father) and cousins in the 1950s and 1960s, 'when the bay was like an aquarium', described a variety of exchange types that typically occurred post-landing.[4] People would gather around when they reached the shore and, by indirect questioning, ascertain whether or not the trip had been successful and what they intended to do with their catch. His grandfather would gift fish to anyone who asked in this way and they also dropped off fish at the homes of close kin and older people. This gifting did not result in direct, immediate or equivalent returns, 'people were skilled in different things. Every family had a taro grower, a hunter ...' and would later return the gift in kind. The grandfather would also go to the local store and barter fish for shop goods such as rice, and on occasion would sell fish at the local Hilo fish auction. With the gifting/ bartering/ selling his take-home catch was often minimal. The grandson and his cousin, in order to appease their *tūtū* (grandmother), would then surreptitiously harvest fish from nearby Puhi Bay.

In the Hawaiian homestead district, and the Kona fishing village, selling fish within the community is largely perceived to transgress cultural norms. A fisherman explained:

> If you look at ancient Hawaiian culture, there used to be *konohiki*, a person responsible for the fishery within an *ahupua'a*, a sliver of land that goes from mountain to the sea and to the nearshore sea, and he'd be responsible for the marine resources there and it would be shared within this community, but, in the next community it would have to be traded and bartered. (See also Kirch and Sahlins 1994)

Sales contemporarily occur outside the communities. Fish is sent to relatives on other islands for the purpose of sale, sold through contacts in the surrounding area, and in the Kona village, a fisher sold *ahi* (tuna) in US$10 or $20 pieces at a tourist destination a few kilometres distant. After trading the *ahi* he gifts the remainder to a number of households in the village, including that of an elder master fisherman. He typically fishes with his son and cousin, using a modern version of a traditional dugout outrigger, an outboard powered three-board style canoe. He also catches *he'e* (octopus) which he keeps for his own consumption as well as gifts. Economic necessity is cited as a reason for sale, and there is a degree of empathy and appreciation for the resourcefulness of such fishermen. In times of financial pressure when wage work is unavailable, or wages are meagre, the possibility of selling fish mitigates hardship to an important degree and reduces the pressure on household economies. Both Hawaiian communities are relatively deprived and poverty is prevalent. For instance, in the Keaukaha homestead community, unemployment is roughly 9.6 percent, 20 percent of people live below the poverty level and about 38 percent of households are dependent on social security (US Census Bureau n.d.). Households typically include an extended family member, often a grandparent, who contributes to childrearing and other household chores. On any given day fishers dot the coastline. A Hawaiian fish seller told me that although she would gift fish she would never sell in the homestead community simply because people there did not have enough money.

The gifting of seafood to extended kin is an important cultural obligation that corresponds to Mauss's identification of a threefold gift sequence: the obligation to give, to receive and to return. These obligations are powerfully embodied. A fisher on a lobster trip to Pohoiki in the Puna district of the Big Island encountered stormy weather and waves that, while prohibiting his dive, enabled him to surf. In order not to return home empty handed he purchased a 10 lb *ahi* for US$20 from boat fishers. He gifted some to the households of his two younger children, to his older daughter and to his cousin and kept some for his sister's household, his present abode. Seafood is a significant food item, traditionally providing the primary protein, an importance recognised in the construction of each *auhupuaʻa* to include access to the shoreline and sea.

Fish is also crucial in ceremonial events. At a wedding of a Native Hawaiian student and her fireman groom in 2012, the 250 guests were served with 17 varieties of reef fish, weighing approximately 45 lb, all of which were fried and served as pre-dinner *pūpūs* (appetisers). The fish had been gathered by the groom and the couple's friends and relatives on diving trips carefully spaced around the Big Island, so as 'not to take from only one place'. The donors were reciprocated with food, beer and invitations to the nuptials.

Seafood is extensively gifted in Hawaii and this sharing is a deeply valued practice. MacGregor (2007) and Glazier et al. (2013) argue that such sharing can be considered an important organising element of local society in general. It is bound up with broader reciprocal exchange networks, an adaptation to the discriminatory effects of a market economy and is deeply culturally significant. The cultural significance of sharing lies in the social relations it references and the cultural values and ethnically distinct identity markers it embodies. Such values and practices include the importance placed on 'ohana (extended family) and one's commitment to it, and the sharing of foods, goods and services.

Resisting enclosure

The United States has proceeded relatively cautiously with the introduction of ITQs, with only four fisheries being incorporated by the late 1990s. Concerns about the distributional impacts, including data on inequities from New Zealand and Iceland, led to the US Congress initiating a moratorium on further introductions of ITQs through the enactment of the Sustainable Fisheries Act of 1996. Congress then asked the National Academy of Sciences, a private, non-profit organisation that advises the US on science, engineering and medicine, to investigate and make recommendations on the social, economic and biological effects of ITQ/IFQ programmes. In 1999 the National Research Council issued a 400-page document, *Sharing the Fish: Toward a National Policy on Individual Fishing Quota*, which contains case studies by 15 international experts, including ITQ critics and anthropologists Gísli Pálsson and Bonnie McCay. While such policy publications necessitate a careful 'balancing' of critics and supporters, the constraint of appearing non-partisan, the report does highlight the problems associated with transferability, consolidation and leasing and a plethora of other social ills. It also recommended lifting the moratorium, a recommendation that came into effect, rather benignly, when it expired in 2002. Rögnvaldur Hannesson, fisheries economist and ITQ zealot, postulated that the moratorium 'delayed and distorted the development toward private use rights in American Fisheries', though it 'did not eliminate the incentives to work towards exclusive use rights, it only channeled them into new directions' (2004: 151). This channelling, through a sleight of hand in nomenclature, led to the baggage-free promotion of the tool 'catch shares' under the Magnuson-Stevens Reauthorization Act 2006.

In 2010 the National Oceanic and Atmospheric Administration (NOAA) released a policy mandate to encourage consideration and adoption of catch shares; a concept understood to encapsulate a suite of programmes defined as fishery management measures that allocate specific portions of the total allowable fishery catch to individuals, cooperatives, communities or other entities. These provisions include limited access privilege programmes (LAPP), individual fishing quota programmes and territorial use rights fisheries (TURFs) (Pan et al. 2014: 1). Despite the appearance of diversity, 'catch shares' are fundamentally premised on some form of privatisation and thus are a variant of ITQs (Pinkerton 2015), though the fishing right may or may not be transferable. Currently there are 16 federal catch share programmes in operation in the US, with six of the eight Federal Management Councils having implemented at least one programme, the highest number being in Alaska. While five programmes were established in the 1990s, eight have been introduced between 2011 and 2016.

Carothers and Chambers, ethnographers of ITQs in Alaska and Iceland respectively, identify a 'growing environmental discourse advocating for individual fishing quotas' as a symptom of a 'recently reinvigorated privatization process' (2012: 40). Indeed, the tension between environmental non-governmental organisations (NGOs) and fishermen is pronounced in Hawaii. To date, however, none of the fisheries in the US Pacific Islands Region[5] operates under a catch share programme, though Hawaii is perceived to be the most likely candidate followed by American Samoa. Federal fisheries staff in Hawaii, in an effort to fulfil the 2010 directive, initiated a variety of measures, including workshops, outreach, research and policy documents. The ultimate determination of these was a considered rejection. That ITQs, or catch shares, are not considered viable is rooted in a mixture of local concerns that can be summarised as: no identified need; insufficient local knowledge of catch shares; incomplete catch records on which to base allocation; inadequate scientific knowledge of fish stocks; resistance by key officials and social unease regarding the questionable morality of privatising a public resource. A commonly ascribed motif that resonates is the sentiment of cultural incommensurability. There is a recognised disjuncture between privatised fishing rights and the established flexibility of an autochthonous gift economy. Severance writes, 'most of our fishermen believe in a widespread sharing of fish and fishing opportunities rather than a narrow sharing of fishing privileges allocated to a few fishermen' (2014: 3).

Drawing on participant observation and interviews with nine people variously involved in fisheries in Hawaii (at a federal and regional level) as scientists, economists, policy analysts and makers, resource managers and commercial fishermen, I will flesh out the general resistance to ITQs in Hawaii through a description of the characteristics of two fisheries, the Hawaii pelagic longline and the Hawaii deep 7 bottomfish fishery, considered to have the highest propensity to be ITQed.

Hawaii deep 7 fishery: no need

The US National Research Council's *Sharing the Fish* report (1999) advises that any fishery that can be managed using a total allowable catch (TAC) is an appropriate contender for individual fishing quota or some form of catch share. Although individual states are not explicitly directed to impose catch shares, they are encouraged to identify characteristics that ITQ advocates see as signalling a need for enclosure. This candidature is rooted in assumptions pertaining to economic efficiency and Hardin's tragedy of the commons thesis. For instance, Eythorsson argues, if the total catching capacity is higher than the TAC 'there will be a problem in the inefficient use of capital resources' (1996: 213) and, in the absence of clearly delineated individual rights, fishermen are predisposed to 'engage in an investment race in order to improve their share of TAC' (Eythorsson 1996: 213). In this idiom the solution to fishermen racing and overcapitalisation is to exclude inefficient operators, that is part-timers and others not fully committed to commercial exploitation, and to privatise fishing rights. A TAC was imposed in the Hawaii deep 7 bottom fishery in 2007. The adage that fishermen race, however, remains unsubstantiated in this instance, irrespective of the absence of individual rights. Neither is the presence of part-timers perceived locally as an inefficient use of capital resources. Rather, the diversity of participants, alongside the historic importance of the fishery, is held to be a definitive strength, for instance, in terms of facilitating food security.

While fishery production in Hawaii is dominated by pelagic fish (such as tuna and swordfish), bottomfish, reef fish and other non-pelagics are culturally and economically significant. The Hawaiian bottomfish fishery targets 14 species of deep-water snappers, groupers and jacks[6] in deep-slope habitats between depths of 50 and 200 fathoms in the seas around the inhabited islands in the Hawaiian archipelago: Hawai'i, Kaho'olawe, Maui, Lana'i, Moloka'i, O'ahu, Kaua'i and Ni'ihau (Hospital and Beavers 2014). Fish are harvested by hook-and-line methods, a relatively selective technology that provides high-quality fish with minimal by-catch. The fishery is historically contiguous; evidence indicates that prior to European settlement and annexation, Native Hawaiians harvested the same species with similar techniques and specialised gear (Spalding

2006). Of the 14 bottomfish species, 6 species of snapper and 1 species of grouper are particularly important. This subgroup is known collectively as the deep 7 and comprises *ehu* (squirrelfish snapper), *gindai* (Bringham's snapper), *kalekale* (von Siebold's snapper), *hapu'upu'u* (Hawaiian black grouper), *onaga* (longtail red snapper), *opakapaka* (pink snapper) and *lehi* (ironjaw snapper), the high-value species which make up the largest share of bottomfish landings and sale.

Bottomfish fishers include a small fraction (approximately 3 percent) of 'high-liners': those who catch more than 2,500 lb per year, and account for nearly 45 percent of all landings. Tellingly, high-liners have higher rates of land-based unemployment than the general population of Hawaii (Hospital and Beavers 2011). The majority of fishers are, however, part-time and seasonal, fishing perhaps once per month, and in December are likely to target the red-coloured 'lucky snappers' to coincide with Christmas festivities. Boats are commonly about 23 ft long, are likely to have been built in the late 1980s and purchased a decade later, though high-liners fish more frequently and on larger and more powerful vessels. The fishery is typically owner operated, with most boats being manned by one or two fishers and fishing trips lasting one day or night, although high-liners spend somewhat longer at sea.

The bottomfish fishery is understood as decidedly 'local', has at least 1,000 participants, around 400 boats with a commercial licence, and reflects the ethnic diversity of contemporary Hawaii and an endogenous mixed economy. Hospital (an NOAA fisheries scientist) and Beavers (a marine scientist with the University of Hawaii), point out:

> Today's MHI [Main Hawaiian Islands] bottomfish fleet is a complex mix of commercial, recreational, cultural and subsistence fishermen whose artisanal fishing behavior, cultural motivations for fishing, and relative ease of market access does not align well with mainland U.S. legal and regulatory frameworks, thus complicating management and monitoring of this fishery. (2011: vii)

Commercial bottomfish fishers are obliged to be in possession of the state's commercial fishing licence and, since 2007, for regulatory purposes, non-commercial bottomfish fishers fishing in federal waters (3 nm out to sea) are required to carry a non-commercial permit. The commercial licence is priced at US$50 per year while the non-commercial licence is free of charge. Holding a commercial licence enables fishers to catch as many fish as they like, while the non-commercial licence holders are subject to daily bag limits. The distinction between commercial and non-commercial operators is, however, decidedly messy. For instance, in a comprehensive survey of bottomfish fishers in 2010, prompted by the NOAA catch share mandate, 19 percent of the 519 respondents provided multiple self-classificatory responses (commercial, non-commercial, recreational, subsistence) and 14 percent identified as subsistence fishers. Of those with commercial licences (477) only 63 percent considered themselves to be either full- or part-time commercial fishers; 30 percent of this group classified themselves as exclusively recreational fishers, though 40 percent of these recreational fishers reported selling catch in the preceding twelve months and 10 percent sold at least half of their catch. Overall, 24 percent of bottomfish catch was consumed at home, 33 percent was gifted and approximately 39 percent was sold (Hospital and Beavers 2014). Only a very small proportion of bottomfish fishers generate a livelihood from the resource.

The fishery has historically been one where open access prevailed. In 1998, as a result of declines in catch, 19 spatial closures prohibiting bottomfish take were enacted. These captured about 20 percent of the habitat around the main Hawaii Islands. Following a determination of overfishing in 2005 and a subsequent emergency closure, a TAC was introduced to the Hawaiian Islands deep 7 bottomfish fishery in 2007; the first such mechanism to be utilised in a small-scale fishery in Hawaii. When the TAC is reached the fishery is closed and closures recurred in the first four years of operation. However, from 2011 to the time of writing (2016) full calendar fishing years have been enjoyed. More recently, as decreed by federal law, the TAC has been replaced by an annual catch limit (ACL). While largely a shift in nomenclature, the new tool has a recovery requirement – overcatch in any given year is deducted from the limit set for the following year. Although unhappy that the ACL does not take account of the biomass in spatial closures and the hardships caused if the ACL is reached and the fishery closed, particularly in the Christmas season, very few bottomfish fishermen are advocates of the catch share system, the touchstone of ITQ-like regulation, or see it as a solution.

A long-time, part-time commercial bottomfish fisher, for whom selling fish at the Honolulu fish market is an important supplement to income, summarises his general opposition to catch shares:

Basically it's a cultural thing. The US constitution says the public has free and open access to our aquatic resource. So that's the premise, a baseline ... When it comes to local, more nearshore coastal fisheries, the bottomfish fishery, it just runs counter to our culture. And the reason we fought against it was, the fishery for us is a generational thing, we pass down from father to son, son to grandson. It's everybody's food, and it should not be just a person's food. It's a public resource, open to the public. And however it is managed, that is the way it is managed, right, but it should not be allocated, the basis for that is we all have an equal opportunity to participate in the fishery. If you start to allocate and Fiona has a share and she chooses not to use it, then I'm not able to capitalise on that portion that's on you. And the fear was that there are some insidious organisations [referring to environmental NGOs] that may find it beneficial to buy shares, or inherit shares and keep it, so they can regulate fisheries and we didn't want that. We fish under an ACL so everyone has an access to that limit.

There were some individuals in the fishery and they were from the mainland US, so they're not local local, and in their culture, their mindset, it was OK to have an individual quota. And we had this discussion after one meeting, two of those guys, they were high-liners, left kind of disgruntled because the rest of us fought against it ... And here's the interesting evolution: the second meeting that we had on the same subject of catch shares, one of those captains sent his deck hand, because he couldn't make the meeting he sent his crew member over. And when his crew member found out that his captain would own his share [in the case of ITQ being introduced], he objected and he quickly got on his phone and he called his captain and said 'screw this, I'm jumping off your ship' because he was the active fisher. The captain owned the boat, the guy that was fishing was not going to get diddly because it's the boat to which the licence accrues or the permit. The commercial captain came back and talked to the other captain and said 'Hey, we've gotta get off this line. It's culturally insensitive. We're two guys and there's about 400 other guys that we need to be mindful of and one is my crew man' ... so that's how it was quietly put to bed.

The longline fishery

The pelagic longline fishery in Hawaii, which targets big-eye tuna and, since the 1980s, swordfish, has a complex management structure, spanning multiple agencies, international treaties and marine property constructs. Hawaiian fishers chase pelagics both inside and outside of the US Exclusive Economic Zone (EEZ), competing with more than 3,000 vessels often using more destructive gear types, with home ports in Japan, Taiwan and Korea among others. It is by far the largest commercial fishery in Hawaii, and indeed the Pacific region: the total value of commercial fish landings from the US Pacific Island regions was around US$101 million in 2011, of which the Hawaii longline fishery accounted for 66 percent. Longliners land on an annual basis about 11.7 million kg of fish valued at about US$75.9 million (Pan 2014).

The longline pelagic fishery dates from at least a century ago, its emergence credited to the initiative of immigrant Okinawan fishermen who developed the precursor flag-line fishery (floats marked with bamboo flags) in 1917. The fishery was suspended during the Second World War as a result of the systematic discrimination practised against US citizens with Japanese ancestry, however it re-emerged after the war. The fleet is perceived as 'large-scale' in Hawaii; however, compared to mainland US and international norms, it is more appropriately described as small-scale. Vessels are typically less than 100 ft in length, the majority measuring about 60 ft. Until recently, they included wooden *aku* and *sampan* boats, introduced by Japanese fishermen in the early 1900s, the predominant vessel types up until the 1980s (Pooley 1993). There are also modern tuna, swordfish longline vessels, converted Gulf shrimpers and a few distant-water albacore trollers in the fleet, the introduction of which coincided with a dramatic increase in the fishery in the late 1970s and 1980s, when it expanded to incorporate migrant fishers. The distant-water albacore trollers arrived in the 1970s from the US west coast, en route to recently discovered fishing grounds north of the Midway Islands (part of the Hawaiian archipelago) (Pooley 1993). In the 1980s, declining catches together with price wars in the Gulf of Mexico between local residents and Vietnamese immigrants made the ongoing viability of the Gulf fishery precarious. Sean Martin, long-time Hawaii longliner, co-owner of six vessels and a marine supply business, describes the Vietnamese arrivals thus:

> Back then the [30–35] longliners used to always operate out of Kewalo Basin, and one day 22 boats from the Gulf of Mexico showed up. They came in a big caravan, traveling across the Pacific from Panama. They were all Vietnamese immigrants who had been displaced by the

Vietnam War and settled on the Gulf Coast. They had been longlining there for yellowfin, so it was a different fishery than ours, but they used similar gear, and I think some of the Vietnamese guys realized there was an opportunity out here, so they got together and said, 'Go west.' That was a kind of the explosion in the industry. (in Hollier 2014)

Today, roughly 46 percent of pelagic boat owners are Vietnamese Americans, 20 percent are Korean-Americans and 34 percent are Euro Americans (Barnes-Mauthe et al. 2013). Although captains are Hawaiian residents, and the vessels are flagged to the US, the three to five crew members are typically foreign nationals from Asia and other Pacific Island states, especially the Philippines, the Republic of Kiribati and the Federal States of Micronesia; a labour source, although controversial,[7] deemed economically necessary by vessel owners (Hospital and Beavers 2011).

Irrespective of the ethnic diversity of captains, boat owners and crew, the restrictions placed around foreign crew movements at port and the relatively recent 'modernisation' in the 1980s, the pelagic fishery is still perceived as local. This localisation is largely contingent on historical relatedness, that Hawaii is home for boat owners and captains, that fuel, bait and ice is purchased locally, and that the catch landed and sold to retailers, wholesalers and the public at the Honolulu fish auction, strategically situated between the major Honolulu docks, is largely consumed in Hawaii. When purchased from fish sellers further down the value chain, tuna is still an affordable local food, particularly compared to tuna prices elsewhere in the world, a situation likely boosted by-catch from the small-boat pelagic fishery. Fresh big-eye and yellowfin tuna, known as *ahi*, are eaten as *ahi poke* or sashimi, and there is perceptible pride in the knowledge that, in spite of the growth of imported goods into the island economy, the majority of this culturally significant food item is produced by a local industry. People are critically conscious of the occasions when their *ahi* is not Hawaiian derived and express disdain for the inferior look, flavour and health benefits of such imports. Longlining is considered a relatively sustainable fishing method and Hawaii's pelagic fishers are known to produce fresh, high-quality, whole fish. It is often noted that, although the Honolulu port is ranked as 32nd in the US in terms of volume, it is sixth in terms of landed value. The fishery is highly regulated and three characteristics of this regulation are of most interest in terms of the development of ITQs, namely, the 'gentleman's agreement', the imposition of ACLs and the use, since 1994, of limited entry permits (LEPs).

The gentleman's agreement

The gentleman's agreement refers to the accord that longliners restrict their fishing activities to waters beyond 50 nm from shore. This agreement was implemented in 1992 and aimed to resolve the growing spatial and gear conflicts between small-boat pelagic fishers and longliners, which occasioned heated disputes in which 'shots were fired'. The agreement explicitly protects the fishing rights, and the cultural and livelihood values this enshrine, of nearer-to-shore pelagic fishers. Similar to the bottomfish fishery, small-boat pelagic fishers are largely part-time, seasonal and move fluidly between commercial and non-commercial categories, selling their catch as well as extensively gifting it. Boats are on average 22.5 ft and fishers predominantly use handline methods known as *palu ahi* (chum-tuna, day time) and *ika shibi* (squid-tuna, night time) to catch yellowfin (Hospital and Beavers 2011). State-funded aggregating devices in nearshore areas, designed to ease the transition from sea to hook, are also indicative of the value of, and protection afforded to, the small-boat pelagic fishery. This custodianship stands in stark contrast to the planned removal of small-boat and part-time fishers from New Zealand's commercial fisheries in 1983 (see chapters 1 and 2).

Annual catch limits

ACLs, a sibling tool to TACs, are deemed to be essential for transitioning to ITQs. They demarcate an overall amount of a fish species, or a total quota, that when reached in a fishing year triggers a closure. The longline fishery operates under an ACL imposed by international agreement for big-eye tuna in the western and central Pacific (since 2009) and in the eastern Pacific (since 2004, imposed on vessels over 24 m). These restrictions are variously honoured by participant fishers and their respective governments. In the case of Hawaii, the Western Pacific Regional Fishery Management Council, colloquially known as the Council, allocates a total of approximately 3,500 metric tonnes (mt) of quota in the western and central Pacific and approximately 500 mt in the eastern Pacific. The Council has enforced closures on the longline fleet fishing in the western central Pacific region on a number of occasions since 2009, for instance, in 2015 the closure was enacted on 5 August and lasted until the end of the year. This region is the world's largest tuna fishery and Hawaiian longliners compete with the industrial and less-discriminatory purse-seiners. Purse-seiners, due to non-commitment by their home governments, are not subject to catch limits. This perceived injustice is keenly felt in the Hawaiian fleet; however, two common practices serve as 'escape valves'. Since 84 percent of the Hawaiian longliner fleet is under 24 m, these vessels can switch to harvesting big-eye in the eastern Pacific, irrespective of whether the quota has been reached in those fishing grounds (Pan 2014). And/or, a deal may be negotiated with the US Pacific territories of Guam, American Samoa and the Northern Mariana Islands, for a transfer of their unused big-eye quota; a trade solidified by an exchange of cash from the Hawaii Longline Association to the particular territorial government, and indicative of a colonial paternal relationship as much as a capitalist commodity one. The presence of these alternatives inhibits the introduction of individualised quota. As Craig Severance notes, however: 'If the safety valve of getting additional quota from the territories is lost (this requires annual NOAA review, and could be subject to an NGO lawsuit), then the incentive for "rationalisation" could strengthen' (personal conversation 2017).

Limited entry permits

LEPs are often viewed as an evolutionary antecedent to ITQs, they are 'sub-optimal' in that they are thought to encourage a race for fish (there is no limit on what a permit holder can catch, subject to a total quota) and overcapitalisation, that is, they do not protect the fishing *Homo economicus* from his innate and rational self. Yet, they seem to be functioning well enough in the Hawaiian longline fleet (Pan 2014).

In order to contain uncontrolled expansion, a limited entry programme was introduced in the longline fleet in 1994, which provided for a cap of 164 permits and restricted vessel size to 101 ft. The permit cap has not been reached and the number of permits has stabilised at around 124–29 (Pan 2014). Under this programme permits are renewable for US$37 in March of each year; no new permits can be created although existing ones can be transferred for a processing fee which is also US$37. Although professing similarities to ITQ technologies in that LEPs can be considered to grant a pseudo property right to a specified number of individuals, and it can be transferred to others for a cost, divergences are more pronounced than analogies.

The way that LEPs are constructed and perceived, together with the relationships they engender, deviates from private property. Young (1983), for instance considers them a restricted common property, not an exclusive property right. As such, emphasis is placed on a community of fishers engaging in a common seascape, subject to structured rules governing their use of the resource. Permits are designed as privileges not perpetual rights: a tenuous and revocable entitlement subject to broader shifts in human–environment relations. They are also decidedly concrete. They refer to a right to hunt fish, not a perpetual claim to a quantity of fish stock, including the as-yet unborn. The dividing lines between restricted common property, privilege and individual property rights are however, legally blurred. There have been a number of instances when judges have decreed that fishing permits meet the definition of property. In 1992, for instance, in a case in Alaska resulting from the non-payment of a federal tax by a permit-holding fisherman for three consecutive years, a determination was reached that a fishing permit was property within the meaning of federal tax lien law (Weiss 1992). Fishing permits have also been considered property in divorce cases in Alaska (*Ferguson vs. Ferguson Alaska* 1996). However, while this legal layer of property is a significant consideration, it is only one layer of complexity that must be considered alongside the social relations, ideologies, cultural context and social practices that equally constitute property (von Benda-Beckman et al. 2006). Importantly, the limited entry system has not resulted in major consolidations in the Hawaii fleet, a consequence which invariably follows the implementation of ITQs.

The longline permits were initially freely allocated in Hawaii, however new entrants now have to 'transfer' them from a previous holder, and the price of such transactions has risen. There is no official data on the current price of a longline permit transfer (the US$37 is a processing fee), though anecdotal evidence suggests the price varies between US$60,000 and $100,000, with the value drifting downwards when closures occur. Longline fishing permits are consequently considered to have an economic value, and thus, they may even be commodity-like. The value, however, arises out of production, and can be conceptualised as a use-value in the Marxist sense. For Marx a 'use-value' is a specific quality arising from the intrinsic usefulness of a commodity in a specific social and historical context from which this value is inseparable (Webster 2016). That LEPs are typologically a use-value is evidenced by the value of the permit decreasing when the fishery is closed. It is the individual labour congealed in a specific social context, for instance harvesting fish from nature, that determines the use-value of a commodity. 'Exchange value', conversely, is a quantity abstracted from the specifics of use-value and is based on the exchange of a quantity of one commodity for a quantity of another. It signifies an entirely quantitative relationship that varies independently of the use-value. And it is the abstracted labour-power in the general context of market exchange that produces the exchange value of a commodity (Webster 2016). ITQs represent an exchange value, a shift from locating value in specific social and historical contexts to value in the marketplace. Further, in contrast to ITQs, fishing permits cannot readily be used as collateral in banks. They cannot be 'perfected', that is, banks do not have absolute rights to permits as secure collateral; Hawaiian permits can at any stage be revoked by the federal government. Fishing permits are thus much less financially pliable than individualised quota and are unlikely to be transformed into financial derivatives.

It is doubtful that catch shares will take hold in Hawaii in the near future, a conclusion that can be gleaned from the following interview excerpts:

When Dr Jane Lubchenco became the NOAA administrator several years ago ... she was a catch shares proponent, and so the regions got money to examine the issue to see how it might work. We spent that money going around talking to all the fishermen on the islands to discuss the pros and cons, we got a lot of feedback. It's like every five years there's a new panacea for fisheries, it used to be Marine Protected Areas, before that ITQs, and then there was catch shares. (NOAA, federal agent)

We've detected no enthusiasm for catch shares. We had the workshop last year and nobody is banging on our door saying please set up a catch shares programme. Even with the [big-eye] fishery closures which probably hurt the fishery, nobody has said we have got to avoid this next year, we need catch shares. It hasn't been that at all, just get the bloody deals done on time with the territories. (NOAA, federal agent)

There are a lot of mom and pop longline operators out there, I think in an ITQ system they might be disadvantaged. (Fisheries biologist, NOAA)

The one thing is once you go down that road [ITQing] you can't get out of it. You're committed. And then your fleet will shrink as happens when quota is consolidated. And you'll have a consolidation of power. It's better to manage effort than manage catch. (NOAA, federal agent).

This region has always been reluctant to engage in any allocated practices, it is just not culturally traditional of the Pacific islands to pick these winners and losers. We do some quasi allocation by virtue of the fact that we do have a limited entry programme for the longline, that's allocative in nature, but when you talk about ITQs or catch shares which are assignments of a property right, a quantitative property right to a specific fishing operation, we'd be very reluctant to do that and I don't see that changing unless we absolutely had to.

To reinforce that, we could [introduce an ITQ], we have the mechanics, we have catch history, what's been allocated, what's left over, that could be auctioned. There's a permit system, there's stock control rules, there's an ability to shut down the fishery, there's an ability to monitor this, that, and the other thing, those are [ITQ] prerequisites. We might argue that, but, here locally an ITQ system is not going to work unless the fishermen want it. It's not a matter of the government shoving it down their throats. It won't happen. In some ways the ground work is there in case something happens down the line that does steer the fishery towards wanting this, but it won't be that the government or the Council are scrambling to provide information and foundational ideas to the fishermen about these concepts. What problem does catch shares in Hawaii solve that is not or can't be solved by the current management machine? What are you trying to conservationally solve? (NOAA, federal agent)

I think it [the resistance to ITQs] is societal driven [rather than by individual actors]. I think that even people who come here that are not from here quickly get acclimated to how things are. When people come from the mainland and try to make things like the mainland, they are quickly ostracised. So they don't get much traction. I think part of it is the individual people. But more so the way the [NOAA and the Council] people understand fisheries, they have been here for a long time and are in upper management. Because of the culture and the importance not just in fisheries but kind of all aspects of Hawaiian society, the host culture is recognised. Not federally, but it is recognised here that there's significance to the concept of host culture, or the philosophy that things don't change much in Hawaii. I don't think I would put the resistance solely on the management, I think it is society as a whole that would be very opposed to that sort of stuff. (Sustainable fisheries officer, Western Pacific Fishery Management Council)

Gifts and commodities

The anthropological tradition of dichotomising gifts and commodities is a powerful means through which to draw attention to the existence of distinctive cultural logics. Noting the prevalence of gift exchange in the distribution of fish in Hawaii makes the point that it is not wholly subsumed to capitalist discipline; non-capitalist social relations, enlivened by tradition, may in fact trump the systematic thrust towards alienation, accumulation and an ever-expanding search for new commodities. The gift as a form of resistance to de-traditionalisation derives from accounts of moral economies and of these being activated when enclosures threaten relationships of reciprocity, moral solidarity, mutual assistance and trust, egalitarianism and a subsistence ethics (Scott 1976; Thompson 1971). The presence of the gift also alerts us to how an object is valued, the meaning and importance a society may embed in particular things, such as a fish (Mauss 1967). This is not to argue that contemporary Hawaii is somehow non-capitalist. Rather, it is to point to the coexistence of non-marketised and marketised sectors of the economy and to suggest that the gift exchange character of fishing is a decisive feature of local society. The pervasiveness of gifting does not, I think, wholly accord with observations regarding the reliance of capitalism on informal economic activity, non-marketised social relations or economic heterogeneity (Fraser 2013; Tsing 2013). The gift is not merely a residual holdover from pre-capitalist times, nor is it on its way out. Neither is it, however, fully premised on capitalism's operational need for 'semi-proletarianised' households (see, for instance, Wallerstein 2002 [1974]). The gift in many ways is antagonistic to capitalism and it may operate to dampen the exigencies of market behaviour and to vitalise traditional alternates.

The fluidity between gifts and commodity-like exchanges is a crucial institutional component, and while this may be more obvious in Hawaii in the case of the subsistence fishing sector and the deep 7 bottom fishery, a tacit gift economy is also manifest in the arrangements of the pelagic longline fishery; a gift-based sociability is apparent among human participants and between humans and the non-human environment. Importantly, unlike in ITQ systems, fishing rights are not privatised. Longline fishers retain an important element of coastal custodianship, they are mere visitors in the ocean commons. In many ways the fish remain hidden until caught, their opaque ocean home defying the machinery of accountancy necessitated in ITQs. Tuna and swordfish are the fishermen's primary targets yet given the difficulty in controlling the ocean's products as private property, other species are attracted to the fishermen's hooks. *Flat opah* (moonfish), *mahimahi* (small dolphin fish), *monchong* (pomfret) and marlin, the longliners 'by-catch', feature at the Honolulu fish auction, capturing good prices for their ocean hunters. For captains and their contracted crew there may be a considerable gift-like quality to their commodity provision – involving the extension of the person and social relations into the product. Fish are a crucial offering at the crew's social gatherings at port (Hospital and Beavers 2011), and the commercial success of each fishing operation is directly measured by the properties of the docked fish. At the auction fish are labelled with a colour-coded tag specific to their captors' vessel and boats get paid daily according to the attributes of their catch. It is the process of valuing at the auction that transforms the gift-like quality of the fish into a commodity, a sensory performance based on sorting fat, temperature, colour and texture. Like Tsing's (2013) mushrooms at the point of sorting, the fish now become commodities of a particular size and grade, ready for use or exchange, work that has to be done again and again.

Gibbs calls attention to the very different social relationships engendered in ITQ fisheries: 'once an individual right holder gains an asset of value (a catch right) then the emphasis of the operation becomes an economic relationship with the objective of maximizing returns on the asset – their catch right to the quota species' (Gibbs 2009: 471); gift-like qualities are removed from the commodity. The political agency of the fisherman changes, from a coastal custodian to a resource owner or lessee, now motivated to protect their private gains, or ensnared to enhance those of the proprietor. This shift has implications for ecosystem governance as associated or dependent species are unequivocally removed from the equation of maximising individual wealth through the value of the commodity, that is, the fishing right to a particular stock in a specific geographic location. The relationship between humans and the environment is reconstructed: fish species for which the extractor has not acquired rights are rendered invisible: dumped and discarded, their non-target flesh adds no value to the asset.

The substitution of a market-based relationship for that of the gift and the attachment of value to the catch right rather than the fish product enables the emergence of novel types of agency. Quota holders are newly empowered as actors in a quota market where transferability is key and the consolidation of fishing rights a sequential occurrence. Although an informal market may have arisen in the Hawaii pelagic fishery whereby LEP transfers occur under the radar of management's accountancy, the fishery retains its 'mom and pop' characteristic – while one company owns seven permits and another owns six, the vast majority of the 144 permit holders own one boat. Importantly, what is transferred in the permit transaction, that is the right to hunt fish, has an important element of the commons.

The presence of the TAC in the pelagic fishery may be perceived to hint at marketisation. Holm and Nielsen suggest that the TAC machinery is a market device, enabling access to fisheries to be produced as a scarce natural resource, and providing the meterology by which the quotas are singularised as commodities (2007: 190–91). Yet while the TAC may be an enabler, it is the actual privatisation of quota that is the commodity catalyst; only when sliced up and shared out as individual quota do catch rights take on their volatile potency, a precarity deflected in Hawaii by the efficacy of the gift.

The increased pressure in neoliberal governance to remove the gift from the commodity is also experienced in the reverse, that is, the commodity is removed from the gift. In New Zealand, Māori fishing under customary regulations are prohibited from exchanging fish, a restriction that pertains not just to cash transactions but also to the quotidian: reciprocating fish for oranges or *kumara* (see chapter 1). This aestheticisation of customary practices means that fishing can only occur for two designated ceremonial events, that is *hui* (meetings) and *tangi* (funerals). The removal of commodities from gifts, or gifts from commodities, however, is never complete. Anecdotal evidence suggests an efflorescence in *hui* and *tangi* in Māori coastal communities.

While this chapter has identified the gift as a central means through which enclosures are resisted, chapter 5 considers how nostalgia might play a similar role in Ireland. In the small-boat sector in particular, nostalgic laments reflect economic and social criteria, but also provide a moral commentary on the present. However, the possibility for nostalgia to challenge hierarchically imposed relations is tempered by a precarious present, creating circumstances often seen as inevitable.

5
Nostalgia:
Laments and Precarity

This chapter considers the potential for assuaging the neoliberal project in fisheries by contextualising quota management technologies within broader debates concerning precarity and nostalgia. I highlight an emergent, though historically contiguous, discourse of nostalgia in Ireland as a means through which hierarchical relations are challenged and describe various strategies designed to temper the exigencies of dispossessions. The analysis in this chapter is, however, anchored in a tension between nihilism and hope. While I would much prefer to follow the anthropological tradition of pointing to alternates, to the indelible potential of human creativity in the face of adversity, the informal power of the non-market sphere and the legacy of reproductive kin, given the current distribution of power between the contending parties in fisheries, there is little to be gained from unchecked idealism. In this year of Brexit and Trump, a particular dominant economic regulation persists irrespective of evidence of its unworkability, its cumulative harmfulness on multiple scales or indeed the integrity of worthy alternatives (Davies 2016: 121). Streeck (2014: 64) points out that on the three frontiers of Polanyian commodification – labour, nature and money (each of which has been made fictitious in individual transferable quota [ITQ] fisheries) – regulatory institutions which kept in check the progression of capitalism for its own good, have all but collapsed. There are 'increasingly demanding claims made by the employment system on human labour, by capitalist production and consumption systems on finite natural resources, and by the financial and banking system on people's confidence in ever more complex pyramids of money, credit and debt' (Streeck 2014: 51).

Streeck considers the global fiscal crisis in 2008 as an indicator of the excessive commodification of money. Financialisation, championed as a strategy to restore growth and profitability to the economy, is now seen as a pyrrhic advance. In terms of labour, commodification may have already reached a critical point: the deregulation of labour markets under international competition, residual unemployment as the new norm and the expansion of sweat shops in the global periphery have made employment more precarious for a growing share of the population (Streeck 2014: 53). In the case of nature, conflict exists between unrelenting capitalist expansion and the finite provision of natural resources. Streeck comments: 'what seems to be taking shape is a race between advancing exhaustion of nature on one hand and technological innovation on the other' (2014: 52). If, as Di Muzio and Robbins assert, 'technology' can be defined as 'simply a skill, art, or manner of doing something connected to a form of rationality or logic and mobilized by definite social forces' (2016: 6), clearly ITQs are advanced by the profit takers to concatenate innovation, sustainability and economic growth. The problem is, as Streeck (2014) observes, such technological advances may be mere place savers, buyers of time, so that we can deny environmental and social deterioration while simultaneously learning to live with it.

Shaw and Byler define precarity as 'an emerging abandonment that pushes us away from a liveable life' (2016). Butler describes it as 'the politically induced conditions in which certain populations suffer from failing social and economic networks … become differentially exposed to injury, violence and death' (2016: 25). Neoliberal induced violence is politically and historically constituted, creating circumstances that, for many, are experienced as inescapable. A small-boat fisherman in Iceland, captures this entrapment: 'You cannot become anything else than a slave. Personal security is not good. The owners of the quota can take it away whenever they want and leave the skipper and crew unemployed' (quoted in Carothers and Chambers 2017: 73). Such precarity is associated with the rising patterns of risk and flexibility in the context of work, the increasing incidence of part-time and zero hour labour contracts, developments which have become characteristic of post-crisis neoliberalism (Smith 2011).

This vulnerability is intensified by ecological threats. Under quota systems governance this includes the eradication of historic relationships with coastal environments and the double bind of retaining fishing as a livelihood while being simultaneously complicit in the destruction of the environment. As noted in chapters 2 and 3, the ITQ commoditisation of nature recreates the ocean ecosystem as a partible complex of commodities to be cherry picked, high-graded in ITQ terms, for consumption, or discarded as valueless. This parcelling out depicts fish as mere units of a resource, as quota stocks inanimate on an accountant's spreadsheet. Emma Cardwell comments 'Stewardship over the environment is very different to stewardship over the right to fish. The first requires responsible ecological behaviour, the second only responsible financial behaviour' (email conversation 2016). This distinction was well understood by the Scottish prawn fishermen participating in her research, who voiced their exasperation at being unable to ban the growth of twin rig gear, understood by all to damage the seabed and deteriorate stock. Though fishers had nominal ownership of the resource, namely, the right to catch prawns, they had none over the means to sustainability. That is, they were powerless when it came to managing the impact of fishing on the environment; a frustration heightened by their own compliance with the tragedy.

I first provide a general background to the fishing industry in Ireland in the context of European Union (EU) reforms and the Irish state's attempts to accommodate the small-scale sector. I then describe, in more specific detail, fishing activities in two sites in Donegal, a county in the north-west of Ireland: Na Cealla Beaga (Killybegs), the largest fishing port in Ireland, and Árainn Mhór (Arranmore), a Gaeltacht (Irish-language-speaking) island formerly famous for salmon fishing. The tension between nostalgia and precarity provides an overarching theme.

Fishing industry in Ireland

> The sea is our identity, our road, our livelihood. Sometimes it takes people, but you take the fishermen off an island, that's it. The life and soul of the island has gone. (Fisherman from Árainn Mhór island, Co. Donegal, Ireland)

The Irish seascape comprises 16 percent of EU waters and contains some of its most important and diverse fishing grounds. While the zone comprising 12 nautical miles (nm) from land is reserved for Irish fishing vessels, the 200 nm Exclusive Economic Zone (EEZ) falls within the International Council for Exploration of the Sea's sub-areas VI and VII and is incorporated in the EU's Common Fisheries Policy (CFP). As noted in chapter 2, the CFP establishes a Total Allowable Catch (TAC) for each fishing zone. The TAC is calculated using maximum sustainable yield (MSY) measurements and users (fishers) are confined to those in possession of quota allocations. Three main methods are used to apportion responsibility for fisheries between the EU and member states: (1) Quota management is implemented based on an annual determination of the TAC followed by the allocation of quota to member states. The amount of quota awarded is calculated on the basis of the average catches of each member state when the CFP was implemented in 1983. This system is assumed to ensure 'relative stability'. Member states are subsequently free to allocate national quota to users as they see fit. (2) Structural policies are set in place that specify member state ceilings for fishing fleet capacity. Member states select policy measures to adjust the sizes of their fleets. (3) Technical rules, which member states have the option to supplement, in relation to closed areas, minimum mesh size, minimum fish size and by-catch rules. Each member state is responsible for the enforcement of CFP regulations in their own waters (Farrell et al. 2010).

In their analysis, Farrell et al. (2010) mount a withering critique of CFP regulations, not only for theoretical failings but also for practical deficiencies in their application. This critique largely mirrors the general assessment of quota management systems (QMS) in terms of: the incompatibility of ecosystem management with MSY measurements; the unsuitability of mixed species management with TAC controls; high incidences of discarding, misreporting, slipping,[1] illegal landing and high-grading as a consequence of altered incentives offered to fishermen arising from quota regulations; and the destruction of fishing communities. Further antagonism is occasioned by the principle of 'relative stability', that is the mechanism by which the EU centralised quota is distributed to member states. The core component of relative stability is catch history, thus member states with a history of fishing off Ireland's coasts (for instance Spanish, French and Dutch fleets) are allocated quota in Irish waters (see chapter 2). In 2013 international fleets harvested more than 1 million tonnes of fish from the waters around Ireland with an estimated value of €1.161 billion (Marine Institute 2013: 6). Ireland's share of the EU's TAC in EU waters is set at 16 percent for demersal (whitefish) species, 23 percent for pelagic species and 23 percent of shellfish (Cawley 2006).

The perceived inadequacies of the relative stability principle include concerns that it encourages quota swapping between member states[2] and out-flagging or 'flags of convenience'; it creates an impetus for inflationary pressure on TACs because a member state that wants to increase its quota must seek an increase of the total EU TAC (European Commission 2009); while ostensibly geared towards certainty, balance and fairness, 'in reality changing ecological circumstances, shifting resource abundance and political compromises flex the boundaries of stable allocations' (Donkersloot and Menzies 2015: 16); and unfairness. In Ireland grievances arises from the perception of inequitable distribution (see chapter 2). This grievance flows from evidence that while it contributes 42 percent of the waters comprising the sub-areas VI and VII, Ireland receives approximately 16 percent of the total demersal catch in these fisheries (Gallagher et al. 2009). A research participant, first mate on a pelagic trawler, articulated a general sense of powerlessness; 'Ireland has not enough quota, Norwegian boats have more mackerel quota than Ireland though the fishery is Irish … it was because of our catch record plus our inability to argue at the level of the EU.'

The CFP underwent reforms in 1992, 2002 and 2014. The most recent reform process considered proposals from the European Commission, the executive body of the EU which proposes legislation, implements decisions, upholds the EU treaties and manages the day-to-day business of the EU. These proposals, which made explicit reference to the notion of MSY as a management objective, were concerned with the implementation of discard bans, increasing the incentives given to strengthen the regionalisation of management, and calling for an increased focus on social sustainability and the promotion of Transferable Fishing Concessions (TFCs). Echoing the exaltation of catch shares in the US Magnuson-Stevens Reauthorization Act 2006 (see chapter 4), TFCs, a euphemism for ITQs, encourage quota to be made individualised and transferable in each member state – a suggestion that was rejected, and vehemently so, by Ireland (as noted in chapter 2). It is of interest to note the alignment of sustainability with TFCs in this recent CFP reform proposal. As argued in chapter 2, this signifies a neoliberal reorganisation of both human and natural worlds and asks that we tolerate the damage done to both.

In Ireland fisheries are divided into four types: deep-water, whitefish, pelagic and shellfish fisheries. Although the contribution of the fisheries sector to Ireland's economy is relatively small, it is much valued because of its decentralised and rural characteristics. Farrell et al. acknowledge this phenomenon: 'maintaining a vibrant fisheries sector (and all of the socio-cultural characteristics associated with the communities that depend on it) is something which receives repeated emphasis in fisheries policy and management debates' (2010: 4). The economic value of the large-scale sector much exceeds that of the inshore, nevertheless, there is a broad understanding of the crucial socioeconomic role fishing plays in coastal communities. Indeed, the Irish fishery is culturally imagined as inshore: that is, as populated by small owner-operator vessels, with labour supplied by family members, comprised of fishermen who fish part-time and on a seasonal basis, and whose livelihood is supplemented by subsistence farming, seaweed and shellfish gathering and turf (peat) digging. This imagery is largely borne out by statistics: of the 1,400 vessels in the Irish fleet, 1,000 operate in the inshore sector, mostly on a part-time and seasonal basis, many of whom now fish non-quota species, such as Irish brown crabs and, until 2006, wild salmon.

These sentiments underlie the social construction of quota as property in Ireland. The Irish Department of Food, Agriculture and the Marine explicitly counterpose quota to private property, stating:

> In Ireland, quota is a public resource managed to ensure that property rights are not granted to individual operators. This is seen as a critical policy in order to ensure that quotas are not concentrated into the hands of large fishing companies whose owners have the financial resources to buy up such rights. In Ireland, any movement towards privatisation and concentration of rights into the hands of large companies would seriously risk fishing vessels losing an economic link with Ireland's coastal communities and undermining the socio-economic importance of the fishing industry in the coastal communities dependant on fishing. (Department of Agriculture, Food and the Marine 2016: 1)

Quota is attached to vessels and, if not used, returned to the state for reallocation. Concessions are made for small boats operating inshore and fishing practices deemed sustainable. The quota for whitefish, for instance, the key stocks of which are cod, haddock, whiting, hake, monk, megrim, nephrops, sole and plaice, are managed on the basis of monthly catch limits. This quota includes a quantity for smaller vessels (those under 55 ft) and an increase in catch limits for vessels using seine gear, since the latter is perceived to be less environmentally destructive than alternative fishing methods. The pelagic quota, which covers eight principal stocks – mackerel, Celtic Sea herring, North West herring, Atlanto-Scandian herring, horse mackerel, blue whiting, boarfish and albacore tuna – is further subdivided for each stock between various sectors of the fleet. Mackerel quota, for example, is proportioned between the large pelagic fleet (refrigerated seawater tank vessels) and polyvalent (multi-purpose) vessels using the ratio of 87 percent to 13 percent. Vessels under 59 ft have access to a periodic boat catch limit which is 2.5 percent of the polyvalent allocation.

The allocation for the autumn Celtic Sea herring fishery is based on fishing history prior to 2010 and catch limits are determined weekly during the season. Eleven percent of this quota is set aside to support a sentinel fishery restricted to vessels under 55 ft off the south-east coast of Ireland, known as the Dunmore Box. A further 5 percent is available for boats smaller than 65 ft. Neither concession employs catch history to restrict access. The number of vessels in the sentinel fleet increased from 4 in 2009 to 16 in 2012 (Le Floc'h et al. 2015). The fishery operates between November and February outside of which non-quota shellfish are targeted. While the aim of the sentinel fishery is to safeguard the interests of small-scale fishing vessels by setting aside a fixed allocation of the quota, it also serves to enhance scientific knowledge; smaller vessels fish inside an otherwise closed area and scientists are able to access samples of catch from that space.

These openings are reflected in a recent softening in the CFP, Article 17, 2014, which states:

> When allocating the fishing opportunities available to them, as referred to in Article 16, Member States shall use transparent and objective criteria including those of an environmental, social and economic nature. The criteria to be used may include, inter alia, the impact of fishing on the environment, the history of compliance, the contribution to the local economy and historic catch levels. Within the fishing opportunities allocated to them, Member States shall endeavour to provide incentives to fishing vessels deploying selective fishing gear or using fishing techniques with reduced environmental impact, such as reduced energy consumption or habitat damage.

Ireland's response to Article 17 includes the following measures:

Mackerel

- Mackerel quota set for under 18m Gill Net fishermen to support Artisanal Gill net fishermen fishing from punts in inshore bays.
- 400t[onnes] Set aside for Hook and Line fishermen operating from small boats primarily used in island communities.

Herring

- Small Boat fishery established to support Artisanal draft ring-net fishing from small punts in inshore bays in the North West.
- The Celtic Sea herring management plan introduced measures which restricts [sic] boats larger than 20m from fishing for herring in the herring spawning box known as the Dunmore Box off Co. Waterford.

Albacore Tuna

- A portion of national quota has been set aside for Surface Longlining and mechanised trolling.

(Department of Agriculture, Food and the Marine 2016: 5–6)

Similar to the accommodations made in Iceland to humanise the fishing economy, to bring about a moral neoliberalism that tempers the market variety, the results are likely to be ambiguous given the existence of an overshadowing EU quota system in which the market is the ultimate distributor of equality. Irrespective of these concessions, there is a palpable crisis in Irish fishing communities (Farrell et al. 2010) and a vocal sense of grievance in the inshore sector. The quota set aside for small boats fishing inshore is perceived to be woefully insufficient and livelihoods are threatened by rising fuel costs, overcapacity and uncertain prices. There is an overarching perception that EU regulations have negatively impacted island fishing communities. While, in general, there is strong support for the EU in Ireland, there is also a consensus that the fisheries sector has been the biggest loser in Ireland's attachment to the European project.

O'Donnchadha et al. (2000), in a study of the Irish fishing industry, found 'quiet despondence, a puzzled desperation and, above all, signs of a pervasive alienation' towards the current fisheries regulations. Historically, coastal waters were governed relatively successfully by local communities. Farrell et al. (2010) point out that, in the 1960s, when fishing escalated and was perceived to threaten stock levels, fishermen's cooperatives were responsible for introducing voluntary measures to restrict catches and effort. This local-based governance was gradually replaced by TAC levels, set initially by the North East Atlantic Fisheries Commission,[3] a development that became fully centralised under the current EU CFP system. Donkersloot and Menzies argue that this recent alienation dovetails with an historic trajectory: 'the Irish fishing industry has been repeatedly undermined through hierarchical integration into larger political economic processes and powers linked to Ireland's colonial encounter with Britain' (2015: 3).

Marine historian John de Courcy Ireland (1981) writes of a thriving and independent commercial fishing sector in Ireland in the 1300s, 1400s and 1500s. Herring and salmon, among other fish species, were included as items for which elites were entitled to levy taxes for the maintenance of their fortifications. Fourteenth-century records indicate that salt was shipped from Brittany to Donegal for curing herring and, by the fifteenth century, the Irish sea fisheries were famous throughout western Europe, attracting foreign interest. Local chieftains benefited opportunistically from this: in the south-west, for instance, chieftain O'Sullivan Beare turned away English applicants for fishing rights along his coasts, preferring instead to pursue an arrangement with Spaniards (1981: 22). As England consolidated its colonial grip from 1536 such independent commercial relations became progressively subjugated to the control of the English monarchy. Much evidence exists to suggest that Irish fisheries under British authority were actively stymied or otherwise sacrificed to colonial interests (Connaghan 1997, 2003; Tucker 1999). Molloy describes the means by which the Irish fisheries industry was propelled to a state of collapse to assuage Scottish and English envy (2004: 50–51). This colonial mismanagement, compounded by famine, greatly increased mortality rates and the ensuing emigration from coastal areas. The number of fishermen decreased by more than 50 percent following the 1845–51 famine (Molloy 2004: 51), fishermen sold their gear to ward off starvation while others were simply too weak to go to sea (Molloy 2004: 34). However, in coastal communities in Donegal, seafood provided an important barrier against starvation (Donkersloot and Menzies 2015).

In 1891 the Congested District Board (CDB), established to address poverty in West Ireland, attempted to organise a fishing industry. The CDB instituted two main advances during its three-decade tenure: first, it undermined the notorious 'gombeen men' (money lenders renowned for high interest rates) by establishing rural banks and cooperatives, buying fish at guaranteed prices directly from fishermen and improving transportation to markets (Molloy 2004); second, improvements were made to catching and processing sectors, including the construction of piers, one of which was in Killybegs, Donegal (Donkersloot and Menzies 2015). The Sea Fisheries Association, established in 1931, continued to improve fishermen's access to markets, a task also undertaken by its successor, the Irish Seafisheries Board (Bord Iascaigh Mhara) in 1952. The major ports were concentrated on the east coast until the 1940s, but in the 1950s a burgeoning interest in pelagics (particularly herring) and shellfish shifted much fishing activity westward. The Irish Seafisheries Board actively encouraged industrialisation as an economic development strategy: boat yards were built, including one in Killybegs, fisheries loans were established and vessel size and design stipulated. The upper limit of vessel size, and for which loans could be approved, was set at 90 ft. The size has since been extended to make the Irish fleet competitive with the European one. Increased fish landings and earnings, market improvements, vessel upgrades and advances in fishing technology characterised the decades leading up to Ireland's integration into the EU in 1972. This marks the point at which a new era of hierarchical governance over Irish waters was ushered in. Harry Browne writes in the *Dublin Review*:

> Joey Murrin, from Killybegs in Donegal, was one of twenty fishermen protesting outside the Department of Foreign Affairs in Dublin as those negotiations drew to a close. With so few protesting, and tens of thousands of farmers marching in enthusiastic support of EEC [European Economic Community] membership, he knew 'we hadn't a hope' of convincing the government that Ireland's seas should be kept for Irishmen to fish. (2008: 2)

In the 1970s Irish fishing grounds were the least over-exploited in Europe (de Courcy Ireland 1981: 149).

Donegal

I was born in a coastal community in Co. Derry, in Northern Ireland, though spent most holidays in a fishing community in Donegal. My parents relocated permanently to Donegal in 2002 and in 2014 I undertook field research in coastal, including island, communities in the south-west of the county. The ethnography in this section is based on participant observation and 15 informal interviews with one or more members of the following fisheries-related occupations and others with a special interest in the industry: inshore fishermen, a harbourmaster, pelagic crew members, fish processors, salmon fishers, crab fishers, fish sellers, fishermen activists, a local Sinn Fein TD,[4] a development officer and an oyster farmer.

Fishing is a particularly embedded way of life in coastal communities in Donegal: more people are employed in fisheries there and seafood consumption rates are higher than in any other county in the Republic of Ireland. Donegal, however, is also the poorest and most socioeconomically disadvantaged county, and this deprivation bears most heavily on its coastal communities. Often referred to as the 'forgotten' county, Donegal consciousness is imbued with sentiments of peripherality, 'remoteness', 'poverty', 'backwardness' and contradictory loyalties due to its historic permeability to the movement of people and ideologies from the troubled North.[5] Although employment in fisheries is declining, it remains enormously significant given the lack of alternative cash earning opportunities and a history of high unemployment rates. Maintaining a viable fishing industry is emotionally charged as any decline is associated with the physical loss of kin. Emigration is an historic wound in Donegal, a place often characterised as an 'emigrant nursery', an employment 'black spot' (MacLaughlin 1994). The recent struggle of many small fishing-dependent communities is experienced locally as an economic and cultural assault and further evidence of the region's marginality. In order to understand the heightened discontent of the last few decades it is important to acknowledge the effect of collective memories of marginality over a much longer period.

In Donegal, the population of fishing communities is in decline. This is seen to be a consequence of the dwindling supply of fish, the EU quota system and, as in Iceland, the fact that large trawlers process on board, thereby bypassing onshore facilities. Fishing villages near Killybegs, the largest fishing port in Ireland, combined small-scale fishing with farming and seasonal employment in the port's fish factories. Fifteen towns in Donegal now have a dwelling vacancy rate of 35 percent or higher: all of them are coastal settlements and there are about 10,000 vacant properties throughout the coastal areas of Donegal (Central Statistics Office 2012). (Some of these are holiday homes and are unoccupied for most of the year but many are not.) A participant pelagic fisherman summarised the local situation as follows: 'many fishing villages are in reality angling villages [that is, geared towards tourist fishing], at Mulligmore Head that's angling, at Teelin, there hasn't been a fishery there for 20 years'.

Killybegs

The port of Killybegs has witnessed a number of booms, busts and population fluctuations. The North West herring fishery, which dominated in the 1970s, was overtaken by the mackerel fishery in the 1980s. The latter is linked to the emergence of 'mackerel millionaires' and occasions of elite corruption, much like the 'sealords' of Icelandic fisheries. The pelagic mackerel is currently the most significant species landed in Killybegs in terms of earnings, onshore employment and exports. This though is a tenuous wealth, subject to the vagaries of climate change, the pelagic mackerel having, since 2008, increasingly migrated north. International quota battles have marked their arrival in Iceland waters (see chapter 3). The Irish pelagic fleet consists of 22 trawlers and 1 factory trawler. The largest of these, between 60 m and 62 m and towing nets with mouth openings of 1,600 m, are termed the 'Big Five' (Donkersloot and Menzies 2015). While the Irish pelagic fleet is only 1 percent of the overall Irish fleet, it makes up 40 percent of the catch capacity (Cawley 2006).

The participants in my research, who come from fishing villages and island communities, largely consider Killybegs to have disproportionately benefited from EU quota. This perception is echoed by a pelagic first mate participant whose assessment of the quota system is: 'it is pretty good, though small boats will have a different story to tell'. While there is substance in this evaluation, particularly when the streets of Killybegs are juxtaposed with the derelict facades of nearby Burtonport, until recently a thriving fishing port, Killybegs is nevertheless subject to the same structural reforms promulgated by EU quota governance, mindful of the tempering facilitated by Ireland's construction of quota as state property and its resistance to transferability. In Killybegs there is a noticeable sense of precarity, of an uncertain future and of relative powerlessness in the face of the EU regulatory system. Donkersloot and Menzies (2015: 8) identify a local consciousness which imagines emigration as the only option for the town's young people and suggest that this is an expression of the pelagic fleet's contested power and peripherality in the sphere of EU fisheries. They refer to a scandal that emerged in 2004 concerning the pelagic fleet's involvement in illegal fishing practices, declining access and rising operational costs as emblematic of economic volatility. The fact that the impact of rising fuel prices is differentially experienced across Europe compounds the perception of Irish peripherality: 'the politically powerful French and Spanish fleets were shored up by state fuel allowances covering 20–25% of fuel costs. Lacking comparable clout, the Irish fishing sector failed to secure similar government support leaving the fleet more vulnerable to escalating operating costs' (Donkersloot and Menzies 2015: 9). Increases in fuel costs may have a detrimental effect on crew wages and the number of people employed. A pelagic fisherman recalled: 'Twenty years ago twelve demersal, whitefish fishing boats were fishing out of Killybegs. There are now maybe two or three. This is a result of the EU quota system, diesel prices and it is hard to get crew.' Killybegs fishers perceive their livelihood as tenuous: they see themselves as having only marginal priority in the overall decision-making process leading to a sense of alienation from the governance of their local fishery resources.

There has also been a spatial shift in fishing grounds. The larger trawlers have increasingly focused their activities in Scottish, Norwegian and other fishing grounds further afield as a consequence of technological advances, EU regulations, ecosystem fluctuations and the improved capacity of vessels; treaties have been struck with non-EU countries, and mackerel have simply relocated. This delocalisation implicates an increasing globalisation of local crew. A fisheries agent observed that while crew on bigger vessels were largely Irish, on smaller boats (likely owner-operator or contracted by factories) they were typically from EU countries such as Poland and Lithuania. A disparity he accounted for by the relative price of labour and the expense of running a vessel. This spatial shift also had strong implications for land-based processing in Killybegs. In the 1980s and 1990s employment in fish factories comprised 83 percent of all employment in the shore-based fishery sector (Donnchadha et al. 2000: 30). The local labour force was supplemented by busloads of workers from surrounding communities who were daily transported to the town's factories (Donkersloot and Menzies 2015). Employment in processing has declined to a level where it is now intermittent, unreliable and reduced to a season of three or four months, with many non-working days throughout. This decline coincided with the closure of the commercial salmon gillnet fishery in 2007, a consequence of an EU Habitats Directive. Up to this point salmon fishing was a traditional alternative livelihood practice for south-west Donegal fish factory workers. When the 'Celtic Tiger' went into steep decline following the financial crash in 2008 an additional layer was added to this economic vulnerability.

The precarity of fishing livelihoods is arguably no longer routinely equated with the perils of the activity itself – long considered the most dangerous of professions – but now tends to refer to the anxieties caused by quota enclosures. Whereas across space and time the ocean has been understood as beyond human control, the present insecurities are firmly rooted in the political economy. It is the latter reality that potentiates hope. Though precariousness implies stasis, this is not necessarily a permanent condition. There may even be a spectrum or an oscillation between precarity and hope along which dissent emerges, becomes thwarted and resurfaces again.

The precarious present evokes what Clifford (2012) describes as 'feeling historical', a looking back to the past even while acknowledging that though certain aspects of it are better left there, it entailed a stable horizon of expectation, the possibility of 'belonging to tomorrow' (Sider in Barber et al. 2012: 9). This retrospection, prompted by economic precarity, is also captured in writings on nostalgia. Anthropologists have long made a connection between a heightened nostalgia and accelerated social trans-formation. Research in Eastern Europe has established a link between nostalgia, the adoption of neoliberal markets and social remembrance of a communal past (Hann 2015; Todorova and Gille 2010). Boym delineates the social construction involved, 'nostalgia becomes a defence mechanism against the accelerated rhythm of change and economic shock therapy' (2002: 64). Such memories are less a commentary on the past than a critique of the present (Reed 2016: 97): a pragmatic nostalgia which works to focus attention on the intersection of the individual, the social and the economic.

Importantly, feeling nostalgic is no longer solely identified with the reminiscences of the diaspora, but has also imbued the rooted, those who have stayed in their now unrecognisable homeland. Memories of a near utopian past may intensify under conditions of imposed austerity. In Ireland the aftermath of the collapse of the 'Celtic Tiger', the trans-formational economic boom that persisted between 1997 and 2007, inspired a popular critique of the fierce immorality of that era, the decided un-Irishness of the decade, a collective folly recognised as 'we who went a bit mad with borrowing' (O'Flynn et al. 2014: 921). It is important, however, to recognise the internalisation of precarity, of being complicit in the excesses, as an insidious form of violence inflicted on populations. O'Flynn et al. draw attention to the subtext of scapegoating in post-crash Ireland, describing it as a 'pervasive political process that is protective of powerful interests and the status quo' (2014: 921). Green (2012) points to the multiple and complex ways in which violence and impunity create cir-cumstances seen overwhelmingly as inevitable. As social processes, these are enabled by silence and memory on the one hand, and by historical amnesia and indifference on the other.

In Irish literature, landscape has historically been associated with nostalgia and loss (Frawley 2005). Post-Celtic Tiger Ireland has added a new material foundation for this imagining. Mianowski (2016) observes how 'the excesses of recent years are made visible, as roads, hotel and housing developments were built frenetically and ghost estates are now scattered across the country' (2016: 1). This disbanded material culture echoes ghost estates of the past, the absentee landlords of previous centuries and the decay of famine cottages still waiting for the return of kin. Seascapes are also ripe for nostalgic extensions as foreign extractors, infuriatingly eyed from shore, replace local livelihoods. In Árainn Mhór graveyards of boats, nets and pots, sit alongside the Marian shrines, seeming to memorialise not only the drowned, but the culture of fishing itself. Lamentations of loss evoke in their wake the resilience of the celebrated traditional values of kin, morality, community, music, 'culture', 'craic', dance and literature, along with the power of heroic myth and legends, and a history of David-style resistance to imperial Goliath encroachment and cultural subjugation. While nostalgia seems to imply sentimentalism, historical fabrication and a politically regressive subject, the opposite is also the case; it may contain a significant political subtext (Louyest and Roberts 2015). Nostalgic laments may be a moral critique of present inequalities and may provide a charter for social change (Parla 2009; Yang 2003). Nostalgia may be creative, may empower agency, may be used as a weapon of the weak, and may have a critical role to play in the field of power and resistance (Angé and Berliner 2015; Berdahl, 1999). Chris Hann (2015) insists that any treatment of nostalgia must take into account the larger socio-political context and must provide a lens through which to interpret contemporary politicisation. Nostalgia, in this sense, can be likened to Polanyi's 'double movement'; it can kindle resistance.

Árainn Mhór

The weight of loss is crystallised on the Gaeltacht (Gaelic/Irish-speaking) island of Árainn Mhór, the largest inhabited island off Donegal,[6] situated in the culturally distinctive Na Rosann parish. In Árainn Mhór fishing is a historically crucial cash and subsistence activity, supplemented by agriculture (though this is tenuous pursuit given the lack of suitable land) and turf cutting. The main species fished were salmon, herring and lobster, though also pollock and dogfish, each of which had its own season. Burtonport, situated 3 miles away on the mainland, served as the port of landing, socialising and marketing of island-caught fish. Deep ties, arising from fishing activities, exist between islanders and mainlanders.

Post-1980 population decline in both Árainn Mhór and Burtonport is associated with a radical change in fisheries, most importantly the implementation of the 1983 European CFP and the reorganisation of fisheries management as a quota regime. This encompassed the herring, pollock and dogfish fisheries. It also had a spatial dimension – the dislocation of commercial fishing rights away from small ports and fishing communities. In Donegal, fishing rights shifted to Killybegs, to large fishing companies and, it is thought, to Spanish and French fleets. This dispossession was compounded by the 2006 nationwide ban on commercial salmon fishing,[7] a move perceived to favour large-scale interests, that is, commercial, mostly Norwegian owned, salmon farms, though also the lucrative angler tourist market. These changes affected numerous fisheries in Árainn Mhór, leaving only lobster and the more recently targeted crab fisheries as going concerns. Such changes have implications for sustainability: they have transformed a multi-species, multi-gear, fishing tradition based on seasonal harvesting into a single-species, single-gear, year-round fishing effort. An oversupplied market and reduced catch per unit of effort has resulted in a shrinking of earnings, and threatened the continuation of fishing as a way of life and source of livelihood. The island's population has now reached a critical survival point: if the population declines any further social services will be cut, for instance, if even one child leaves one of the two primary schools, the school will be forced to close. Meanwhile Burtonport, formerly famous for its herring fishery, has become, in the words of participants, a 'ghost town'.

The following extracts from an interview with a woman in her mid-50s, a former Burtonport resident, captures how nostalgia reflects economic and social criteria, but also provides a moral commentary on the present:

> I was born and bred in Burtonport; there were seven fish factories then and six pubs, over one hundred in the fleet of boats. Families, entire families were involved. My father and brothers fished, and me and my sisters worked in the processing factories. I started at 13 years of age. Burtonport was a booming fishing village then. Boats used to land from Greencastle, all over Ireland and Scotland. Fisheries used to be a great living, you could live comfortably. I enjoyed the work. It was a great laugh. We worked long hours.
>
> It is not because the fish have gone, they haven't. The French and Spanish can fish but we can't. Irish fishermen are being done left, right and centre because of the stupidity of our politicians. Going to Burtonport makes me very sad now. We lost all our buses. All our fishermen. The men there were always working, fixing nets and all.

Now it is a ghost town. In some places people didn't know anything else but fishing. People feel shoved out, people haven't the freedom.

A loss of control over the future and a restriction of former freedoms were powerfully expressed by this participant through the imagery of imprisoned salmon:

It's like the farmed salmon, what are they feeding the fish? Look at the colour of them. They are hemmed in, just like us now. With prey you have to give them a chance, poor old bloody salmon. It's not fishing, there is no fun in it, not even for the salmon.

Nostalgia for a pre-neoliberal past juxtaposes the individualism of the present with memories of a former moral economy:

Back then people didn't exploit the resource, they used what they needed. Most people lived off the sea – dillisk, winkles, barnacles, crabs, all boiled or fried out. About 7 or 8 o'clock in the evening me Da would say, come on, let's go fishing. The fish used to go round. We all helped each other out. Our family had more land than other families, so we could grow more potatoes. Our neighbours with less land grew vegetables like cabbage. No money ever changed hands. They had very little, but at the same time they had everything. Today we live by the clock, we never looked at the clock back then, only to see if it was time to go to bed. Time meant nothing.

Nostalgic discourse also provides a means through which seemingly powerless people can expresses the social and phenomenological disruptions that accompany economic transformations:

Back then the sea was another city at night. You could look out and see the light, now you see nothing. My family were all fishermen, not one of them fish any more, where has all that knowledge gone? Most people lived off the sea, I miss that food, the salt water taste, I miss the freshness. *Cèilidh* – it means going to visit people. Music and dancing carried on into the wee hours. People danced on slate floors and sparks would come flying off their shoes, you know, with the nails in them for Irish dancing. I have never had that happiness again.

In Burtonport there was a great attachment to Árainn Mhór Island. There was a grand nightlife over there. We used to go to the hall and dance until all hours, we could see the fishermen coming in and we kept on dancing. The atmosphere was great, the bars didn't shut. We would play gaelic [football] against the island, that was the only time of rivalry. People on the island used to come across and work in the fish factories. They would come home with us if they worked on a late shift. (former Burtonport resident)

The cultural identity of an Árainn Mhór islander is synonymous with fishing activity and the knowledge required, not just to be a successful producer, but also to survive on and with the sea.

The sea is the fabric of what and who we are. I end up crying when I talk about it. There is a sadness. What will I do with this knowledge that I was given freely and with generosity? There is nowhere to go with it. I can't pass it on to my children. Knowledge of the weather, the ocean swells, the moon when it is lying on its back. Our grandfathers and fathers gave this to us. No one taught us to fish only one species of fish. They taught as to go fishing on a seasonal basis. That is sustainable. That is reading nature. Now we buy our fish from Killybegs. We are living on an island and have to buy our fish from the mainland. When tourists ask whether the fish was caught locally, I am ashamed. (Árainn Mhór generational fisher)

Many people think that island people are stupid, that we don't know anything about the world, but in reality we are highly articulate people. We know that our fisheries have been systematically broken down. We know that the rich are always rewarded. We know that islanders are the peasants of the system. (Árainn Mhór generational fisher)

Nostalgia may be a weapon at the disposal of the poor. It is bound up with perceptions of crisis and of uncertainties around the viability of cultural transmission (Berliner 2015); it can provide an alternative to confront social change and in this sense can empower resistance. For island fishermen in Donegal, the mobilising potential of nostalgia has been married to an indigenous rights rhetoric to provide a critique of economic and cultural dispossession, and leverage through which to envision an alternative future. The following extract, from a presentation by Árainn Mhór fisherman, Jerry Early, given to the Joint Committee on Agriculture, Foods and the Marine Debate at the *Tithe an Oireachtais* (Irish parliament), in 2012, captures this rhetoric:[8]

We call for the fair treatment of small island communities and respect for fishermen as custodians of our fisheries and the sea. We ask for the responsibility and right to practise traditional livelihoods that are ecologically sustainable, socially just and culturally diverse and pass down our traditions, knowledge and skills to future generations ... Our islands have characteristics that are intrinsically valuable and play an important role in the mixture that forms Europe's diverse coastal economy. Islands should be maintained not as museum pieces, but as vibrant and critical elements of modern Europe ... if islands can gain consideration and return to the traditional way of life ... we can foresee the return of the emigrant, the need for more schools, the possibility of small businesses growing ... [a] return to self-sufficiency, practising traditional, small-scale fishing and supported by a diversity of livelihoods ... The island man has been given a task to keep this way of life alive. We are different, a breed apart. We are part of a whole yet, at times, undeniably alone and separate. Ireland has entrusted its islanders to keep the lights burning, keep the traditions and be at the forefront of the culture, the language, the skills, the crafts ... island fishermen will happily undertake the responsibilities involved in preserving the traditions held in high esteem throughout Europe and beyond.

Jerry Early and John O'Brien (of Árainn Mhór and Inis Bo Finne islands) are founders of the Donegal Islands Marine Resource Organisations (DIMRO) and both generously participated in this research. They now navigate national and international political forums to agitate for special recognition of their fishing traditions and livelihood rights. This politicisation has international traction: the involvement of non-governmental organisations such as the indigenous knowledge promoter, the Gaia Foundation; the International Collective in Support of Fishworkers; the European Small Islands Federation; Alyne Delaney, EU fisheries social scientist; Scottish Crofting Federation member, Iain MacKinnon; and French documentary filmmaker, Loïc Jourdaine.[9] The group has also garnered political recognition in Ireland. A Joint Sub-committee on Fisheries was formed by the Irish government in December 2012 to examine the socioeconomic challenges facing rural coastal and island communities. The committee's 2014 report acknowledges the impetus provided by island fishermen in Donegal:

> The identification of this priority came, in part, from sections of the fishing community who had earned their livelihood from mixed stock salmon fishing (using drift nets) off the coast of Árainn Mhór in the Donegal Gaeltacht who felt that no alternative had been provided for them following the ban on this form of fishing. (Joint Sub-committee on Fisheries 2014: 5)

> The scale of the socio-economic challenge facing many island and rural coastal communities was encapsulated by the Donegal Islands Fishermen (DIF) in their presentation to the Sub-committee on Fisheries ... (2014: 18)

A briefing paper for the report details the decline of Altantic salmon since their peak in the 1970s, which is ascribed to rising sea temperatures, changes in oceans' circulation, overfishing, technological advances, poor water quality, loss of riverine habitat, predations from seals, marine parasites and diseases, by-catches in pelagic fisheries and the secondary effects of aquaculture (the impact of sea lice, chemical treatments, and escaped farmed fish). The ban of drift net fishing for salmon brought Ireland into line with the EU Habitats Directive; Ireland was the last country in the EU to comply. The briefing paper acknowledges that since the ban salmon numbers have continued to fall, and while fishermen in Gaeltacht island communities have sustained economic loss, the recreation and tourism industry associated with angling has experienced beneficial economic growth (Joint Sub-committee on Fisheries 2014: 222–24). Britton's research on the loss of salmon rights in Greencastle Donegal highlights the cultural significance of salmon, a species celebrated in legends, folksongs and in the distinctive ecological knowledge of those who pursue them. Salmon driftnet fishing is also, and importantly, tied up with a strong sense of identity and attachment to place (Britton 2014: 144). Three recommendations from the sub-committee's report are worth citing:

> **Recommendation 10:** The sub-Committee recommends that the Government examine the feasibility of the issuance of 'heritage licences' to rural coastal and island communities. Such licences would optimally

facilitate traditional fishing practices in conjunction with the establishment of a producer organisation representing vessels under a certain
length overall in designated areas.

Recommendation 11: The sub-Committee recommends that a more
flexible legislative approach to minor fishing infractions be introduced
to ensure that they are dealt with in a way that reflects the scale of the
infractions i.e. based on the length overall and the potential impact of
the vessel concerned on fish stocks.

Recommendation 12: The sub-Committee recommends that if salmon
stocks are increasing, innovative technologies should be used so that all
fishermen including drift fishermen can harvest them in a controlled
and managed way that will not endanger stocks. Pilot projects should
be initiated and Ireland should lead the way in this area. (Joint
Sub-committee on Fisheries 2014: 11)

However, these accommodations are overshadowed in the report by an
explicit emphasis on aquaculture as a means to develop rural and island
communities. This proposal endorses an economic orientation that,
particularly in the case of the symbolic salmon, evokes deep antagonism
in Donegal. The following vignette, adapted from fieldnotes, illustrates
some of these tensions:

Marti [pseudonym], a former salmon fisher insisted I see what happened
to Castleberg [pseudonym], a small village in Donegal through which
flows an historic and culturally significant salmon river. The village is
also renowned for: hosting one of the counties first salmon farms; a
mysterious and massive death of farmed fish in 2003; reports of sea lice
infestations in 2013 and 2014 and the escape of 83,000 salmon from a
giant fish cage during a stormy night in 2015. Driving into the village
Marti warns: 'They won't talk to you here. They feed into themselves.
They were expert inshore fishers, now they are aqua farmers, they sold
all that 20 odd years ago for a handful of jobs. And these are getting less
as the technology improves. It's a loss of fisheries.' There was obvious
wealth creation in the village, and a splattering of well-to-do homes.
Marti explained that while 'local fellows have houses and the farm's
employees, it is surmised, are paid well and get training in diving and
it is less precarious than fishing, the owners can up and move at any
time, just leave and close it all down'. Walking out onto the small pier

I counted 25 circular cages in the water, the stench from which was overwhelming.

While the DIMRO has had successes to date, thorny economic and social issues remain unresolved, a situation that is likely to become increasingly fraught given the pressure to make quota transferable, the mooted European conservation directive to designate the seascape surrounding Árainn Mhór a nature protected area (under the EU programme Natura 2000), the invigoration of the 'Blue Economy' (see chapter 3) and the tendency of neoliberal governance to discipline dissent. The promotion of salmon farms as an alternative economy is fraught with complexity. It raises moral, political and environmental concerns about a heightened era of enclosures, human–environment destructions and the loss of cultural knowledge.

The local lament of small-scale producers cannot be understood simply as an irrational inability to modernise, an attempt to cling on to traditional values (as Icelandic ITQ opponents were satirised for doing by Runolfsson and Arnason 1999). Making sense of these anxieties and uncertainties, of people losing control over their own fate and that of their communities, is to engage with the mechanics of a particularly recent alienation, a particularly recent curtailment of freedom. In the context of such economic transformations, nostalgic memories of a pre-neoliberal era can serve to activate an alternative future trajectory. To argue for a return to a system of commoning (Linebaugh 2012), for an egalitarian distribution of resource rights, is no more romantic than the capitalist utopia of free markets operating in entirely privatised space.

Epilogue: ITQs, Neoliberalism and the Anthropocene

Individual transferable quotas (ITQs) are a central actor in this book, a key technology through which enclosures are actioned, natural and social realms are reconstructed, catch rights are divorced from labour and precarity is unleashed on fishing peoples. They are intertwined with neoliberal restructuring and a heightened search for new environmental commodities, those that can be parcelled as ecosystem services and become amenable to the mechanics of auditing. The mutation of ITQs over time can usefully be contextualised within Davies (2016) demarcation of the three phases of neoliberalism.

The first era, lasting from 1979 to 1989, he terms combative neoliberalism for its insistence on an absolute dichotomy between market capitalism and everything else and the introduction of a friend–enemy distinction to economic policy making. Graeber succinctly states this obliteration of alternatives: 'whenever there is a choice between one option that makes capitalism seem the only possible economic system, and another that would actually make capitalism a more viable economic system, neoliberalism means always choosing the former' (2013: 7). With the systemic demise of state socialism, neoliberalism firmly entrenched political hopes and identities in non-socialist economic forms (Davies 2016: 127). It is noteworthy that, during this time frame, ITQs were introduced in New Zealand and Iceland as the only possible methodology for managing the fisheries resource. This development aligned wealth creation with privatisation, instigated the abrupt removal of part-time and small-scale fishers from the seascape and has, as one of its consequences, the destruction of fishing communities. It is also the era in which the interim settlement of Māori fisheries, actualised in the Māori Fisheries Act 1989, facilitated the carving up of indigenous fishing rights into commercial and non-commercial concerns and assigned different levels of Māori kinship (*iwi* and *hapu*) as the appropriate entity to engage with each. This cut across *rangatiratanga* (sovereignty) and removed any semblance of market exchange from customary fishing livelihoods. The ultimately unsuccessful challenge of the *koha* fishers described in chapter 1 illustrates the propensity of ITQ regimes to disallow alternative means to organise the economy.

The second era, normative neoliberalism, incorporated the golden age of neoliberalism in the 1990s, ended with the global fiscal crisis in 2007 and is associated with centre-left governments. With the absence of a socialist 'other', the period is noteworthy for attempting to render the system 'fair',[1] hence the extension of market instruments and metrics as the measure of human worth to non-market social and natural domains, the opening up of neoliberal spaces. Davies points out that this gave rise to ideas of legitimate inequality. Competition became constitutionally important and 'its moral vision hung ultimately on the authority of the audits, economic tests and methodologies that various agencies used to judge and calculate value across society at large' (2016: 129). The Blue Economy in general, and ecosystem services tools in particular, facilitate an evaluation of both human and natural worlds through the practices of ecological auditing. Such an audit culture elides accountancy with policing (Shore and Wright 1999: 557) and reduces social and natural phenomenon to crude, quantifiable and, in particular, 'inspectable templates' (Strathern 1997).

Given the emphasis on competition and the market as a distinguisher of equality, it is notable that Māori Treaty claims to fisheries were fully and finally resolved in this era and community quotas, a neoliberal opening, were instituted in both Iceland and New Zealand. In chapter 1, I traced the incorporation of Māori claims to fisheries into the ITQ system, a development that led to a 'generalisation' of property such that individual quota became a substitute for indigenous customary tenure regimes, and the mechanism through which colonial alienations were repatriated. While community quotas suggest an element of equitable distribution, they are equally a conglomeration of individual quota and encompass none of the fluidity and flexibility inherent in common property regimes. That the community quota allocated to Māori *iwi*, for instance, largely functions in a virtual market, where catch rights are divorced from production and wealth is created through abstracted trading activities, challenges the pretension to commons of this property construct. This situation is illustrated in chapter 3 where the leasing of Māori quota to consolidated companies and foreign charter vessels is juxtaposed to the demise of fishing livelihoods in coastal communities. In Iceland, similarly, community quotas have done little to reverse the exigencies of dispossessions.

The ensuing dispossession in Māori society cannot simply be explained as an elite capture of Treaty settlement assets; rather, I argue, that this development is entangled with the distributional effects of a market-based fisheries regime. Harvey's (2005) work on 'accumulation by dispossession' argues that neoliberalism extends the reach of classical primitive accumulation in contradictory ways and opens the door for subsequent dispossessions. The latter are accomplished, critically, through the market. In chapter 3 I focus on the transferability aspect of ITQs, the mechanism designed to unleash the potency of market trading relationships, and through which ITQs became bound up with financialisation and crisis. In Iceland the role of fishing quota in the financial crash of 2008 is illustrative of the capacity of finance to innovate, to securitise and to alienate what was once perceived as a common and constitutional right to a natural resource. It also indicates how great fortunes and escalating inequality are generated in a process that is only tangentially related to the production of physical commodities. Marketising the environment, which, while never complete, importantly directs the production and exchange of fish, coerces the behaviour of actors within the sector, elevates the status of quota traders and devalues the knowledge associated with harvesting. In this sense, ITQs can be problematised as a 'total social fact' in the fisheries in which they operate. They occasion 'manners of acting, thinking and feeling external to the individual, which are invested with a coercive power by virtue of which they exercise control over him' (Durkheim 1982: 52).

The rendering of neoliberalism as fair can also be identified in ITQ claims to sustainability, a concept that introduces an aura of morality, and additionally, in its neoliberal invocation, confers an ideological legitimacy on further enclosures. In chapter 2 I refer to the lexical history of sustainability as a means to engage with these darker semantics. I argue that sustainability is implicated not only in extending privatisations, along the lines of Hardin's (1968) solution to the apparent lack of stewardship in commonly owned resources, but also in the re-creation of ocean ecosystems as an environment-in-waiting for capital infusion. The privatisation accomplished in individual quota, a subjugation of the social, has a frightful symmetry in the establishment of regional entities in the sea that can be compared with each other, and scientific assessments of species boundaries and species productivity. Both forms of enclosure are, I suggest, premised on capital accumulation.

Davies's description of the third and current post-2008 phase of neoliberalism is fraught with accounts of unreason, disbelief and economic nonsense. It would appear, he declares, 'that neoliberalism has entered some sort of post-hegemonic phase, in which systems and routines of power survive, but without normative or democratic authority' (2016: 122). The key characteristics of this phase of neoliberalism are vindictive varieties of policy making and the disciplining of vulnerable populations. This is a 'punitive neoliberalism' when debt, whose cumulation was secreted during the first two eras, came crashing onto centre stage. The current period is distinguished by an ethos of heavily moralised punishment fixated on the politically, and now indebted, weak. Davies comments: 'economic dependency and moral failure become entangled in the form of debt, producing a melancholic condition in which governments and societies unleash hatred and violence upon members of their own populations' (2016: 130). In Davies's description what has changed in neoliberalism is not so much the techniques of power, but rather their ethical orientation.

This is also an embodied neoliberalism, one played out in individual bodies and psyches and one in which it is not at all clear why measures such as austerity, for instance, are introduced. The crash of the Irish Celtic Tiger in 2007, followed by an era of austerity, evoked a subtext of scapegoating; the infliction of insidious violence on already marginalised populations and the simultaneous protection of powerful interests and the status quo. The extension of neoliberalism to the psychosomatic segues with a recent concern with precarity. In chapter 5 I argue that precarity is now a characteristic of fishing livelihoods, not so much because of the dangers implicit in the activity itself, the sea conceived of as a life force outside of human control, nor so much as a result of a decline in resource abundance, but rather as a consequence of quota enclosures. In Ireland the propertisation characteristic of quota management hits up against local memories and small-scale livelihoods. Here, contemporary enclosures sit alongside historical acts of incorporation into outside powerful entities. The implementation of the 1983 European Common Fisheries Policy (CFP) reorganised national fisheries as a quota regime and diverted fishing rights away from small ports and fishing communities. This reorganisation has been compounded by a ban on drift-net fishing for salmon and the designation of the seascape surrounding parts of Donegal as a marine protected site. These directives, arguably, subjugate fishing livelihoods to conservation imperatives and aquaculture production, and implicate a new round of dispossessions. Ireland has thus far, however, resisted the momentum to make quota transferable, a proposal rejected in the recent 2014 CFP reforms.

Davies's temporal analysis of neoliberalism, while convincing, has an all-encompassing character, one in which the diversity of cultural actors, the richness of histories and economies, is all but annihilated. As the ethnographic encounters in this book suggest, neoliberalism is neither monolithic nor does it produce seemingly inevitable results. Each chapter is careful to highlight neoliberal impurities, the different ways in which accommodations are made for local cultural contexts, and the types of resistances that shape the policies, programmes and practices of neoliberalism as it hits the ground running. While Māori had little option but to accept the implementation of ITQs, with Jim Bolger, the prime minister of the time, stipulating that 'no other proposal [is] on the horizon for settling commercial fisheries claims', the manner in which propertisation proceeded confronted long-standing opposition. Beginning with the Oyster Fisheries Act 1866, wherein Māori were prohibited from selling oysters from beds reserved for them, there was a concerted effort to redefine Māori interests in fisheries as non-commercial activities at best. Chapter 1 highlights the complexities of indigenous engagements with colonial settlerism in New Zealand, the power dynamics that are both explicit and implicit, the intricacies of Māori politicking and the absolute determination of Māori to maintain their relationship with their *moana* (sea) and its resources. In this, they were successful, as is evidenced by the 1992 treaty settlement and the subsequent distribution of quota to tribal groups; a property construct that, while it has overtly individualist characteristics as noted above, also contains an important element of social justice. That Māori now own some 50 percent of quota is a remarkable indigenous achievement.

In Hawaii, resistance to privatisation achieves its most axiomatic expression, a resistance I conceptualise in terms of the antagonistic relationship between gifts and commodities. The increased pressure in neoliberal governance to remove the gift from the commodity, to privatise the commons, has not, or at least not yet, been achieved in the case of fisheries in Hawaii. Local values, institutional arrangements of gifting and the sea as a crucial site of identification continue to affect human–environmental relationships. In New Zealand, the legislation of Māori customary fisheries, while symptomatic of a softening of neoliberal agendas, can be thought of as having instigated further dispossessions by removing the commodity from the gift. As illustrated in chapter 2, this was facilitated by the ascription of sustainability to the wealth-generating practices of quota holders. The removal of the commodity from the gift, however, is never stable; *koha* still provides a means through which Māori fishers negotiate the dichotomisation of livelihoods into commercial and non-commercial spheres. And, as noted, anecdotal evidence suggests an increase in ceremonial events in coastal communities in which seafood is harvested and distributed.

In Iceland, a fishery-dependent nation, the financialisation of ITQs is perhaps the most distinctive feature of the system and one which aligns with a description of neoliberalism as hyper-capitalism. This enclosure, however, is countered by a vocal local discourse peppered with feudal metaphors and rooted in conceptions of a transgressed moral economy. Financialisation also has its limits, as is evidenced by the crash of the Icelandic economy in 2008, leaving a tide of unevenly, if not unethically, distributed debt in its wake. A second discernible characteristic of ITQ in Iceland, however, is the post-financial crash attempts to temper dispossessions, to simulate ITQ as having a commons touch through, for instance, the implementation of catch fees. There has also been an effort to reverse enclosures and establish an open access, derby-style summer fishery. Evidence suggests, however, that ITQ systems are characteristically 'sticky'; that is, they create institutional lock-ins, occasioning problems in a world of dynamic ecosystems. It is, simply, very difficult to reverse enclosures. These tensions, the difficulties in neoliberalising nature, in particular the ocean commons, are symbolically embodied in the pelagic mackerel – a species which, having recently boomed in Icelandic waters, has enabled a new round of contestations over property, ownership and commoditisation, and the possibility of new human–environment configurations, to come to the fore.

In the fifth chapter I illustrate how nostalgia can be interpreted as a critique of the precarious present. In Donegal, island fishermen have married a 'looking back to the past' with an indigenous rights rhetoric, a strategy which has garnered widespread recognition. This momentum, however, is likely to be dampened by, for instance, the mooted establishment of a marine protected area as well as Ireland's recent enthusiasm for the Blue Economy. As argued in chapter 3, the Blue Economy has the propensity to accentuate the centuries-long process of enclosures in the world's fisheries by identifying a new wave of 'growth opportunities' in marine and coastal ecosystems. This augurs an expansion of privatisations and the stimulation of speculation-driven trade through newly created markets.

This re-scaling of activities from the privatisation of national fishing rights to a global Blue Economy is echoed in recent articulations of the Anthropocene. While emerging pragmatically out of a genuine distress with environmental destruction in which humans are considered to be a force of nature (Crutzen and Stoermer 2000), the term, is, as noted by Latour (2014), a 'poisonous' gift for anthropologists. My concern is not so much with the Anthropocene as an immutable fact, inevitable event or definitive period of time, but rather the political, social and ethnographic implications of the idea itself. Capitalocene, as a refined theorisation, is relevant here. By emphasising the networks of capital and power that have given rise to the current state of planetary change, it foregrounds the inequity of lumping into one undifferentiated 'Anthropos' all the human agents responsible for shaping the planet (Haraway 2015; Moore 2014). Haraway et al.'s (2016) proposition that the Anthropocene has the propensity to be captured by an elite with the global pretensions to cure the ills, has particular relevance to my argument.

Like the Blue Economy, the Anthropocene operates on a global scale: conjuring the world's oceans, atmospheres, climates, rivers, forests, lakes and so on. As Tsing (2011) points out, the scale is global because the models are global. This both intimates a modernist, telescopic, view of the Earth, that is, man's control *over* nature, irrespective of the emphasis on human–nature feedbacks, and elevates the role of one species, the Anthropos, as holding the key to the new geological epoch. It also implies the appearance of a network of actors, the 'good Anthropocenes' (Haraway et al. 2016), opportunistically situated at the global nexus, to lead the charge. The term suggests an ethnocentric and lineal view of time, one entwined with the biblical ages of 'Chaos, Eden, the Fallen Present, Apocalypse, Earthly Paradise and Judgment' (Haraway et al. 2016: 540) and the great chain of being – the age of fish, the age of reptiles, the age of mammals, culminating now in the age of the human. A shepherding omnipresence is implicit is both accounts. The term also is apposite to an era dominated by crisis: of fisheries, climates, economies, banking, housing markets, refugees, mental health, obesity, the Eurozone and so on. Narratives of crisis evoke stories of ruin and renewal and of a fabled morality. Thus enter ecosystem services, designed to counter the ruination of the Earth, make visible our reliance on natural resources and similarly dismantle the nature–culture divide (see Daily et al. 1997). The Earth, although in a grievous condition, can be redeemed by costing and accounting for its services. This is where the Anthropocene is at its most dangerous: at the same time as creating possibilities for reimagining human–environment relations, there is a not unsubstantiated fear that the opportunities for doing so are already foreclosed. This is not so much because the damage humans have inflicted is irreversible, though this may well be the case, but because our imaginings are likely to be limited. The same actors and ideologies that already purport to sustain and conserve marine and terrestrial spaces, and the marginalised groups that rely most on these environments, are strategically positioned to entrap the Anthropocene into extending enclosures through making ever more pieces and aspects of nature transferable.

Market approaches to fisheries are characteristically ahistorical, in that they tend to invisibilise the political and technological changes that drive over-exploitation. Hence, privatisation and marketisation as the panacea posits capital accumulation as both problem and solution. ITQ fisheries management, with its species designations, total allowable catch, maximum sustainable yield and quota management areas accountancy, endeavours to flatten what is for fishermen a multi-dimensional, featureful, saltwater seascape; a generative environment imbued with their own, and often their kin's, history, and one in which humans and non-humans are interfused. Though not only is there an attempted enclosure of the seascape to better produce an environment-in-waiting for capital infusion, this process is also mirrored on land: in the consolidation of quota shares, the difficulty in beginning or maintaining a fishing livelihood, in value having shifted from production to quota trading, in a perception of losing control of the resource and in the relative powerlessness of fishermen to influence the care of their ecosystem. The following vignette comes from early on in my fieldwork with Māori fishers in Wainui Bay, on the North Island of Aotearoa/New Zealand:

A conflict surfaced at a *hui* (meeting) in connection with a local Māori family who had managed to gather enough capital to purchase crayfish (lobster) quota. The family members complained that their crayfish pots had been removed and equipment destroyed, the implication being that the action had been carried out by some of their own *hapū* members. Other *hui* participants countered by branding the family's crayfish venture as antithetical to Māori 'lore'. The quota management system was described as encouraging a particular type of fishing that fostered unremitting expansion, which was said to be a necessary condition for survival within capitalist economies. A fisher predicted that ITQs would lead to stock depletion and hunger for the local *hapū*, and described it as an 'immoral' system. A *kaumatua* (elder) suggested that ITQs reflect the imposition of outside illegitimate 'law', creating an opposition with 'lore' and causing rifts 'between *whanau* (extended family) and *hapū* within the same *whakapapa* (genealogical descent)'. Another fisher stated that most *whanau* fishermen could not afford the commercial quota nor the equipment and sophisticated technology needed to comply with the quota system. A *kaumatua* then recommended a return to fishing practices governed by Māori 'lore'. This would, he believed, end conflicts within the *hapū* as fishermen realised their reliance on one another and would, as well, reignite their traditional knowledge of their fisheries.

Notes

Introduction: neoliberalising the environment – the case of fisheries quota

1. Participants included: Daniel Bromley, Oran Young, Ross Virginia, Niels Einarsson, Emma Cardwell, Jesper Raakjær, Einar Eythorsson, Lau Blaxekjær, Courtney Carothers, Richard Howarth, D.G. Webster and myself.
2. Fisheries were at this stage administered conjointly with agriculture. In 1995 fisheries were allocated their own ministry (the Ministry of Fisheries, Mfish) and in 2012 this ministry became incorporated into the current Ministry for Primary Industries (MPI).
3. The New Zealand government asserts that the security offered by the introduction of the QMS was responsible for quota holders investing in deep-water fishing vessels in the 1990s and in the growth of foreign exports.

1 Disciplining and incorporating dissent: neoliberalism and indigeneity

1. This was a landmark case that established that traditional Māori fishing rights could override European laws; see *Te Weehi v Regional Fisheries Officer* [1986] 1 NZLR 680, 691–92.
2. Ngāi Tahu and Muriwhenua are tribes in the tip of the North and South Islands in New Zealand. Both groups lodged fisheries claims with the Waitangi Tribunal in the 1980s. The tribunal hearings and subsequent reports (Waitangi Tribunal 1992a, 1992b) emphasise the extent of Māori fishing activities and their commercial worth, and government failure to protect them.
3. This put the QMS in place for inshore fisheries and established ITQs.
4. The Treaty of Waitangi has two texts, an English and Māori version. Much contestation exists over differences between the two texts.
5. Many coastal *hapū* were opposed to the fisheries settlement.
6. A *hui* held typically one year after a person has been buried during which their memorial marker is unveiled.
7. *Ministry of Agriculture and Fisheries (Lyell) v John Hikuwai*, 22 Sept. 1997, In the District Court, Kaikohe CRN: 620900474-8.
8. *Ministry of Agriculture and Fisheries v Reedy*, 28 November 1997 in District Court Gisbourne, CRN701600609/570.
9. *Manukau v Ministry of Fisheries*, 29 July 1998, M984/97 High Court Auckland, Salmon J.

10. *Ministry of Fisheries v John Hikuwai*, CRN 8004044264,65.

11. See, for instance, *Northern Advocate* (8 January 1998: 1–3), *Nelson Mail* (9 January 1998: 2) and *New Zealand Herald* (10 January 1998: 3).

12. *New Zealand Herald* (9 January 1998).

13. TV One Network News, 21 January 1998.

14. Letter from Nga iwi o te Ika to John Luxton, Minister of Fisheries, 8 January 1997.

15. *Northern Advocate* (12 January 1998: 1).

16. 23 November 1998, in District Court, Kaikohe, CRN8027006005-6.

17. National Radio, *Nine to Noon*, 21 January 1998: Measures to halt the abuse of customary rights, 9.07 am.

18. ZB City Edition (20 January 1998, 5.14 pm).

19. One of the main leaders in the Irish war of independence in the early 20th century.

2 Sustainability: a malleable concept

1. In 2012 fisheries were incorporated into The Ministry of Primary Industries (MPI). The new ministry incorporates farming, fishing, food, animal welfare, biosecurity, and forestry and has an explicit focus on export opportunities, sector productivity, resource sustainability and biosecurity.

2. BMSY, is the biomass (total weight of fish) that can support harvest of the maximum sustainable yield.

3. In Larkin's seminal paper (1977) he criticised the concept of single-species MSY and argued that optimum sustainable yield should replace this as other goals needed optimising as well. Sissenwine (1978) also contested the concept in 1978. These critiques did little to hinder its incorporation in policy in New Zealand at least.

4. The 1995 Code of Conduct is a non-binding, though significant, international agreement.

5. The Fisheries Act 1996 gives the governor-general (on recommendation of the minister) the ability to amalgamate or split QMAs. Factors that need to be taken into account in the decision include the stock's biological characteristics and the interests of non-commercial fishers, stakeholders and quota holders. An amendment in 1999 gives the minister the ability to alter a QMA without the agreement of quota owners.

6. Section 7.2.1 of the 1995 FAO Code of Conduct for Responsible Fisheries states:

   Recognizing that long-term sustainable use of fisheries resources is the overriding objective of conservation and management, States and sub-regional or regional fisheries management organizations and arrangements should, inter alia, adopt appropriate measures, based on the best scientific evidence available, which are designed to maintain or restore stocks at levels capable of producing maximum sustainable yield, as qualified by relevant environmental and economic factors, including the special requirements of developing countries.

7. TACs were implemented in 1997 alongside the designation of an EEZ.

8. A fact known by Scott, which influenced his argument for ITQs as the final solution.

9. Quota was allocated based on 'fishing commitment' measured in terms of catch levels, the companies' degree of investment in onshore processing, employment and fishing capital. Allocations of quota were only made where commitment equalled at least 2,000 tonnes per company. Smaller operators were allowed to combine into consortia to achieve this level in order to attract allocations. The remaining smaller participants were able to continue to fish under competitive TACs comprising more than the sum of their historical catches. This was perceived to encourage further development of these operators and the industry at large (Connor 2001: 229).

10. Though over NZ$300 million has been paid in subsidies since the late 1990s through Seafood Innovations and Project Preparation Grants (PPGs).

3   Transferability and markets

1. Customary allowance does not act as a cap, the 50 tonnes figure is based on information about the current level of catch.

2. Recreational fishing is not governed by the quota management system (QMS), rather by restrictions on gear, bag limits and so on. It is estimated that the recreational catch exceeds the combined non-commercial catch (MPI, 2013).

3. Calculated from the FishServe database.

4. I use the New Zealand term ACE (Annual Catch Entitlements) to highlight the similarities of these trading mechanisms.

5. Since the Fisheries Act 1996, many registry-based QMS services are devolved or contracted to Seafood New Zealand (SNZ, the commercial industry organisation funded by quota owner levies), as an approved government provider. FishServe is the trading name of Commercial Fisheries Services, which is a wholly owned subsidiary of SNZ.

6. Sanford Ltd, **Aotearoa Fisheries Ltd, Sealord Ltd**, Talley's Fisheries Ltd, **Ngai Tahu Fisheries Settlement Ltd** (the names in bold are Māori owned). The companies combine harvesting, farming, processing, storage and marketing operations.

7. Now rebranded as Moana New Zealand (the Māori word for the sea), a move described as: signalling a move from fisheries, which implies food processing, to premium seafood and direct connections with consumers and showing responsibility to the environment.
8. Kin groups are organised around *marae* (Sissons 2010). These meeting house complexes are considered a crucial material marker of Māori identity and cultural practice. *Marae* are commonly set up as charitable trusts and thus have become the site where settlement dividends are channelled.
9. Only one New Zealand company is not using FCVs to harvest deep-water fish.
10. In a derby-style fishery, a season opens for a few months and fishermen 'race' to land their catch before it is closed again.
11. The Coastal Fisheries Initiative (CFI) is a partnership of six organizations under the auspices of the FAO (Conservation International, UN Development Programme, UN Environment Programme, World Bank, World Wildlife Fund, Global Environment Facility). It has been developed and is funded within the Global Environment Facility (GEF) framework of safeguarding the world oceans and the marine environment.
12. Indonesia, Ecuador and Peru (Latin America), and Cabo Verde, Côte d'Ivoire and Senegal (West Africa).

4   Gifts and commodities: Hawaiian fisheries

1. A local delicacy and a culturally important dish generally made of *'ahi* (tuna) sashimi, sea salt, soy sauce, kukui nut (candlenut), limu (seaweed) and chopped chilli pepper (many variations of this recipe exist).
2. Recreational fishermen in the Hawaiian region harvested 11.7 million lb of finfish in 2011 (compared to 29.3 million pounds of fish caught by commercial fishermen) and spent over US$284.9 million. Including multiplier effects, these purchases resulted in more than US$309.9 million in sales, US$101.2 million in income, US$156.6 million in value added (GDP), and supported 2,948 jobs (Southwick Associates 2013).
3. Within 'local' are the emergent categories of 'Native Hawaiian' and 'local *haole*'. Hawaiians increasingly distinguish themselves from other locals. Although 'local' is often opposed to '*haole*' on a racial basis, the term 'local *haole*' refers to local behaviour and contradicts the racial opposition (Kale Langlas, personal conversation, November 2016).
4. They used different boat and shore techniques: throw net, spearfishing, netting and also gathered *opihi*, a ceremonially significant limpet.
5. This incorporates American Samoa, Guam, Hawaii, the Northern Mariana Islands and Pacific remote island areas (Wake Island, Johnston, Howland and Baker, Palmyra and Jarvis). It is the largest geographical area managed by NOAA with an EEZ of more than 1.5 million square nautical miles. It includes

people typically ethnologically classified by anthropologists as Polynesian and Micronesian and, since 2003, the regional management office has been based in Honolulu, Hawaii.

6. Seven of which are under the joint state and federal quota.

7. A recent newspaper series in the *Honolulu Star-Advertiser* highlights the mistreatment of foreign nationals (see, for instance, 'How U.S. laws trap foreign workers on Hawaii's fishing boats', Associated Press, 8 September 2016).

5   Nostalgia: laments and precarity

1. This occurs when a catch contains the wrong mix, size, type or condition of fish. The net, which does not leave the water, is opened to release the fish, the majority of which are already dead.

2. For instance, Irish pelagic vessels can ask Scottish vessels for 100 tonnes of a particular quota stock, but then must swap this for another quota stock. They cannot buy quota outright from Scottish or English vessels as, unlike in both these places, Irish quota is not an ITQ.

3. The NEAFC, established in 1980, replaced a 1959 commission of the same name. It aims to ensure the conservation and utilisation of the fisheries resources in the area which stretches from the southern tip of Greenland, east to the Barents sea and south to Portugal.

4. *Teachta Dala*, a member of *Dail Eireann* the lower house of the *Oireachtas*, the Irish Parliament. A TD is equivalent to an MP – Member of Parliament.

5. 'The North' is a colloquialism for Northern Ireland, which is part of the United Kingdom.

6. At 18 sq. km it is the second largest island in Ireland. Two-thirds of the island is covered by peat land.

7. Eighteen Árainn Mhór vessels held salmon licences at the time of the ban, half of which were held independent of any other licence, thus effectively proscribing these vessels from fishing (Nautilus Consultants 2007).

8. See: http://oireachtasdebates.oireachtas.ie/debates%20authoring/debates webpack.nsf/committeetakes/AGJ2012070300004 (accessed 17 May 2017).

9. Jourdaine's 2015 film, *A Turning Tide in the Life of Man*, documents the communities of Árainn Mhór, Inis Bo Finne and Oileán who together with world experts, including anthropologists, have been fighting against restrictive fishing policies. Jourdaine follows the personal politicisation of fisherman John O'Brien over eight years as he engages with national and European politicians, and other island communities from around Europe. The 2015 documentary, *Atlantic*, directed by Risteard Ó Domhnaill, also documents the struggles of fishermen from the Donegal Island of Árainn Mhór.

6   Epilogue: ITQs, neoliberalism and the anthropocene

1. The notion of fairness in this schema does not refer to equality, rather a type of equality of opportunity which is blind to origins.

Bibliography

Agardi, T. (2008) 'Individual fisheries quotas (ITQs and IFQs)', in Forest Trends, the Ecosystem Marketplace and PROFOR (eds) *Payments for Ecosystem Services: Market Profiles*, pp. 26–28. Available at: www.dcnanature.org/wp-content/uploads/fundraising/Payments-Ecosystem-Services-PROFOR.pdf (accessed 25 January 2017).

Agnarsson, S., Matthiasson, T. and Giry, F. (2016) 'Consolidation and distribution of quota holdings in the Icelandic fisheries', *Marine Policy*, 72: 263–70.

Akroyd, P. and Walshe, K. (2000) *Subsistence Fishers in New Zealand*. Project SEC 2000-02. Wellington, NZ: Ministry of Fisheries.

Allison, A. and Piot, C. (2014) 'Editors' note on "Neoliberal Futures"', *Cultural Anthropology*, 29(1): 3–7.

Angé, O. and Berliner, D. (2015) 'Introduction: Anthropology of nostalgia – anthropology as nostalgia', in O. Angé and D. Berliner (eds) *Anthropology and Nostalgia*. Oxford: Berghahn Books, pp. 1–16.

Aotearoa Fisheries Limited (n.d.) *Maximising the Value of Maori Fisheries Assets*. Available at: www.afl.maori.nz/ (accessed 13 March 2013).

Arnason, R. (1993) 'The Icelandic individual transferable quota system: a descriptive account', *Marine Resource Economics*, 8: 201–18.

—— (2008) 'Iceland's ITQ system creates new wealth', *Electronic Journal of Sustainable Development*, 1(2): 35–41.

Arrighi, G. (1994) *The Long Twentieth Century: Money, Power and the Origins of Our Times*. London: Verso.

Bakker, K. (2010) 'The limits of "neoliberal natures": debating green neoliberalism', *Progress in Human Geography*, 34(6): 715–35.

Ballara, A. (1998) *Iwi: The Dynamics of Māori Tribal Organisation from c. 1769 to c. 1945*. Wellington: Victoria University Press.

Barber, P.G., Leach, B. and Lem, W. (eds) (2012) *Confronting Capital: Critique and Engagement in Anthropology*. Abingdon: Routledge.

Barbesgaard, M. (2015) 'Blue growth: saviour or ocean grabbing?', paper presented at: 'Global Governance/Politics, Climate Justice and Agrarian/Social Justice: Linkages and Challenges – An International Colloquium', The Hague, Netherlands, 4–5 February. Available at: www.iss.nl/fileadmin/ASSETS/iss/Research_and_projects/Research_networks/ICAS/5-ICAS_CP_Barbesgaard.pdf

Bargh, M. (2014) 'A blue economy for Aotearoa New Zealand?', *Environment, Development and Sustainability*, 16(3): 459–70.

Barnes-Mauthe, M., Arita, S., Allen, S.D., Gray, S.A. and Leung, P. (2013) 'The influence of ethnic diversity on social network structure in a common-pool resource system: implications for collaborative management', *Ecology and Society*, 18(1): 23.

Begg, G. and Waldman, J. (1999) 'An holistic approach to fish stock identification', *Fisheries Research*, 43(1): 35–44.

Bender, B. (2002) 'Time and landscape', *Current Anthropology*, 43(S4): S103–S112.

Benediktsson, K. and Karlsdóttir, A. (2011) 'Iceland crisis and regional development – thanks for all the fish?', *European Urban and Regional Studies*, 18(2): 228–35.

Berdahl, D. (1999). '(N)ostalgie for the present: memory, longing and East German things', *Ethnos* 64(2): 192–211.

Berkes, F. (1988) 'Subsistence fishing in Canada: a note on terminology', *Arctic*, 41(4): 319–20.

Berliner, D. (2015) 'Are anthropologists nostalgists?', in O. Angé and D. Berliner (eds) *Anthropology and Nostalgia*. London: Berghahn Books, pp. 17–34.

Bess, R. and Rallapudi, R. (2007) 'Spatial conflicts in New Zealand fisheries: the rights of fishers and protection of the marine environment', *Marine Policy*, 31(6): 719–29.

Boast, R. (1998) 'Lawyers, historians, ethnics and the judicial process', *Victoria University of Wellington Law Review*, 28(1): 87–112.

Bodwitch, H. (2017) 'Challenges for New Zealand's individual transferable quota system: processor consolidation, fisher exclusion, and Māori quota rights', *Marine Policy*, 80: 88–95.

Bord Iascaigh Mhara (n.d.) *Ireland's Response to the European Commission's Green Paper on the Reform of the Common Fisheries Policy*. Available at: www.bim.ie/media/bim/content/bim4.0%20Irelands%20CFP%20green%20paper%20response.pdf (accessed 25 January 2017).

Boyd, J. (2010) 'Fishing for the big boys: competing interests under the Fisheries Act 1996', *Victoria University of Wellington Law Review*, 41: 761.

Boym, S. (2002). *The Future of Nostalgia*. New York: Basic Books.

Bräuer, I., Müssner, R., Marsden, K., Oosterhuis, F., Rayment, M., Miller, C. and Dodoková, A. (2006) *The Use of Market Incentives to Preserve Biodiversity*. Ecologic Institute, DG Environment. Available at: http://ecologic.eu/sites/files/download/projekte/1750-1799/1750/1750-11_use_of_market_incentives_to_preserve_biodiversity.pdf (accessed 25 January 2017).

Britton, E. (2014). 'Ghost boats and human freight: the social wellbeing impacts of the salmon ban on Lough Foyle's fishing communities', in J. Urquhart, T. Acott, D. Symes and M. Zhao (eds) *Social Issues in Sustainable Fisheries Management*. The Netherlands: Springer, pp. 143–64.

Bromley, D. (2008) 'The crisis in ocean governance: conceptual confusion, spurious economics, political indifference', *Maritime Studies (MAST)*, 6(2): 7–22.

Brown, R., Xu, X. and Toth, J. (1998) 'Lifestyle options and economic strategies: subsistence activities in the Mississippi Delta', *Rural Sociology*, 63(4): 599–623.

Brown, W. (2003) 'Neoliberalism and the end of liberal democracy', *Theory and Event*, 7: 1–19.

Browne, H. (2008) 'Where will they get the fish?', *Dublin Review*, 33. Available at: http://thedublinreview.com/article/where-will-they-get-the-fish/ (accessed 5 January 2017).

Büscher, B. (2009) 'Letters of gold: enabling primitive accumulation through neoliberal conservation', *Human Geography*, 2(3): 91–93.

Büscher, B., Sullivan, S., Neves, K., Igoe, J. and Brockington, D. (2012) 'Towards a synthesized critique of neoliberal biodiversity conservation', *Capitalism Nature Socialism*, 23(2): 4–30.

Butler, J. (2016) *Frames of War: When Is Life Grievable?* London: Verso.

Carothers, C. and Chambers, C. (2017) 'Thirty years after privatization: a survey of Icelandic small-boat fishermen', *Marine Policy*, 80: 69–80.

Carrier, J.G. (1995) 'Maussian occidentalism: gift and commodity systems', in J.G. Carrier (ed.) *Occidentalism: Images of the West*. Oxford: Clarendon Press, pp. 85–108.

Castree, N. (2010a) 'Neoliberalism and the biophysical environment: a synthesis and evaluation of the research', *Environment and Society: Advances in Research*, 1: 5–45.

——(2010b) 'Neoliberalism and the biophysical environment 1: what "neoliberalism" is, and what difference nature makes to it', *Geography Compass*, 4(12): 1725–33.

Cawley, N. (2006) *Steering a New Course: Report of the Seafood Industry Strategy Review Group*. Dublin: Bord Iascaigh Mhara/ Irish Sea Fisheries Board.

Central Statistics Office (2012) *Profile 4: The Roof over Our Heads – Housing in Ireland, 2012*. Dublin: The Stationery Office.

Chambers, C. and Carothers, C. (2017) 'Thirty years after privatization: a survey of Icelandic small-boat fishermen', *Marine Policy*, 80: 69–80.

Christensen, A.-S., Hegland, T. and Oddsson, G. (2009) 'The Icelandic ITQ system', in H.K. Hauge and C.D. Wilson (eds) *Comparative Evaluations of Innovative Fisheries Management*. Dordrecht: Springer, pp. 97–118.

Christy, F.T. and Scott, A. (1965) *The Common Wealth in Ocean Fisheries: Some Problems of Growth and Economic Allocation*. Baltimore, MD: Johns Hopkins University Press.

Chu, C. (2009) 'Thirty years later: the global growth of ITQs and their influence on stock status in marine fisheries', *Fish and Fisheries*, 10(2): 217–30.

Clark, N., Major, P. and Mollett, N. (1988) 'The development and implementation of New Zealand's ITQ management system', *Marine Resource Economics*, 5: 325–49.

Clarke, J. (2004) *Changing Welfare, Changing States: New Directions in Social Policy*. London: Sage.

Clarke, W. (1990) 'Learning from the past: traditional knowledge and sustainable development', *Contemporary Pacific*, 2(2): 233–51.

Clifford, J. (2012) 'Feeling historical', *Cultural Anthropology*, 27(3): 417–26.

Connaghan, P. (1997) *The Great Famine in South-west Donegal, 1845–1850*. Enniscrone, Co. Sligo: Westprint Ltd.

Connor, R. (2001) 'Initial allocation of individual transferable quota in New Zealand fisheries', in R. Shotton (ed.) *Case Studies on the Allocation of Transferable Quota Rights in Fisheries*. Fisheries technical paper 411. Rome: FAO.

Costanza, R., d'Arge, R., De Groot, R., Faber, S., Grasso, M., Hannon, B. et al. (1997) 'The value of the world's ecosystem services and natural capital', *Nature*, 387: 253–60.

Costanza, R., de Groot, R., Sutton, P., van der Ploeg, S., Anderson, S.J., Kubiszewski, I. et al. (2014) 'Changes in the global value of ecosystem services', *Global Environmental Change*, 26: 152–58.

Costello, C., Lynham, J., Lester, S.E. and Gaines, S.D. (2010) 'Economic incentives and global fisheries sustainability', *Annual Review of Resource Economics*, 2(1): 299–318.

Crutzen, P.J. and Stoermer, E.F. (2000) 'Global change newsletter', *The Anthropocene*, 41: 17–18.

Daily, G.C. (1997) *Nature's Services: Societal Dependence on Natural Ecosystems*. Washington, DC: Island Press.

Daily, G.C., Alexander, S., Ehrlich, P.R., Goulder, L., Lubchenco, J., Matson, P.A. et al. (1997) 'Ecosystem services: benefits supplied to human societies by natural ecosystems', *Issues in Ecology*, 2: 1–16.

Davidson, K. (2011) 'Reporting systems for sustainability: what are they measuring?', *Social Indicators Research*, 100(2): 351–65.

Davies, W. (2016) 'The new neoliberalism', *New Left Review*, 101: 121–34.

de Courcy Ireland, J. (1981) *Ireland's Sea Fisheries: A History*. Dublin: Glendale Publishing.

de Freitas, C. and Perry, M. (2012) *New Environmentalism: Managing New Zealand's Environmental Diversity*. Dordrecht: Springer Science & Business Media.

Degnbol, P., Gislason, H., Hanna, S., Jentoft, S., Raakjær, J., Sten, N. et al. (2006) 'Painting the floor with a hammer: technical fixes in fisheries management', *Marine Policy*, 30(5): 534–43.

Department of Agriculture, Food and the Marine (2016) 'Fisheries quota management in Ireland', available at: https://webcache.googleusercontent.com/search?q=cache:7CW-wbUXwXAJ:www.agriculture.gov.ie/media/migration/seafood/sea-fisheriespolicymanagementdivision/QuotaMgmtPolicyApril 16250416.doc+&cd=1&hl=en&ct=clnk&gl=nz&client=safari (accessed 5 January 2017).

Di Muzio, T. and Robbins, R.H. (2016) *Debt as Power*. Manchester: Manchester University Press.

Donkersloot, R. and Menzies, C. (2015) 'Place-based fishing livelihoods and the global ocean: the Irish pelagic fleet at home and abroad', *Maritime Studies*, 14(1): 1–19.

Durkheim, E. (1982) *The Rules of Sociological Method and Selected Texts on Sociology and Its Method*. New York: The Free Press.

Einarsson, N. (2011) *Culture, Conflict and Crises in the Icelandic Fisheries: An Anthropological Study of People, Policy and Marine Resources in the North Atlantic Arctic.* PhD thesis, Uppsala Universitet.

Epstein, G. (2002) 'Financialisation, rentier interests and central bank policy', Privatization in Education Research Initiative (PERI) Conference on 'Financialisation of the World Economy', University of Massachusetts, Amherst, 7–8 December.

Eriksen, T.H. (2016) 'Overheating: the world since 1991', *History and Anthropology*, 27(5): 469–87.

Errington, F. and Gewertz, D. (1995) *Articulating Change in the 'Last Unknown'.* Boulder, CO: Westview Press.

Escobar, A. (1996) *Constructing Nature.* New York: Routledge.

European Commission (2009) Green Paper: Reform of the Common Fisheries Policy. Available at: http://eur-lex.europa.eu/LexUriServ/LexUriServ.do?uri= COM:2009:0163:FIN:EN:PDF (accessed 5 January 2017).

Eversole, R. (2003) 'My business pays me: labourers and entrepreneurs among the self-employed poor in Latin America', *Bulletin of Latin American Research*, 22(1): 102–116.

Eythórsson, E. (1996) 'Coastal communities and ITQ management: the case of Icelandic fisheries', *Sociologia Ruralis*, 36(2): 212–23.

—— (2000) 'A decade of ITQ-management in Icelandic fisheries: consolidation without consensus', *Marine Policy*, 24(6): 483–92.

Fairgray, J. (1985) *ITQ Implications Study: First Report, Northland Fishing Communities 1984.* FMP Series 1. Wellington: Fisheries Management Division, MAF.

—— (1986) *ITQ Implications Study: Second Report, Community Issues.* FMP Series 20. Wellington: Fisheries Management Division, MAF.

Fairhead, J., Leach, M. and Scoones, I. (2012) 'Green grabbing: a new appropriation of nature?', *Journal of Peasant Studies*, 39(2): 237–61.

FAO (Food and Agriculture Organization) (2015) *FAO Contribution to part 1 of the Report of the Secretary-General on Oceans and the Law of the Sea.* Available at: www.un.org/depts/los/general_assembly/contributions_2015/FAO.pdf (accessed 21 October 2016).

Farrell, N., Breen, B., Cuddy, M. and Hynes, S. (2010) *Sustainable Fishing in Irish Waters: Assessment of Current Practices, Policies and Alternative Approaches.* Working Paper 165. Discipline of Economics, National University of Ireland, Galway.

Feige, E. (1990) 'Defining and estimating underground and informal economies: the new institutional economics approach', *World Development*, 18(7): 989–1002.

Ferguson, J. (2010) 'The uses of neoliberalism', *Antipode*, 41(s1): 166–84.

Finley, C. and Oreskes, N. (2013) 'Maximum sustained yield: a policy disguised as science', *ICES Journal of Marine Science: Journal du Conseil*, 70(2): 245–50.

Flaaten, O. (2010) 'Fisheries rent creation and distribution: the imaginary case of Codland', *Marine Policy*, 34(6): 1268–72.

Fontaine, P. (2015) 'Iceland struggles to settle the fishing quota dispute', available at: http://grapevine.is/mag/articles/2015/06/22/iceland-struggles-to-settle-the-fishing-quota-dispute/ (accessed 25 January 2017).

Forest Trends and the Katoomba Group (2010) *Payments for Ecosystem Services: Getting Started in Marine and Coastal Ecosystems: A Primer*. Available at: www.forest-trends.org/documents/files/doc_2374.pdf (accessed 27 January 2017).

Fraser, N. (2013) 'A triple movement? Parsing the politics of crisis after Polanyi', *New Left Review*, 81(81): 119–32.

Frawley, O. (2005) *Irish Pastoral*. Dublin: Irish Academic Press.

Freeman, M. (1993) 'The International Whaling Commission, small-type whaling, and coming to terms with subsistence', *Human Organization*, 52: 243–51.

Friedlander, A. and Parrish. J. (1997) 'Fisheries harvest and standing stock in a Hawaiian bay', *Fisheries Research*, 32: 33–50.

Gallagher, P. and DiNovelli-Lang, D. (2014) 'Introduction: Nature and knowledge: contemporary ecologies of value', *Environment and Society: Advances in Research*, 5(1): 1–6.

Gallagher, P., Crowley, B. and Aylward, L. (2009). The Green Paper on the Reform of the Common Fisheries Policy: Response of the three Fianna Fail MEPs. Available at: https://ec.europa.eu/fisheries/sites/fisheries/files/docs/body/3_fianna_fail_meps_en.pdf (accessed 5 January 2017).

Ganti, T. (2014) 'Neoliberalism', *Annual Review of Anthropology*, 43: 89–104.

Garcia, S.M. and Staples, D.J. (2000) 'Sustainability reference systems and indicators for responsible marine capture series: a review of concepts and elements for a set of guidelines', *Marine and Freshwater Research*, 51: 385–426.

Geslani, C., Loke, M., Takenaka, B. and Leung, P. (2012) *Hawaii's Seafood Consumption and Its Supply Sources*. SOEST publication 12-01. Hawai'i: Joint Institute for Marine and Atmospheric Research.

Gibbs, M. (2008) 'The historical development of fisheries in New Zealand with respect to sustainable development principles', *Electronic Journal of Sustainable Development*, 1(2): 23–33.

—— (2009) 'Individual transferable quotas and ecosystem-based fisheries management: it's all in the T', *Fish and Fisheries*, 10(4): 470–74.

Glazier, E. (2009) 'Supply, demand and distribution of pelagic seafood on Oahu: select results from the PFRP seafood distribution project', *PFRP News*, 14(1): 13–17.

Glazier, E., Carothers, C., Milne, N. and Iwamoto. M. (2013) 'Seafood and society on O'ahu in the main Hawaiian islands', *Pacific Science*, 13(3): 345–59.

Goldstein, D.M. (2012) 'Decolonialising "actually existing neoliberalism"', *Social Anthropology*, 20(3): 304–9.

Gómez-Baggethun, E. and Muradian, R. (2015) 'In markets we trust? Setting the boundaries of market-based instruments in ecosystem services governance', *Ecological Economics*, 117: 217–24.

Gordon, H.S. (1954) 'The economic theory of a common-property resource: the fishery', in C. Gopalakrishnan (ed.) *Classic Papers in Natural Resource Economics.* London: Palgrave Macmillan, pp. 178–203.

Graeber, D. (2013) 'A practical utopian's guide to the coming collapse', *The Baffler* 22: 53–58.

Gray, J. (1998) *False Dawn: The Illusions of Global Capital.* London: Granta Publications.

Green, L. (2012) 'To die in the silence of history', in P. Barber, B. Leach and W. Lem (eds) *Confronting Capital: Critique and Engagement in Anthropology.* Abingdon: Routledge, pp. 97–113.

Greensill, A. (2010) 'Inside the Resource Management Act: A Tainui case study', Master's thesis, University of Waikato.

Habib, G. (1985) *Maori Involvement in the New Zealand Fishing Industry: Report for the Maori Economic Development Commission.* Auckland: Southpac Fisheries Consultants.

Hale, C.R. (2005) 'Neoliberal multiculturalism', *PoLAR: Political and Legal Anthropology Review,* 28(1): 10–19.

Hamnett, M., Liu, M. and Johnson. D. (2004) *Fishing, Ocean Recreation, and Threats to Hawaii's Coral Reefs: Results from a December 2004 household survey.* Honolulu: Hawai'i Coral Reef Initiative. Available at: www.hcri.ssri.hawaii.edu/files/education/fishingbrochure.pdf (accessed 11 May 2015).

Hann, C.M. (1998) 'Introduction: The embeddedness of property', in C.M. Hann (ed.) *Property Relations: Renewing the Anthropological Tradition.* Cambridge: Cambridge University Press, pp. 1–47.

—— (2015) 'Why post-imperial trumps post-socialist: crying back the national past in Hungary', in O. Angé and D. Berliner (eds) *Anthropology and Nostalgia.* London: Berghahn Books, pp. 96–122.

Hannesson, R. (2004) *The Privatization of the Oceans.* Cambridge, MA: MIT Press.

Haraway, D. (2015) 'Anthropocene, capitalocene, plantationocene, chthulucene: making kin', *Environmental Humanities,* 6(1): 159–65.

Haraway, D., Ishikawa, N., Gilbert, S.F., Olwig, K., Tsing, A.L. and Bubandt, N. (2016) 'Anthropologists are talking – about the anthropocene', *Ethnos,* 81(3): 535–64.

Hardin, G. (1968) 'The tragedy of the commons', *Science,* 162(3859): 1243–48.

Harrison, G. (2010) 'Post-neoliberalism?', *Review of African Political Economy,* 37(123): 1–5.

Harrison, S. (2000) 'From prestige goods to legacies: property and the objectification of culture in Melanesia', *Society for the Comparative Study of Society and History,* 42: 662–79.

Harvey, D. (2003) *The New Imperialism.* New York: Oxford University Press.

—— (2005) *A Brief History of Neoliberalism.* Oxford: Oxford University Press.

—— (2007) 'Neoliberalism as creative destruction', *Annals of the American Academy of Political and Social Science,* 610(1): 21–44.

Hau'ofa, E. (1994) 'Our sea of islands', *Contemporary Pacific*, 6(1): 147–61.

Hawkey, D. (1994) *Property Rights, ITQs, and the Slice of the Fish Pie: An Appraisal of Fishery Culture and Conflict in the Northland Region*. Auckland: University of Auckland.

HDAR (Hawaii Division of Aquatic Resources) (n.d.) 'Commercial marine license'. Available at: http://dlnr.hawaii.gov/dar/fishing/commercial-fishing/ (accessed 19 May 2017).

Helgason, A. and Pálsson, G. (1997) 'Contested commodities: the moral landscape of modernist regimes', *Journal of the Royal Anthropological Institute*, 3(3): 451–71.

Hilgers, M. (2012) 'The historicity of the neoliberal state', *Social Anthropology*, 20(1): 80–94.

Hollier, D. (2014) 'How fish get from the sea to your plate', *Hawaii Business*, February. Available at: www.hawaiibusiness.com/how-fish-get-from-the-sea-to-your-plate/ (accessed 27 January 2017).

Holm, P. (2003) 'Crossing the border: on the relationship between science and fishermen's knowledge in a resource management context', *MAST*, 2(1): 5–33.

Holm, P. and Nielsen, K.N. (2007) 'Framing fish, making markets: the construction of Individual Transferable Quotas (ITQs)', *Sociological Review*, 55(s2): 173–95.

Hopa, N.K. (1999) 'Land and Re-empowerment', in A. Cheater (ed.) *The Anthropology of Power: Empowerment and Disempowerment in Changing Structures*. London: Routledge, pp. 101–16.

Hospital, J. and Beavers, C. (2011) *Management of the Main Hawaii Islands Bottomfish Fishery: Fishers' Attitudes, Perceptions, and Comments*. Administrative Report H-11-06. Honolulu, HI: Pacific Islands Fisheries Science Center, NOAA.

——(2014) 'Catch shares and the main Hawaiian Islands bottomfish fishery: linking fishery conditions and fisher perceptions', *Marine Policy*, 44: 9–17.

Hospital, J., Bruce, S. and Pan, M. (2011) *Economics and Social Characteristics of the Hawai'i Small Boat Pelagic Fishery*. Administrative report H-11-01. Honolulu, HI: Pacific Islands Fisheries Science Centre, National Oceanic and Atmospheric Administration (NOAA).

Humphrey, C. and Verdery, K. (2004) 'Introduction: Raising questions about property', in K. Verdery and C. Humphrey (eds) *Property in Question: Value Transformation in the Global Economy*. Oxford: Berg, pp. 1–25.

Hviding, E. (1996) *Guardians of Marovo Lagoon: Practice, Place, and Politics in Maritime Melanesia*. Honolulu: University of Hawai'i Press.

Ingold, T. (2000) *The Perception of the Environment: Essays on Livelihood, Dwelling and Skill*. New York: Routledge.

Inland Revenue, Te Tari Taake (1998) *Payments and Gifts in the Māori Community IR278*. Available at: www.ird.govt.nz/resources/7/1/7158386f-d86e-4f8b-a9c8-6559c42aaf7f/ir278.pdf (accessed 21 April 1998).

Innes, J. (2013) *Maori in the Seafood Sector (Fisheries and Aquaculture): The Year in Review*. Available at: http://maorilawreview.co.nz/2013/06/maori-in-the-seafood-sector-fisheries-and-aquaculture-the-year-in-review/ (accessed 25 January 2017).

Irish Marine Development Office (2012) *Harnessing Our Ocean Wealth: An Integrated Marine Plan for Ireland*, IMD, Ireland. Available at: www.seai.ie/Publications/ Renewables_Publications_/Ocean/Harnessing-Our-Oceans-Wealth-report-2012. pdf (accessed 25 January 2017).

Johannes, R. (1981) *Words of the Lagoon: Fishing and Marine Lore in Palau District of Micronesia*. Berkeley: University of California Press.

Johannsen, B. (2012) 'A tool for marine and coastal conservation: lessons learned from terrestrial payments for ecosystem services', Master's thesis, Universiteit Utrecht.

Joint Sub-committee on Fisheries (2014) *Tuarascáil ar Phobail Thuaithe Inmharthana ar an gCósta agus ar na hOileáin a Chur chun Cinn: Report on Promoting Sustainable Rural Coastal and Island Communities*. Available at: www.oireachtas.ie/parliament/ media/Draft-3-Final-Report-on-Promoting-Sustainable-Rural-Coastal-and-Island-Communities.pdf (accessed 5 January 2017).

Jolly, M. (2015) 'Braed Praes in Vanuatu: both gifts and commodities?', *Oceania*, 85(1): 63–78.

Kaiser, B. and Roumasset, J. (2004) 'Coasean economics and the evolution of marine property in Hawai'i', *Scientific Commons*. Available at: https://ideas.repec. org/p/hai/wpaper/200407.html (accessed 19 May 2017).

Kalb, D.P. (2012) 'Thinking about neoliberalism as if the crisis was actually happening', *Social Anthropology*, 20(3): 318–30.

Kalb, D.P. and Visser, O. (2012) 'The Soviet revenge: how the unrecognized Soviet-style mechanisms of contemporary finance cause social crisis and catastrophe in the West', in P.G. Barber, B. Leach and W. Lem (eds) *Confronting Capital: Critique and Engagement in Anthropology*. London: Routledge, pp. 76–96.

Kallis, G., Gómez-Baggethun, E. and Zografos, C. (2013) 'To value or not to value? That is not the question', *Ecological Economics*, 94: 97–105.

Karlsdóttir, A. (2008) 'Not sure about the shore! Transformation effects of Individual Transferable Quotas on Iceland's fishing economy and communities', in M. Lowe and C. Carothers (eds) *Enclosing the Fisheries: People, Places and Power*. Bethesda, MD: American Fisheries Society, pp. 99–117.

Kelsey, J. (2002) *At the Crossroads: Three Essays*. Wellington, NZ: Bridget Williams Books.

Kingfisher, C. and Maskovsky, J. (2008) Introduction: the limits of neoliberalism. *Critique of Anthropology*, 28: 115–26.

Kirch, P.V. and Sahlins, M. (1994) *Anahulu: The Anthropology of History in the Kingdom of Hawaii: Historical Ethnography*, vol. 1. Chicago: University of Chicago Press.

Kokorsch, M., Karlsdóttir, A. and Benediktsson, K. (2015) 'Improving or overturning the ITQ system? Views of stakeholders in Icelandic fisheries', *Maritime Studies*, 14(1).

Kotz, D. (2010) 'Financialization and neoliberalism', in G. Teeple and S. McBride (eds) *Relations of Global Power: Neoliberal Order and Disorder*. Toronto: University of Toronto Press, pp. 1–18.

Larkin, P.A. (1977) 'An epitaph for the concept of maximum sustained yield', *Transactions of the American Fisheries Society*, 106(1): 1–11.

Lashley, M.E. (2000) 'Implementing treaty settlements via indigenous institutions: social justice and detribalisation in New Zealand', *Contemporary Pacific*, 12(1): 1–55.

Latour, B. (2014) 'Anthropology at the time of the Anthropocene: a personal view of what is to be studied', American Anthropological Association annual meeting, Washington, DC, 6 December. Available at: http://www.bruno-latour.fr/sites/default/files/139-AAA-Washington.pdf (accessed 17 May 2017).

Law Commission (1989) *The Treaty of Waitangi and Māori Fisheries – Mataitai nga tikanga Māori me te Tiriti o Waitangi*, Preliminary Paper, Wellington.

Le Floc'h, P., Murillas, A., Aranda, M., Daurès, F., Fitzpatrick, M., Guyader, O. et al. (2015) 'The regional management of fisheries in European western waters', *Marine Policy*, 51: 375–84.

Linebaugh, P. (2012) *Ned Ludd and Queen Mab: Machine-breaking, Romanticism, and the Several Commons of 1811–1812*. Retort Pamphlet Series 001. Oakland, CA: PM Press.

Lock, K. and Leslie, S. (2007) *New Zealand's Quota Management System: A History of the First 20 Years*. Motu Working Paper 07-02. Wellington, NZ: Ministry of Fisheries. Available at: http://tinyurl.com/zyorddn (accessed 25 January 2017).

Loftsdóttir, K. (2010) 'The loss of innocence: the Icelandic financial crisis and colonial past', *Anthropology Today*, 26(6): 9–13.

Longo, S.B., Clausen, R. and Clark, B. (2015) *The Tragedy of the Commodity: Oceans, Fisheries, and Aquaculture*. New Brunswick, NJ: Rutgers University Press.

Louyest, A. and Roberts, G.H. (2015) 'Guest editors' introduction: Nostalgia, culture and identity in Central and Eastern Europe', *Canadian Slavonic Papers*, 57(3–4): 175–79.

Mace, P. (2012) 'Evolution of New Zealand's fisheries management frameworks to prevent overfishing, ICES Document CM2012/L:09. Available at: http://www.ices.dk/sites/pub/CM%20Doccuments/CM-2012/L/L0912.pdf (accessed 22 May 2017).

Mace, P.M. and Sissenwine, M.P. (2002) 'Coping with uncertainty: evolution of the relationship between science and management', in J.M. Berkson, L.L. Kline and D.J. Orth (eds) *Incorporating Uncertainty into Fishery Models*. American Fisheries Society Symposium, 27. Bethesda, MD: American Fisheries Society, pp. 9–28.

Mace, P., Sullivan, K. and Cryer, M. (2014) 'The evolution of New Zealand's fisheries science and management systems under ITQs', *ICES Journal of Marine Science*, 71(2): 204–15.

MacGregor, D. (2007) *Na kua'aina: living Hawaiian culture*. Honolulu: University of Hawai'i Press.

MacLaughlin, J. (1994) *Ireland: The Emigrant Nursery and the World Economy*. Cork: Cork University Press.

Maguire, J. (2014) 'Virtual fish stink too', in P. Durrenberger and G. Palsson (eds) *Gambling Debt: Iceland's Rise and Fall in the Global Economy*. Boulder, CO: University Press of Colorado, pp. 121–36.

Manderscheid, K. (2012) 'Planning sustainability: intergenerational and intragenerational justice in spatial planning strategies', *Antipode*, 44(1): 197–216.

Mansfield, B. (2004) 'Neoliberalism in the oceans: "rationalization," property rights, and the commons question', *Geoforum*, 35(3): 313–26.

—— (2011) '"Modern" industrial fisheries and the crisis of overfishing', in R. Peet, P. Robbins and M. Watts (eds) *Global Political Ecology*. London: Routledge, pp. 84–99.

Marine Institute (2013) *The Stock Book 2013: Annual Review of Fish Stocks in 2013 with Management Advice for 2014*. Available at: http://hdl.handle.net/10793/918 (accessed 5 January 2017).

Martin, B. (2000) *Sub-national Income Differentials: 1986–1999*, Population Studies Centre, 35, University of Waikato.

Matthiasson, T. (2008) 'Rent collection, rent distribution, and cost recovery: an analysis of Iceland's ITQ catch fee experiment', *Marine Resource Economics*, 23(1): 105–17.

Matthiasson, T. and Agnarsson, S. (2010) 'Property rights in Icelandic fisheries', in R.Q. Grafton, R. Hilborn, D. Squires, M. Tait and M. Williams (eds) *Handbook of Marine Fisheries Conservation and Management*. New York: Oxford University Press, pp. 299–309.

Matthiasson, T., Giry, F. and Agnarsson, S. (2015) 'Individual transferable quotas allocation in Icelandic Fisheries: a community-oriented inequality analysis', *Rannsóknir í félagsvísindum XVI*. Reykjavik, Iceland, October 2015. Available at: http://skemman.is/stream/get/1946/23151/52659/4/HAG_%C3%9E%C3%B3r%C3%B3lfurMatth%C3%ADasson_FlorentGry_SveinnAgnarsson.pdf (accessed 15 May 2017).

Mauss, M. (1967) *The Gift: Forms and Functions of Exchange in Archaic Societies*. New York: Norton.

McAfee, K. (2012) 'The contradictory logic of global ecosystem services markets', *Development and Change*, 43(1): 105–31.

Mccarthy, A., Hepburn, C., Scott, N., Schweikert, K., Turner, R. and Moller, H. (2014) 'Local people see and care most? Severe depletion of inshore fisheries and its consequences for Māori communities in New Zealand', *Aquatic Conservation: Marine and Freshwater Ecosystems*, 24(3): 369–90.

McCarthy, J. and Prudham, S. (2004) 'Neoliberal nature and the nature of neoliberalism', *Geoforum*, 35(3): 275–83.

McCormack, F. (2010) 'Fish is my daily bread: owning and transacting in Māori fisheries', *Anthropological Forum*, 20(1): 19–39.

—— (2012) 'The reconstitution of property relations in New Zealand fisheries', *Anthropological Quarterly*, 85(1): 171–201.

—— (2016) 'Indigenous claims: hearings, settlements, and neoliberal silencing', *PoLAR: Political and Legal Anthropology Review*, 39(2): 226–43.

McCormack, F. and Barclay, K. (2013) 'Insights on capitalism from Oceania', *Research in Economic Anthropology*, 33(1): 1–27.

Medovoi, L. (2010) 'A contribution to the critique of political ecology: sustainability as disavowal', *New Formations*, 69(1): 129–43.

Merlan, F. (2009) 'Indigeneity', *Current Anthropology*, 50(3): 303–33.

Mianowski, M. (2016) *Post-Celtic Tiger Landscapes in Irish Fiction*. Abingdon: Routledge.

Ministry of Agriculture and Fisheries (MAF) (1984) *Inshore Finfish Fisheries: Proposed Policy for Future Management: Public Consultation Document*, Wellington: New Zealand Ministry of Agriculture and Fisheries, Wellington.

Ministry for the Environment (2010) *Fishing activity: Fish stocks*. Available at: www.mfe.govt.nz/sites/default/files/media/Environmental%20reporting/fish- stocks-report-card-nov-2010.pdf (accessed 24 March 2016).

Ministry for Primary Industries (2010) *New Zealand fisheries at a glance*. Available at: www.fish.govt.nz/en-nz/Fisheries + at + a + glance/default.htm (accessed 24 March 2016).

—— (2013) *Review of sustainability and other management controls for snapper 1 (SNA 1)*. (MPI Discussion Paper No.2013/31). Ministry for Primary Industries, New Zealand. Available at: www.legasea.co.nz/documents/SNA1-IPP-MPI-Jul13.pdf (accessed 25 January 2017).

—— (2014) *Quota Management System*. Available at: http://fs.fish.govt.nz/Page.aspx?pk=81 (accessed 25 January 2017).

Mirowski, P. and Plehwe, D. (eds) (2009) *The Road from Mont Pelerin: The Making of Neoliberal Thought Collective*. Cambridge, MA: Harvard College.

Molloy, J. (2004) *The Irish Mackerel Fishery*. Galway: Killybegs Fishermen's Organization and the Marine Institute, Ireland.

Moore, J.W. (2000) 'Environmental crises and the metabolic rift in world-historical perspective', *Organization & Environment*, 13(2): 123–57.

—— (2014) *The Capitalocene, Part I: On the Nature and Origins of Our Ecological Crisis*. Fernand Braudel Center and Department of Sociology Binghamton University. Available at: www.jasonwmoore.com/uploads/The_Capitalocene__Part_I__June_2014.pdf (accessed 25 January 2017).

Moss, M.L. (2010) 'Rethinking subsistence in Southeast Alaska: the potential of zooarchaeology', *Alaska Journal of Anthropology*, 8(1): 121–35.

Muehlebach, A. (2012) *The Moral Neoliberal: Welfare and Citizenship in Italy*. Chicago: University of Chicago Press.

Mulrennan, Monica and Scott, Colin. (2000) 'Indigenous rights in saltwater environments', *Development and Change*, 31(3): 681–708.

Muru-Lanning, M. (2011) 'The analogous boundaries of Ngaati Mahuta, Waikato-Tainui and Kiingitanga', *Journal of the Polynesian Society*, 120(1): 9–41.

NOAA (National Oceanic and Atmospheric Administration) (n.d.) 'Subsistence artisanal barter and trade fisheries definitions and management issues'. Available at: www.pifsc.noaa.gov/human_dimensions/subsistence_artisanal_barter_and_ trade_fisheries_definitions_ and_management_issues.php (accessed 27 March 2015).

National Research Council (1999) *Sharing the Fish: Toward a National Policy on Individual Fishing Quota*. Washington, DC: National Academy Press.

New Zealand News (1996) 'Urban Maori win share of fisheries', 8 May (2515):23.

Neveling, P. (2014) 'Structural contingencies and untimely coincidences in the making of neoliberal India the Kandla free trade zone, 1965–91', *Contributions to Indian Sociology*, 48(1): 17–43.

Niezen, R. (2002) *The Origins of Indigenism*. Berkeley: University of California Press.

NRAC (National Research Advisory Council) (1980) *'Commercial Fisheries'. New Zealand: Commercial Marine Fisheries Working Party, National Research Advisory*, Wellington, NZ: NRAC.

O'Donnchadha, G., O'Callaghan, T. and Niland, C. (2000) *A Socio-economic Study of Fisheries in Counties Cork, Donegal, Kerry and Galway*. Marine Institute. Available at: http://oar.marine.ie/bitstream/10793/210/1/No%2011%20Marine%20 Resources%20Series.PDF (accessed 25 January 2017).

O'Flynn, M., Monaghan, L.F. and Power, M.J. (2014) 'Scapegoating during a time of crisis: a critique of post-Celtic Tiger Ireland', *Sociology*, 48(5): 921–37.

O'Regan, T. (1996) 'Video interview with Jerry Morris', Fishing Industry Association Conference, 11 April.

Oxford English Dictionary (2012) 3rd edn (accessed online via subscription: www. oed.com.ezproxy.waikato.ac.nz/view/Entry/195212?redirected From=sustainer +#eid).

Pálsson, G. and Helgason, A. (2000) *Quota Systems and Resource Management: Icelandic Fishing*. Available at: www.thearctic.is/articles/cases/quotasystems/ enska/index.htm (accessed 25 January 2017).

Pan, M. (2014) 'Economic characteristics and management challenges of the Hawaii pelagic longline fisheries: will a catch share program help?', *Marine Policy*, 44: 18–26.

Pan, M., Criddle, K. and Severance, C. (2014) 'Guest editors' introduction: catch shares and Pacific Islands region fisheries', *Marine Policy*, 44: 1–2.

Parla, A. (2009) 'Remembering across the border: postsocialist nostalgia among Turkish immigrants from Bulgaria', *American Ethnologist* 36(4): 750–67.

Pauli, G. (2010) The blue economy. *Our Planet*, February. Available at: www.unep. org/ourplanet (accessed May 2017).

Pawson, M. and Jennings, S. (1996) 'A critique of methods for stock identification in marine capture fisheries', *Fisheries Research*, 25(3–4): 203–17.

Pearce, D.W. (1998) 'Auditing the earth: the value of the world's ecosystem services and natural capital', *Environment: Science and Policy for Sustainable Development*, 40(2): 23–28.

Pearce, D.W. and Atkinson, G. (1992) *Are National Economies Sustainable*. Working Paper, GEC 92-11. London: Centre for Social and Economic Research on the Global Environment (CSERGE).

Peck, J. and Theodore, N. (2012) 'Reanimating neoliberalism: process geographies of neoliberalisation', *Social Anthropology*, 20(2): 177–85.

Peebles, G. (2010) 'The anthropology of credit and debt', *Annual Review of Anthropology*, 39(1): 225–40.

Pihama, L. (1998) 'Reflections of a fisheries court case', in *Fisheries and Commodifying Iwi: Economics, Politics and Colonisation*, vol. 3. Auckland: IRI/Moko Productions, pp. 67–70.

Pinkerton, E. (2013) 'Alternatives to ITQs in equity–efficiency–effectiveness trade-offs: how the lay-up system spread effort in the BC halibut fishery', *Marine Policy*, 42: 5–13.

—— (2014) 'Groundtruthing individual transferable quotas', in E. Paul Durrenberger and Gísli Pálsson (eds) *Gambling Debt: Iceland's Rise and Fall in the Global Economy*. Boulder, CO: University Press of Colorado, pp. 109–20.

—— (2015) 'The role of moral economy in two British Columbia fisheries: confronting neoliberal policies', *Marine Policy*, 61: 410–19.

Pinkerton, E. and Davis, R. (2015) 'Neoliberalism and the politics of enclosure in North American small-scale fisheries', *Marine Policy*, 61: 303–12.

Pinkerton, E. and Edwards, D.N. (2009) 'The elephant in the room: the hidden costs of leasing individual transferable fishing quotas', *Marine Policy*, 33(4): 707–13.

Pirard, R. and Lapeyre, R. (2014) 'Classifying market-based instruments for ecosystem services: a guide to the literature jungle', *Ecosystem Services*, 9: 106–14.

Pooley, S. (1993) 'Hawaii's marine fisheries: some history, long-term trends, and recent developments', *Marine Fisheries Review*, 55(2): 7–19.

Prudham, S. (2009) 'Pimping climate change: Richard Branson, global warming, and the performance of green capitalism', *Environment and Planning A*, 41(7): 1594–613.

Quiggan, J. (1998) 'Social democracy and market reform in Australia and New Zealand', *Oxford Review of Economic Policy*, 14: 76–95.

Raco, M. (2005) 'Sustainable development, rolled-out neoliberalism and sustainable communities', *Antipode*, 37(2): 324–47.

Rata, E. (2011) 'Discursive strategies of the Maori tribal elite', *Critique of Anthropology*, 31(4): 359–80.

—— (2013) 'Tribalism, democracy, incompatible', *New Zealand Herald*, 29 January. Available at: www.nzherald.co.nz/nz/news/article.cfm?c_id=1&objectid=10861949 (accessed 25 January 2017).

Redclift, M. (2005) 'Sustainable development (1987–2005): an oxymoron comes of age', *Sustainable Development*, 13(4): 212–27.

Reed, A.R. (2016). 'Nostalgia in the post-apartheid state', *Anthropology Southern Africa*, 39(2): 97–109.

Robbins, J. (2007) 'Afterword: Possessive individualism and cultural change in the Western Pacific', *Anthropological Forum*, 17(3): 299–308.

Roepstorff, A. (2000) 'The double interface of environmental knowledge: fishing for Greenland halibut', in L. Feld and B. Neis (eds) *Finding Our Sea Legs: Linking Fishery People and their Knowledge with Science and Management*. St John's: ISER Books, pp. 165–88.

Roitman, J. (2005) *Fiscal Disobedience: An Anthropology of Economic Regulation in Central Africa*. Princeton, NJ: Princeton University Press.

Rumbles, W. (1999) 'Treaty of Waitangi settlement process: new relationship or new mask', paper presented at Compr(om)ising Post/Colonialism(s) Challenging Narratives and Practices conference, Wollongong, Australia, 10–13 February.

Runolfsson, B. and Arnason, R. (1999) *Evolution and Performance of the Icelandic ITQ System*. Available at: https://notendur.hi.is/bthru/iceitq1.html (accessed 27 April 2016).

Sahlins, M.D. (1974) *Stone Age Economics*. Abingdon: Routledge.

Sanchirico, J., Holland, D., Quigley, K. and Fina, M. (2006) 'Catch-quota balancing in multispecies individual fishing quotas', *Marine Policy*, 30(6): 767–85.

Sassen, S. (2014) *Expulsions: Brutality and Complexity in the Global Economy*. Cambridge, MA: The Belknap Press of Harvard University Press.

Scheiber, H.N. and Carr, C.J. (1998) 'From extended jurisdiction to privatization: international law, biology, and economics in the marine fisheries debates, 1937–1976', *Berkeley Journal of International Law*, 16(1): 10–54.

Scott, A. (1955) 'The fishery: the objectives of sole ownership', *Journal of Political Economy*, 63(2): 116–24.

—— (1993) 'Obstacles to fishery self-government', *Marine Resource Economics*, 8(3): 187–99.

Scott, J.C. (1976) *The Moral Economy of the Peasant: Subsistence and Rebellion in Southeast Asia*. New Haven, CT: Yale University Press.

Severance, C. (2010) 'Customary exchange maintains cultural continuity', in *Pacific Islands fishery news: Newsletter of the Western Pacific Regional Fishery Management Council*, University of Hawaii, Hilo, pp. 1–2.

—— (2014) 'Sharing the catch or catching the shares: catch shares for the western Pacific region?', *Marine Policy*, 44: 3–8.

Severance, C., Franco, R., Hamnett, M., Anderson, C. and Aitaoto, F. (2013) 'Effort triggers, fish flow, and customary exchange in American Samoa and the Marianas: fleshing out the human dimension in western Pacific fisheries', *Pacific Science*, 67: 383–93.

Sharp, B. (2008) 'Designing property rights for achieving sustainable development of the oceans', in M. Patterson and B. Glavovic (eds) *Ecological Economics of the Oceans and Coasts*. Cheltenham: Edward Elgar.

Shaw, J. and Byler, D. (2016) 'Precarity', *Cultural Anthropology*. Available at: https://culanth.org/curated_collections/21-precarity (accessed 25 January 2017).

Shore, C. and Wright, S. (1999) 'Audit culture and anthropology: neo-liberalism in British higher education', *Journal of the Royal Anthropological Institute*, 5(4): 557–75.

Shotton, Ross (ed.) (1999) *Use of Property Rights in Fisheries Management, Proceedings of FishRights 99 Conference*, FAO Fisheries Technical Paper 404/1, Freemantle, Western Australia, 11–19 November.

Simmons, G. and Stringer, C. (2014) 'New Zealand's fisheries management system: forced labour an ignored or overlooked dimension?', *Marine Policy*, 50: 74–80.

Simmons G., Bremner, G., Stringer, C., Torkington, B., Teh, L., Zylich, K. et al. (2015) *Preliminary Reconstructions of Marine Fisheries Catches for New Zealand (1950–2010)*. Working Paper 2015-87, Fisheries Center, University of British Columbia, Canada. Available at: http://www.seaaroundus.org/doc/PageContent/OtherWPContent/Simmons+et+al+2016+-+NZ+Catch+Reconstruction+-+May+11.pdf (accessed 25 January 2017).

Sissenwine, M. (1978) 'Is MSY an adequate foundation for optimum yield?', *Fisheries*, 3(6): 22–42.

Sissenwine, M. and Mace, P. (2003) 'Governance for responsible fisheries: an ecosystem approach', in M. Sinclair and G. Valdimarsson (eds) *Responsible Fisheries in the Marine Ecosystem*. Wallingford, UK: CABI Publishing.

Sissons, J. (2010) 'Building a house society: the reorganization of Maori communities around meeting houses', *Journal of the Royal Anthropological Institute*, 16(2): 372–86.

Smith, C. (1998) 'Commodification of fisheries timeline', in *Fisheries and Commodifying Iwi, Economics, Politics and Colonisation*, vol. 3. Auckland: IRI/Moko Productions, pp. 32–36.

Smith, G.A. (2011) 'Selective hegemony and beyond-populations with "no productive function": a framework for enquiry'. *Identities*, 18(1): 2–38.

Smith, N. (2007) 'Nature as accumulation strategy', *Socialist Register*, 43: 19–41.

Soini, K. and Birkeland, I. (2014) 'Exploring the scientific discourse on cultural sustainability', *Geoforum*, 51: 213–23.

Southwick Associates (2013) *Comparing NOAA's Recreational and Commercial Fishing Data*, American Sportfishing Association. Available at: http://asafishing.org/wp-content/uploads/Comparing_Recreational_and_Commercial_Marine_Fishing_Data_Report_Summary_May_2013.pdf (accessed 25 January 2017).

Spalding, S. (2006) 'History of the Hawaii bottomfish fishery', *Hawaii Fishing News*, 32(1): 16–18.

Strathern, M. (1992) 'Qualified value: the perspective of gift exchange', in C. Humphrey (ed.) *Barter, Exchange and Value: An Anthropological Approach*. Cambridge: Cambridge University Press, pp. 169–91.

—— (1997) '"Improving ratings": audit in the British university system', *European Review*, 5(03): 305–21.

Strathern, M. and Hirsch, E. (2004) 'Introduction', in E. Hirsch and M. Strathern (eds) *Transactions and Creations: Property Debates and the Stimulus of Melanesia*. New York: Berghahn, pp. 1–8.

Streeck, W. (2014) 'How will capitalism end?', *New Left Review*, 87: 35–64.

Stringer, C., Simmons, G. and Rees, E. (2011) 'Shifting post-production patterns: exploring changes in New Zealand's seafood processing industry', *New Zealand Geographer*, 67(3): 161–73.

Sullivan, S. (2013) 'Banking nature? The spectacular financialisation of environmental conservation', *Antipode*, 45(1): 198–217.

TGH (Tainui Group Holdings) and Waikato-Tainui Fisheries Ltd (2011) *Annual Report*, New Zealand. Available at: www.versite.co.nz/~2011/15861/#/1/ (accessed 27 March 2015).

The Economist Intelligence Unit (2015) 'The blue economy: growth, opportunity and a sustainable ocean economy', World Ocean Summit, the Oitavos, Cascais, Portugal, 4–5 June.

The Press (1997) 'Chief judge vexed', 19 November.

Thompson, E.P. (1971) 'The moral economy of the English crowd in the eighteenth century', *Past & Present*, 50: 76–136.

Thornton, T.F. and Hebert, J. (2015) 'Neoliberal and neo-communal herring fisheries in southeast Alaska: reframing sustainability in marine ecosystems', *Marine Policy*, 61: 366–75.

Todorova, M. and Gille, Z. (eds) (2010) *Post-communist Nostalgia*. New York: Berghahn.

TOKM (Te Ohu Kai Moana; Treaty of Waitangi Fisheries Commission) (1998) Policy Brief, November.

Townsend, R. (2008) 'Transaction costs and fisheries self-governance in New Zealand', *ASB House*. Available at: http://nzae.org.nz/wp-content/uploads/2011/08/nr1215398635.pdf (accessed 25 January 2017).

Trigger, D. and Dalley, C. (2010) 'Negotiating indigeneity: culture, identity, and politics', *Reviews in Anthropology*, 39(1): 46–65.

Tsing, A. (2003) 'Agrarian allegory and global futures', in P. Greenough and A. Tsing (eds) *Nature in the Global South*. Durham, NC: Duke University Press.

—— (2011) *Friction: An Ethnography of Global Connection*. Princeton, NJ: Princeton University Press.

—— (2013) 'Sorting out commodities: how capitalist value is made through gifts', *HAU: Journal of Ethnographic Theory*, 3(1): 21–43.

US Census Bureau (n.d.) *Keaukaha Hawaiian Homeland, HI. Population and Housing Narrative Profile: Data Set 2005–2009*, American Community Survey. Available at: http://tinyurl.com/z66y8tj (accessed 25 January 2017).

Van Meijl, T. (2006) 'Who owns the fisheries? Changing views of property and its redistribution in post-colonial Maori society', in F. von Benda-Beckmann, K. von Benda-Beckmann and M. Wiber (eds) *Changing Properties of Property*. Oxford: Berghahn, pp. 170–93.

—— (2013) 'Ownership and distribution in the settlement of Maori grievances: balancing historical and social justice between classes', in F. McCormack and K. Barclay (eds) *Engaging with Capitalism: Cases from Oceania*. Bingley: Emerald, pp. 29–52.

Vázquez-Arroyo, A. (2008) 'Liberal democracy and neoliberalism: a critical juxtaposition', *New Political Science*, 30: 127–59.

Verdery, K. (2003) *The Vanishing Hectare: Property and Value in Postsocialist Transylvania*. Ithaca, NY: Cornell University Press.

von Benda-Beckmann, F., K. von Benda-Beckmann and M. Wiber (eds) (2006) *Changing Property of Properties*. Oxford: Berghahn.

Wacquant, L. (2012) 'Three steps to a historical anthropology of actually existing neoliberalism', *Caderno CRH*, 25(66): 505–18.

Waikato-Tainui (2015) *Waikato Raupatu Lands Trust Guide to the Financial Statements for the Year Ended 31 March 2015*, New Zealand. Available at: www.waikatotainui. com/wp-content/uploads/APPROVED-Waikato-Tainui-2015-Guide-to-the-Financial-Statements.pdf (accessed 25 January 2017).

—— (2016) *Puurongo-aa-Tau o Waikato-Tainui*, New Zealand. Available at: www. versite.co.nz/~2016/19210/files/assets/basic-html/page-1.html# (accessed 25 January 2017).

Waitangi Tribunal (1988) *Muriwhenua Fishing Claims Report (Wai 22)*. Wellington: New Zealand Department of Justice.

—— (1992a) *Ngai Tahu sea fisheries report (Wai 27)*. Wellington: New Zealand Department of Justice.

—— (1992b) *The Fisheries Settlment Report (Wai 307)*. Wellington: New Zealand Department of Justice.

Walker, R. (1990) *Ka whawhai tonu matou* (Struggle without End). Harmondsworth: Penguin.

Walker, S. and R. Townsend (2008) 'Economic analysis of New Zealand's deemed value system', 14th IIFET (Institute of Fisheries Economics and Trade) Conference, Nha Trang, Vietnam, 22–25 July.

Wallerstein, I. (2002 [1994]) 'Development: lodestar or illusion?', in L. Sklair (ed.) *Capitalism and Development*. London: Routledge, pp. 3–20.

Wanner, T. (2015) 'The new "passive revolution" of the green economy and growth discourse: maintaining the "sustainable development" of neoliberal capitalism', *New Political Economy*, 20(1): 21–41.

Warming, J. (1911) 'On the rent of fishing grounds', *History of Political Economy*, 15(3): 391–96.

WCED (World Commission on Environment and Development) (1987) *Our Common Future*. Oxford: Oxford University Press.

Webster, S. (1998) 'Maori hapu as a whole way of struggle: 1840s–50s before the land wars', *Oceania*, 69(1): 4–35.

—— (2002) 'Maori retribalization and treaty rights to the New Zealand fisheries', *Contemporary Pacific*, 14(2): 341–76.

—— (2016) 'Māori indigeneity and commodity fetishism', *Sites: a Journal of Social Anthropology and Cultural Studies*, 13(2): 1–18.

Weiss, J.D. (1992) 'Taxing issue: are limited entry fishing permits property?', *Alaska Law Review*, 9(1): 93–112.

Wu, J.-G., Guo, X.-C., Yang, J., Qian, G.-X., Niu, J.-M., Liang, C.-Z. et al. (2014) 'What is sustainability science?', *Journal of Applied Ecology*, 25(1): 1–11.

Yandle, T. (2008) 'The promise and perils of building a co-management regime: an institutional assessment of New Zealand fisheries management between 1999 and 2005', *Marine Policy*, 32(1): 132–41.

Yang, G. (2003) 'China's Zhiqing generation: nostalgia, identity, and cultural resistance in the 1990s', *Modern China*, 29(3): 267–96.

Young, O.R. (1983) 'Fishing by permit: restricted common property in practice', *Ocean Development & International Law*, 13(2): 121–70.

Zeller, D., Booth, S. and Pauly, D. (2006) 'Fisheries contributions to the gross domestic product: underestimating small-scale fisheries in the Pacific', *Marine Resource Economics*, 21(4): 355–74.

Index